Konrad Graf

Shadow Work For A Nation

A Journey from Collective Ego

to Democratic Consciousness

INTRODUCTION 1

THE DEMOCRACY WE'VE NEVER HAD 9

I. SELF-AWARENESS AND IDENTIFICATION 21

FREEDOM.. 21

THE ILLUSION OF CHOICE 23

THE REACTIVE MACHINE 24

THE PRICE OF WAKING UP 26

FEAR... 31

THE MECHANICS OF COLLECTIVE HIJACKING......... 32

THE TWO FEARS NOBODY ADMITS TO 35

THE WIRING BENEATH THE ALARM 38

CONTROL... 43

THE ROOTS OF CONTROL-SEEKING 44

THE PSYCHOLOGY OF CONTROL......................... 46

THE ILLUSION AND THE ADDICTION 51

MODERN CONTROL MECHANISMS 54

THE COST AND THE ALTERNATIVE........................ 57

SHAME AND GUILT 63

MANIFESTATION OF SHAME AND GUILT................. 64

The Cultural Cost and Benefit 68

Projection...**73**

The Cheapest Psychology 74

Projection in Action 76

Reclaiming the Shadow 81

Responsibility **87**

Why We Run From It 88

Who Decides, Who Pays 94

The Superiority-Victimhood Delusion.........**99**

The Ladder 100

The Ladder Goes National 105

Stepping Off.. 109

Group Think...**115**

The Obedience Machine 116

Draw the Line 118

Software You Didn't Install 121

Denial **127**

The Nations That Never Looked Back 129

The Scale of Evil....................................... 131

II. EXPLORATION AND ACKNOWLEDGMENT 143

COLLECTIVE TRUTH TELLING..........................**143**

MAKING LIES EXPENSIVE................................. 146

POWER MONOPOLY..................................**151**

THE MONOPOLY ISN'T NATURAL 153

DEMOCRACY AS PERFORMANCE 160

THE DIRECTION OUT 163

MEDIA & CONSPIRACY **167**

THE MONOPOLY ON REALITY............................ 169

THE INTELLIGENCE LAYER 171

MANUFACTURING WARS................................. 175

THE BURIED RECORD 178

THE SOCIAL MEDIA BATTLEFIELD 184

WHAT TO DO WITH THIS................................. 188

MONEY IS A LEASH **191**

WORSHIPPING WHAT WE MADE UP 193

THE PARADOX OF CONTROL 197

THE REDISTRIBUTION PROBLEM....................... 199

RESTRUCTURING, NOT REPLACING 202

TAKING OFF THE LEASH 205

DOMINATION VS TRUE LEADERSHIP 209

THE ANATOMY OF DOMINATION 211

THE PATH TO TYRANNY 218

TRUE LEADERSHIP: SERVICE, NOT CONTROL 222

CONQUERING EVERYTHING 226

CONSCIOUSNESS BEFORE SYSTEMS 229

DIVIDE AND CONQUER 233

ANATOMY OF DIVISION 234

THE DELIBERATE FRAGMENTATION OF OCCUPY WALL STREET 239

PATTERN RECOGNITION 245

THE DIVIDE BETWEEN BLACK AND WHITE 249

IT'S JUST SUNLIGHT, BABY! 249

THE TWO TESTIMONIES 253

THE DIVIDE BETWEEN LEFT AND RIGHT 257

THE PERFORMANCE OF OPPOSITION 258

THE CONTROLLED SPECTRUM 260

THE EXHAUSTION STRATEGY 263

THE ATTITUDE NETWORK 264

BEYOND THE PARTY SYSTEM 271

THE DIVIDE BETWEEN MEN AND WOMEN..........**275**

THE PHYSICAL REALITY 277

THE DIVINE COLLABORATION............................ 280

WHEN THE SAME GIFTS BECOME WEAPONS........ 287

MATE CHOICE SHAPES POWER 290

THE CRISIS OF ROLE MODELS 295

WHO BENEFITS FROM THE WAR 300

THE UNPRECEDENTED CURRENT DIVIDE 304

INTEGRATION, NOT PROJECTION....................... 306

CLARITY, DIRECTION, PURPOSE 308

WHY PARTNERSHIP MATTERS FOR DEMOCRACY... 312

BUILDING WHAT'S BEEN DESTROYED 316

THE WINDOW **319**

WHEN SYSTEMS FALL...................................... 320

FOR THOSE WHO ARE AWAKE........................... 325

III. INTEGRATION AND HEALING..............**329**

HEALTH **329**

YOUR GUT IS RUNNING YOUR GOVERNMENT........ 329

POLITICS ON GOOD HARDWARE 333

EDUCATION..**337**

THE FACTORY MODEL IN ACTION 338

TEACHING TO THINK 342

SCHOOLS THAT GOT IT RIGHT 348

PROOF OF CONCEPT.....................................352

THE GROUND HAS BEEN PREPARED **355**

DIRECT POWER IN PRACTICE...........................358

RANDOM SELECTION AND EXPERTISE.................360

DELIBERATION WITHOUT TEETH.......................364

DELEGATES, NOT REPRESENTATIVES..................366

THE PARTS ALREADY EXIST 371

A SYSTEM OF ACCOUNTABILITY **373**

THE MINIMAL SHIFT 375

THE ARCHITECTURE: SUBJECT MATTER EXECUTIVES
....379

THE BREAKER SWITCH—REVOCABLE DELEGATION 401

THE TECHNICAL INFRASTRUCTURE 406

THE ARCHITECTURE OF LAWS: FROM STONE TABLETS
TO LIVING CODE 408

THE ARCHITECTURE OF TAXATION 421

THE ARCHITECTURE OF JUSTICE.......................427

The Necessary Monster of Defense 430

The Infrastructure 435

The Bet 438

Objections **441**

„But Won't The Majority Tyrannize Minorities?"
.... 441

„Demagogues Will Manipulate The System". 444

„It's Too Slow For Modern Crises" 446

„People Will Vote For Short-Term Benefits
Over Long-Term Needs" 448

„Tribalism Will Tear It Apart" 451

„Economic Power Will Still Dominate" 453

„People Will Be Overwhelmed By Decision
Fatigue" 456

„The Technology Will Fail Or Be Compromised"
.... 459

„Theocratic Ideologies Will Destroy The
System From Within" 461

The Standard We Must Meet 464

Economy **467**

The W.L. Gore Model 473

A Speculative Merit Alternative........ 476

ECONOMIC VISION 478

CULTURE 481

THE CONSCIOUSNESS DEMOCRACY REQUIRES 483

THE SLOW GROWTH OF CULTURE 490

IV. ONGOING PRACTICE AND MAINTENANCE 493

SUSTAINABLE ENGAGEMENT 493

THE TEMPTATION TO ABANDON RESPONSIBILITY ... 495

THE QUIET COST OF LOOKING AWAY 498

BOUNDARIES 501

NUCLEAR DETERRENCE 505

WHEN COMPASSION GETS WEAPONIZED 507

EVOLUTION, NOT OSSIFICATION 515

WHEN CITIZENS BECOME THE LEGISLATURE 528

WHEN SILICON REPLACES MINISTERS 528

BEYOND THE OBVIOUS 528

THE ONLY IMPERATIVE 528

THE WORK NEVER ENDS 529

THE ETERNAL DANCE WITH DOMINATION 529

THE SHADOW YOU'RE STILL CARRYING 530

THE CAGE HAS NO LOCK.................................. 534

Introduction

„If there is to be peace in the world,
There must be peace in the nations.

If there is to be peace in the nations,
There must be peace in the cities.

If there is to be peace in the cities,
There must be peace between neighbors.

If there is to be peace between neighbors,
There must be peace in the home.

If there is to be peace in the home,
There must be peace in the heart."

— Lao-Tsu

Thanks for reading my book on how to fix a nation!

Before you close this book thinking you've gotten the complete solution in a single ancient quote, hang on a minute. Lao-Tsu was right that a healthy society needs healthy parts. But rightfully diagnosing the problem and actually solving it are two very different things. Solving it requires deep, uncomfortable work. It means looking honestly at the things we'd rather ignore. And here is the real question worth sitting with: what is it about our societies that makes both their parts and the whole fail, again and again, across cultures and centuries?

Consider that you were born into a system you never designed. You didn't choose the economic structures that shape your daily life, the political frameworks that govern your society, or the cultural narratives that inform your understanding of how the world works. These were already in place before you took your first breath. You inherited them the way you inherited your native language, absorbing their logic and assumptions long before you developed the capacity to question them.

Yet despite having no hand in creating these systems, you are likely deeply committed to them. Not because you consciously evaluated alternatives and chose what seemed best, but because the water you swim in rarely announces itself as water. Challenge someone's economic beliefs and watch how quickly it becomes personal. Question their political framework and notice the defensiveness that arises, as if you've attacked not just their ideas but their identity. We defend systems we didn't create with the fervor of their architects, never pausing to ask why we feel so invested in structures that were imposed upon us without our consent.

When we do contemplate change, we often just trade one pre-packaged system for another. Move to a different country, adopt a distinct political ideology, embrace a different economic model. We shuffle the deck chairs, convinced we're steering the ship. But this unconscious allegiance to inherited systems points to something deeper, something that operates beneath our awareness and shapes our collective behavior in ways we rarely examine.

Every nation has a shadow. Carl Jung observed that individuals carry unconscious aspects of themselves that they deny, repress, or project onto others. The same holds true at the collective level. Entire societies harbor blind spots, unhealed traumas, and disowned parts of their national identity. Germany spent decades unable to speak honestly about the Third Reich. America's founding mythology of freedom coexists uneasily with its history of slavery and displacement. Britain's imperial nostalgia persists alongside willful amnesia about what empire actually meant for those who lived under it. These are not ancient history. They are active psychological forces shaping policy, identity, and conflict today.

When these shadows remain unacknowledged, a nation begins to fracture in predictable ways. The pattern mirrors what happens in individuals caught between narcissism and echoism. The louder parts of the collective psyche grow obsessed with control and appearance, consuming resources and demanding constant recognition. The quieter parts retreat into silence, suppressing their needs until they become invisible. Think of how national discourse works in practice: a small number of voices dominate, performing outrage and certainty, while the majority withdraws, sensing that honest conversation has become impossible. In this imbalance, what is denied festers. What is silenced grows weak. What is indulged grows hollow.

Lasting peace and national flourishing demand more than good intentions or policy reforms. They require a nation willing to do its shadow work, to acknowledge uncomfortable truths and transform defensiveness into curiosity. The peace we seek is not merely the absence of conflict. It is the presence of an authentic relationship with reality. And that requires the collective courage to be honest about our past and present while learning to hold complexity without collapsing into denial.

This is not about shame or national self-flagellation. It is about wholeness. It is about moving from unconscious reactivity to conscious response. The journey begins exactly where Lao-Tsu suggested, in the heart. But it extends outward, because personal and collective transformation are intimately connected. A society capable of facing its shadow creates space for individuals to do the same, just as conscious individuals create the foundation for national healing.

Perhaps the most compelling evidence for this connection between inner and outer transformation comes from unexpected research. In 1978, a study in Merseyside, Great Britain, found that when a group of practitioners engaged in Transcendental Meditation, crime rates in the area decreased by 16%. In Washington, D.C., in 1993, researchers documented significant reductions in violent crime when a coherence group meditated together with the intention of creating peace.

Leaving only one conclusion: these damn meditators were responsible for all the crime. Once they got busy sitting quietly with their eyes closed, they simply didn't have time for their criminal enterprise anymore.

There might be a more likely explanation. Whether through direct effects on collective consciousness, as Jung's own work on synchronicity might suggest, or through the subtler ripple effects of individual change spreading through social networks, inner transformation appears to have measurable impacts on the collective environment. The quality of consciousness we cultivate within ourselves does not stay contained within ourselves. It influences the fabric of our communities in ways that controlled studies have begun to capture, even if the mechanisms remain debated.

If these studies intrigue you, consider a simple experiment: dedicate just a few minutes each day to sitting quietly and holding the intention of peace. Peace within yourself, peace in your community, peace in your nation. You don't need special training or techniques. Simply find a quiet moment, breathe deeply, and let your consciousness rest in the possibility of harmony. If enough of us take up this small practice, we may discover that the peace Lao-Tsu wrote about begins to manifest not just as a poetic ideal but as something tangible.

The chapters ahead explore what shadow work looks like on a national scale. They examine the historical patterns of resistance, the mechanisms by which societies avoid self-knowledge, and the profound healing that becomes possible when a nation commits to seeing itself clearly. This work is difficult. It is also the most important work we can do. It begins here, in our own hearts, and extends outward to transform the very soul of a nation.

A Note to Readers

A necessary warning before we go further: this book will make you uncomfortable regardless of where you sit on the political spectrum. If you consider yourself left-leaning, you will find critiques here that challenge sacred assumptions of progressive thought. If you lean right, the same applies. In our polarized moment, readers instinctively assume that criticism of their tribe means the author belongs to the opposing camp.

Let me be clear from the outset: I hold no loyalty to any political faction.

Both left and right-wing movements, despite their stated intentions, operate within systems that have been fundamentally compromised. The endless battle between these camps is not the profound ideological struggle it appears to be. It is largely manufactured theater, a manifestation of the very groupthink this book examines, serving to divide populations while deeper systemic issues go unaddressed. Continuing to participate in these systems on their terms, regardless of which side you choose, only accelerates the trajectory toward collapse that we seem collectively unwilling to acknowledge.

True shadow work requires stepping outside these tribal allegiances entirely. It demands that we examine not just the obvious flaws in our political opponents but the blind spots and contradictions within our own preferred worldviews. It asks us to consider that both sides are partially right and fundamentally limited, and that real solutions exist beyond the narrow confines of our current political imagination.

If you're willing to question everything you've been taught about how nations should function, if you're ready to examine your own psychological investment in systems that may not serve you, then read on. This journey demands intellectual honesty and emotional courage. It will be uncomfortable. It will also be necessary.

The Democracy We've Never Had

In November 2022, Isabel Vaughan-Spruce stood silently on a public street in Birmingham. She held no signs. She spoke no words. She wasn't protesting or demonstrating. She was praying. Silently. In her mind.

Police approached and asked what she was doing. When she said she might be praying, they arrested her.

Officers interrogated her about the „nature of her prayer." They showed her photographs of herself standing quietly on a public street and asked if she had been praying in those specific moments. They charged her with violating a Public Space Protection Order. She was taken to court. The magistrate acquitted her. The prosecution couldn't offer evidence that thinking constituted a crime.

Three weeks later, police arrested her again. For the same silent prayer. In the same location. Six officers this time.

This happened in Britain in 2022 and 2023. A country that calls itself a free democracy.

Six officers for a woman standing silently on a street. But this isn't just another civil liberties story gone wrong. It's the timing that matters. Because while Isabel stood in Birmingham, facing charges for the contents of her mind, similar patterns were emerging across the Western world.

In Canada, Tamara Lich sat in jail for weeks without bail. Her crime was organizing a protest convoy. Not participating in violence. Not destroying property. Organizing. The Canadian government invoked emergency powers for the first time in the nation's history, freezing the bank accounts of protesters and donors without trial or conviction. Peaceful assembly met with financial destruction, carried out not by courts but by executive decree.

In the United States, a 30-year-old woman was driving to her local church to donate clothing when an unmarked car with a fake rideshare sticker sideswiped her vehicle. Three masked men in camouflage jumped out. They were immigration agents. One of them shot her five times. She was an American citizen, on her way to church, in her own country. ProPublica has since documented over 170 U.S. citizens detained by immigration agents. DHS Secretary Kristi Noem's on-camera response: "No American citizens have been arrested or detained."

These are not isolated incidents. They form a pattern. Across the United States, the United Kingdom, France, Germany, Australia, and

Canada, citizens are being arrested for social media posts. Protesters face criminal charges for exercising what were supposedly fundamental rights. Governments expand surveillance while eliminating privacy. Digital IDs track movements. Central bank digital currencies are being prepared to monitor every transaction. Laws criminalize speech, assembly, and resistance.

Nations that built their identities on freedom and democracy are systematically dismantling both, often using those very words to justify the demolition. Most citizens either don't notice or accept it as necessary. Safety requires sacrifice. Complex problems need expert management. The threats are too great for messy democratic processes.

Six officers to arrest a praying woman. Emergency powers to freeze bank accounts. A citizen shot five times on her way to church. And before you assign blame to your preferred political villain, note the governments responsible: Conservative in Britain, Liberal in Canada, Republican in America. The tools of repression have no party loyalty. In each case, the state acted as if these measures were both reasonable and temporary. The measures remain. The surveillance expands. The criminalization of dissent continues.

Why is this happening everywhere at once?

The easy answer is that crises demand coordination. Terrorism, pandemics, climate change, and misinformation require unprecedented government action. Individual rights must bend when collective survival is at stake. Every authoritarian measure comes wrapped in emergency language, presented as temporary necessity rather than permanent transformation.

But there's another possibility, one that requires looking at what these systems have always been rather than what we've been told they are.

What if representative democracy has never actually been a democracy? What if calling yourself democratic while operating as an oligarchy is not a recent corruption but the original design?

You might think that's an exaggeration. After all, you vote. Elections happen. Power transfers peacefully. Isn't that democracy?

Consider the American founding. The Constitutional Convention of 1787 occurred behind closed doors, in secret. The fifty-five men who attended represented less than 1% of the population. They were property owners, merchants, and slaveholders. Their explicit goal was not to create democracy but to contain it.

Alexander Hamilton stated this plainly in Federalist No. 35: „The idea of an actual representation of all classes of the people, by persons of each class, is altogether visionary." John Adams wrote that democracy „never lasts long" because it „wastes, exhausts, and murders itself." The founders feared popular control of government. They designed a system to filter that control through elites who would, as James Madison put it, „refine and enlarge the public views."

Refine and enlarge. A pleasant way of saying that what you want must pass through better people who will correct your misguided impulses.

The Constitution's structure reflects this intention precisely. The Senate was not initially elected by popular vote but appointed by state legislatures, creating a buffer between citizens and federal power. The Electoral College was designed explicitly to override popular votes when the masses chose poorly. Property requirements for voting excluded the majority of adult men, and of course all women and enslaved people. The system was not democratic. It was a republic designed to protect property and power from democratic demands.

And the American founding was not exceptional in this regard. Britain's parliamentary system evolved not from a desire to empower citizens but from negotiations between monarchs and landed aristocracy over who would control taxation. France's republican tradition, born in revolution, cycled through empires, restorations, and republics before stabilizing into a system where a narrow political class circulates through the same elite institutions. The democratic language changed. The power structures remained remarkably consistent.

This is not ancient history overcome by progressive reform. The structural logic persists. Political parties act as gatekeepers, filtering who can run for office and ensuring only candidates acceptable to existing power structures reach the ballot. You choose between pre-approved options, not genuine alternatives. Executive power concentrates in single individuals or small groups. Presidents and prime ministers wield enormous authority with minimal accountability, creating conditions for inevitable capture by special interests. Representatives serve fixed terms regardless of performance, insulated from consequences until the next election cycle, when they campaign on new promises while facing no penalty for broken ones.

The system is not failing. It is working exactly as designed.

The authoritarian drift you're witnessing isn't democracy being corrupted. It's an oligarchy revealing itself when the democratic pretense becomes inconvenient. As long as populations accepted the illusion, the aesthetic of freedom could be maintained. Now that crises expose failures and legitimacy weakens, the mask drops. The pattern repeats everywhere because these systems share the same fundamental structure: concentrate power among elites while giving populations the appearance of control through periodic voting rituals that change nothing about who actually governs.

But the problem runs deeper than structural flaws in representative systems. Throughout history, we've experimented with capitalism, communism, socialism, fascism, monarchies, theocracies, and every hybrid variation imaginable. Each promised to solve the fundamental problems of human organization. Each delivered genuine insights alongside catastrophic blind spots.

Capitalism recognized the power of individual initiative and decentralized decision-making, then elevated self-interest from a human tendency into a governing principle, treating greed as a human characteristic. Communist systems recognized the exploitation inherent in unchecked capital accumulation, then assumed that restructuring ownership would fundamentally alter human behavior, and acted surprised when corruption and power-hoarding persisted under new names. Both focused obsessively on distributing goods and resources while assuming that proper distribution mechanisms would automatically solve human problems.

They missed what should have been obvious. Human behavior stems from consciousness. A system created by unconscious people produces unconscious results, regardless of its theoretical sophistication.

This is not an abstract philosophical claim. Watch it play out in real time. The same people who design systems to promote equality end up creating new hierarchies. The same revolutionaries who overthrow tyrants become tyrants themselves. The same constitutions that enshrine rights get reinterpreted to eliminate them. The documents don't govern. The consciousness of the people operating within them does.

Every political theory ignores this. Every revolution forgets it. And so we keep replacing one dysfunctional system with another and acting surprised when the new one also fails.

Now, the problem with current representative systems isn't representation itself. Professional governance requires expertise, specialization, and dedicated focus that most citizens cannot provide while living their lives. The average person cannot dedicate forty hours per week to understanding agricultural subsidies, nuclear regulatory frameworks, or international trade agreements. Nor should they have to. The problem is that representation has been structured to serve oligarchic control rather than citizen welfare.

But simply restructuring representation without addressing human consciousness would produce its own disaster. You could redesign the entire system to give citizens genuine control over who governs them. Hand that power to populations incapable of wise judgment, and the results would be predictable.

Citizens who cannot think critically will choose demagogues. Citizens who project their shadows will scapegoat minorities. Citizens who avoid responsibility will demand leaders promising easy solutions to complex problems. The oligarchy would point to the catastrophe as proof that people cannot handle genuine power. Under current conditions, they would have a point.

Those conditions, however, are not fixed. They are produced by systems deliberately designed to keep populations dependent, distracted, and incapable of the very discernment that genuine self-governance requires.

True democratic representation requires populations capable of evaluating those who would govern them. Citizens must be able to assess professional competence rather than respond to charisma, distinguish between populist manipulation and genuine expertise, and hold representatives accountable rather than blindly trusting authority.

These capacities do not develop accidentally. They require something most political theories never mention: shadow work.

Consider a simple analogy. When you need surgery, you don't elect your surgeon every four years based on campaign promises. You choose a professional based on demonstrated competence, credentials verified by independent bodies, and ongoing performance evaluated by peers and patients. If the surgeon proves incompetent, they lose their license. They don't get to keep operating until the next election cycle. Governance involves value judgments that surgery does not, but the principle of professional accountability applies: hire for competence, evaluate continuously, fire for failure.

Imagine applying this to governance. Professional administrators hired for expertise and evaluated on performance. Not politicians making promises, but specialists solving problems, with citizens empowered to hire and fire based on results rather than rhetoric. This would require mechanisms for continuous accountability rather than waiting for election cycles. It would require genuine citizen control over who can serve rather than party gatekeepers deciding who reaches the ballot. It would require distributing executive power across multiple roles rather than concentrating it in single individuals who inevitably become captured by special interests.

The details of such a system matter enormously, and we will explore them thoroughly in Section III. Designing governance that serves citizens without creating new forms of tyranny requires careful thought.

But those details are meaningless without the foundation. You cannot choose competent administrators if you cannot see through manipulation. You cannot hold professional governance accountable if you avoid responsibility in your own life. You cannot build a system that serves citizen welfare if you refuse to face your own shadows.

The global authoritarian drift is not inevitable. It is the predictable outcome of oligarchic systems operating on populations that have not developed the consciousness to resist. Isabel Vaughan-Spruce was arrested for praying silently on a street, and the nation shrugged. Tamara Lich was jailed for organizing a protest, and most citizens looked away. A pregnant woman was handcuffed in front of her children for a Facebook post, and the public accepted it as a reasonable response to extraordinary circumstances.

These were not failures of law or policy. They were failures of collective consciousness. A population capable of recognizing authoritarianism would not tolerate it, regardless of the emergency language used to justify it.

Change those conditions, and different outcomes become possible. But changing them requires seeing clearly what we are actually dealing with, not the story we've been told.

That seeing begins now.

I. Self-Awareness and Identification

Freedom

In 1989, millions of people watched the Berlin Wall fall. Strangers embraced in the streets, champagne corks flew, and the word on everyone's lips was *Freiheit*. Freedom. Within a decade, researchers began documenting a phenomenon so widespread it earned its own name: *Ostalgie*, a nostalgia for the very system people had risked their lives to escape. Former East Germans, now free to travel anywhere, buy anything, say anything, found themselves longing for the predictability of the regime that had imprisoned them. Not because the regime was good. Because freedom, it turned out, was more terrifying than they had imagined.

This is not a story about German reunification. It is a story about what happens when human beings get what they say they want and discover they were never prepared to handle it.

Most nations proudly proclaim their commitment to freedom in constitutions, anthems, and political speeches. Yet the very fact that a book about collective shadow work needs to exist reveals something uncomfortable: there is a fundamental disconnect between the freedom we celebrate and the freedom we actually practice. That gap is where this chapter lives.

Real freedom is not merely the absence of external constraints. This sounds like a greeting card sentiment until you watch it play out in practice. Consider the United States after the Civil Rights Act of 1964. Legal barriers to racial equality were dismantled. Formal segregation ended. Yet decades later, residential segregation patterns in American cities remained remarkably similar to those that existed under Jim Crow. No law required it. People simply continued the pattern, driven by unconscious biases and inherited fears so deeply embedded they operated without anyone needing to enforce them. The external chains were removed. The internal ones kept working just fine.

The same principle scales to entire civilizations. A nation may boast of its democratic institutions while remaining enslaved to collective patterns, historical traumas, and systemic dynamics that no one voted for and no one knows how to stop. These are not signs of hypocrisy. They are symptoms of unconscious programming operating the machinery while the conscious mind believes it is steering.

True freedom begins with a paradox most people would rather not hear: we are not as free as we think we are. For a society, this means developing the capacity to observe its own automatic reactions, its default responses to crises, its unquestioned assumptions about how the world works. Without that capacity, freedom is just a word on a monument.

The Illusion of Choice

Walk into any American supermarket and you will find roughly 30,000 products on the shelves. You can choose between 47 varieties of toothpaste and hundreds of breakfast cereals, each in its own brightly colored box. This abundance feels like freedom. It is marketed as freedom. But here is the question no cereal box will ever ask you: Why are you eating cereal for breakfast in the first place?

The menu may be enormous, but if you never examine who wrote it, you remain inside someone else's framework for your life. You are free in the way a hamster is free to choose which wheel to run on.

Political systems operate within this same illusion, and this is where it stops being funny. Citizens in democratic nations choose between competing parties and platforms. The ritual of voting creates a genuine feeling of participation.

But when the range of „acceptable" policy positions is quietly defined by donors and media gatekeepers rather than by citizens themselves, the freedom to choose starts looking more like a management technique than genuine self-determination.

This does not require a conspiracy. It only requires a system that has evolved to protect its own continuation, which is what all systems do.

Shadow work for a nation must begin with an honest examination of these invisible constraints. What assumptions does a society hold so deeply that questioning them feels not just wrong but unthinkable? What power dynamics are so woven into the culture that pointing them out makes you sound crazy?

Every society has these invisible walls. The work begins when you start walking into them.

The Reactive Machine

The most practical definition of freedom is the ability to choose your response rather than react automatically. An individual who can pause between stimulus and response possesses a freedom that no government can grant and no tyrant can take away. A society with this capacity could face crises with something resembling wisdom rather than sleepwalking through the same catastrophic sequences that have destroyed civilizations since the Bronze Age.

But that is not what societies typically do.

In the summer of 1914, the assassination of Archduke Franz Ferdinand triggered a chain of events that reads, in retrospect, like a script no one had the power to deviate from. Austria-Hungary issued an ultimatum. Russia mobilized. Germany activated its war plans. France followed. Britain entered because of a treaty obligation most of its citizens had never heard of. Within weeks, Europe was locked into a war that would kill 20 million people, and nearly every leader involved later admitted they had not actually wanted it.

Provocation led to outrage. Outrage led to retaliation. Retaliation led to escalation. The societies involved believed they were making free choices at every step. They were following ancient scripts written by unprocessed trauma and inherited patterns of dominance running on autopilot for centuries.

The terrifying part is not that this happened in 1914. The terrifying part is that the same sequence is recognizable in conflicts happening right now, as you read this sentence. The technology changes. The uniforms change. The script does not.

A free society would interrupt these patterns. It would recognize when old wounds are being triggered and choose a different response. No society in history has fully achieved this. But some have come closer than others, and the difference is not genetic or cultural. It is a difference in awareness.

The Price of Waking Up

True freedom cannot be separated from responsibility. They arrive as a package deal, and most people want to return the second item.

A society that wants real freedom must be willing to look at its own history without flinching, to own its current dysfunctions without blaming them entirely on external enemies, and to take responsibility for its future without waiting for a savior.

This is where many liberation movements stumble. Post-colonial nations that rightly fought for independence sometimes discover, decades later, that they have replicated the very hierarchies they overthrew. The Democratic Republic of the Congo gained independence from Belgium in 1960 after nearly a century of brutal colonial exploitation. What followed was not freedom but a series of authoritarian regimes that mirrored the extractive logic of the colonial system itself. The external oppressor was removed. The internalized pattern of oppression continued.

This is not a failure unique to any one nation. It is a universal tendency. We fight for freedom from the thing that controls us while remaining blind to how deeply we have absorbed its methods. The revolutionary who becomes a dictator. The nation that overthrows tyranny and rebuilds it under a different flag.

The most profound freedom comes from taking responsibility for your own unconscious patterns. When a society can honestly examine how its victim mentality generates new victimization, how its fear manufactures the very threats it fears, how its obsessive pursuit of security produces the exact insecurity it was trying to escape, it begins to access a power that no military budget can provide: the power to actually change.

Freedom understood this way becomes the necessary foundation for all shadow work. You cannot examine what you refuse to see, and you cannot see what you are unconsciously merged with. A society convinced it is already free has no reason to look deeper. Why would it? Everything is fine. The dashboard lights are all green. Never mind the smoke coming from under the hood.

Recognition typically arrives through crisis. When a nation's usual strategies stop working, when the gap between official narrative and lived reality becomes too wide to bridge with rhetoric, the trance of unconscious functioning breaks. Crisis does not guarantee awakening. But it creates the opening.

The question is whether a society has the prerequisites to walk through that opening: the willingness to question assumptions that feel sacred, the courage to face truths that are genuinely painful, the humility to admit the story you have been telling about yourself might be wrong, and the discipline to keep doing this work when the initial crisis fades and the temptation to fall back asleep returns.

Freedom is not a destination you arrive at and defend with a flag. It is a practice. A daily, unglamorous, sometimes infuriating practice that requires choosing consciousness over comfort, over and over again. A free society is not one that has solved all its problems. It is one that meets each problem with open eyes rather than closed fists.

Any system that demands the permanent sacrifice of freedom in exchange for other benefits, no matter how eloquently it justifies itself, has chosen a slow death over the difficult work of being alive. History is littered with the remains of civilizations that made that trade and called it wisdom.

The path of *shadow work for a nation* begins here. With the uncomfortable admission that we are not as free as our anthems claim. With the willingness to look at what runs beneath the surface. With the understanding that genuine freedom is both what makes this work possible and what this work ultimately produces.

We start by telling the truth about where we actually stand. Everything else follows from that.

Fear

In the weeks after September 11th, 2001, Americans surrendered civil liberties their ancestors had fought wars to protect. The Patriot Act sailed through Congress with minimal debate. Torture became a policy discussion rather than a moral impossibility. Entire populations accepted surveillance that would have sparked revolution a decade earlier. Looking back, many people struggle to explain why they supported measures they now find abhorrent.

Fear was making the decisions. Not as a minor contributing factor. Fear was running the entire operation.

Most of what we call rational decision-making is fear in disguise. It doesn't show up wearing a nametag. It arrives dressed as prudence, common sense, patriotism, tradition, or moral conviction, and it sits at the head of the table like it owns the place. When fear starts calling the shots at a collective level, entire nations can make decisions that destroy the very things they were trying to protect.

Before any society can do meaningful shadow work, it has to get honest about how fear controls behavior. Not the fear people admit to, but the fear they dress up as something else.

The fear that masquerades as strength, wisdom, or virtue while quietly steering the ship toward the iceberg.

The Mechanics of Collective Hijacking

Neuroscientist Joseph LeDoux's research revealed an uncomfortable fact about who's actually in charge: the amygdala, our brain's alarm system, can trigger a fear response before our conscious mind has even registered what's happening. The brain's fast subcortical pathway processes threat signals in roughly 100 milliseconds, well before the slower cortical route, the one responsible for actual thinking, catches up around 500 milliseconds later.

This isn't a neurological glitch. It's an evolutionary survival strategy. When you hear a rustling bush, you don't want to stop and write a risk assessment. You want to react first and analyze later. The problem is that this same lightning-fast response, the one that saved our ancestors from tigers, now gets triggered by tax policy, cultural change, and people who vote differently. The amygdala cannot tell the difference between a predator and a parliamentary procedure. It treats them both like existential threats.

Our nervous systems evolved to outrun lions. Instead we're using them to evaluate cable news. Evolution did not anticipate this use case.

Daniel Goleman coined the term „amygdala hijack" to describe what happens when this ancient alarm system takes over modern decision-making. Suddenly, intelligent people start making choices that seem completely irrational to outside observers. They're not stupid. They're scared. And scared brains don't think clearly. At a national scale, mass amygdala hijack can drive entire populations into decisions that historians later struggle to explain. The answer is almost always the same: fear, dressed up as patriotism, security, or moral righteousness.

The hijacking gets considerably more powerful when combined with another cognitive vulnerability. Psychologists Amos Tversky and Daniel Kahneman discovered that people judge the likelihood of events based on how easily they can remember examples, a pattern they called the „availability heuristic." Vivid, recent, or heavily reported events feel more probable than they actually are. Quiet, statistical dangers feel remote even when they're far more likely to kill you.

Consider what this means for political life. A shark attack makes national news. Heart disease, which kills roughly 650,000 Americans every year, does not. Terrorism generates months of coverage. Car accidents, which kill around 40,000 Americans annually, are reported locally and forgotten by Tuesday. Rare but dramatic events crowd out accurate risk perception, and politicians who understand this dynamic can manufacture fear about almost anything by controlling what gets attention and what doesn't. The availability heuristic isn't just a cognitive quirk. It's a security vulnerability that sophisticated actors exploit deliberately.

Once fear gets manufactured and amplified, it doesn't just change what people are afraid of. It changes who they're willing to become. Stanley Milgram's obedience experiments revealed this in disturbing detail: participants weren't simply following orders when they administered what they believed were painful electric shocks to strangers. They were terrified of challenging authority. The fear of social rejection, professional consequences, or being seen as difficult overrode their moral concerns about hurting another person.

When Milgram varied his experiments, obedience dropped dramatically when the authority figure wasn't physically present, when the victim was in the same room, or when other participants refused to comply. These variations demonstrate that people's compliance wasn't driven by fear of the authority figure's power to punish. It was social fear, the fear of standing alone, the fear of being different from everyone else in the room.

The implications extend well beyond laboratory settings. People don't necessarily support harmful policies because they think they're good ideas. They support them because they're afraid of the social consequences of saying otherwise. The fear of being ostracized, labeled, or excluded from the group becomes more powerful than individual moral judgment. History's great enthusiasms for terrible ideas were never purely ideological. They were significantly social. Most people simply didn't want to be the one who raised their hand.

The Two Fears Nobody Admits To

Every mechanism described above, amygdala hijacks, conditioned fears, obedience to authority, social conformity, is ultimately a defense against the same thing. The fear underneath all other fears. Death.

Ernest Becker's landmark work „The Denial of Death" argued that human civilization is essentially one enormous distraction from mortality. Psychologists Sheldon Solomon, Jeff Greenberg, and Tom Pyszczynski spent decades testing this claim through what became Terror Management Theory. Their experiments consistently showed that when people were reminded of their own mortality, even briefly and subconsciously, they became more aggressive toward those who challenged their worldview, more rigidly committed to cultural beliefs, and more hostile to outsiders.

In one representative study, participants who had written about their own death showed measurably increased prejudice and conformity to group norms compared to those who had written about a neutral topic like dental pain. The reminder of death didn't make people more philosophical. It made them more tribal.

The implications for societies in crisis are direct. Every terrorist attack, pandemic, economic collapse, or natural disaster activates collective death anxiety at scale. People don't consciously think, „I'm afraid of dying, so I'm going to support authoritarian policies." They think, „We need strong leadership to protect our way of life." The conscious thought is genuine. The engine running underneath it is death anxiety.

Death anxiety is basically humanity's master override switch. Remind people they're mortal, and they'll hand power to almost anyone who promises safety. It's the Konami cheat code for authoritarianism, and it's been entered successfully in every century on record.

But death anxiety reveals an even stranger paradox: sometimes the thing people fear most isn't death itself, but the freedom that comes with fully living. Psychologist Erich Fromm's analysis of fascism identified something counterintuitive about why people voluntarily surrender liberty. Freedom requires making choices, owning the consequences, and tolerating uncertainty without anyone to blame. For many people, that burden becomes genuinely unbearable. They seek escape into authoritarianism, fundamentalism, or simple conformity, not because they were forced, but because certainty, even someone else's certainty, feels better than the responsibility of their own.

Fromm called this „escape from freedom." People rarely announce it. Instead they say, „We need strong leadership," or „Traditional values are under attack," or „You can't trust ordinary people to make good decisions." Underneath, much of this is fear of the psychological weight that real freedom requires. Any society attempting serious shadow work needs to reckon with this honestly. The process of examining collective shadows demands exactly the kind of tolerance for uncertainty and responsibility that many people are fleeing.

Resistance to shadow work isn't always ideological disagreement. Sometimes it's terror of the process itself.

The Wiring Beneath the Alarm

The question isn't whether societies develop irrational fears. The question is how those fears get installed in the first place, and why they persist across generations long after the original threat has disappeared.

John Watson's infamous Little Albert experiment, conducted in 1920 and now serving as a textbook example of how not to treat research subjects, demonstrated how efficiently fear can be manufactured from scratch. Watson took an infant who showed no fear of white rats and repeatedly paired the rat with a sudden, loud noise. The result was predictable and horrifying: the child became terrified not just of rats, but of anything white and furry. Rabbits. Dogs. A Santa Claus beard.

One child. One experimenter. A few weeks of conditioning. What Watson demonstrated, perhaps without fully grasping the implications, was a blueprint for manufacturing collective terror at industrial scale. Most national fears aren't based on direct experience or rational risk assessment. They are conditioned responses built by pairing neutral things with frightening images or narratives, repeated often enough, across enough channels, to make the association feel like common sense. Modern media conducts Little Albert experiments on entire populations every single day. Pair a particular group with threatening imagery consistently enough, and millions of people develop visceral fear responses toward things they've never directly encountered, based entirely on learned association.

Conditioned fears are one layer. Beneath them sits something harder to dislodge: collective trauma. Trauma researcher Bessel van der Kolk's work on how traumatic experience gets encoded in the body explains why certain fears persist not just within individuals but across generations. Traumatic events don't create memories in the ordinary sense. They create ongoing physiological responses that can be triggered by anything resembling the original threat, even remotely, even symbolically.

Nations that have survived invasion, genocide, famine, or economic catastrophe often develop hypervigilant cultural nervous systems. The original events pass. The fear response remains, transmitted through family stories, institutional memory, cultural narratives, and sometimes, as emerging epigenetic research suggests, through biology itself. A society shaped by historical trauma may react with wildly disproportionate fear to situations that vaguely resemble what happened generations ago, even when the present circumstances are entirely different. Acknowledging this pattern isn't weakness. It's the beginning of understanding why certain political buttons produce such reliable results on certain populations, and who has learned to press them.

But conditioning and trauma explain how fear gets installed, not what it's actually pointing at. Strip away the amygdala hijacks, the conditioned associations, the death anxiety, the generational trauma, and something more fundamental appears. At the deepest level, most fears are fears of encountering our own shadow material. Not other people. Not foreign threats. The parts of ourselves we refuse to acknowledge: the capacity for selfishness, violence, irrationality, and failure that every human being carries and most prefer not to examine.

Carl Jung put it plainly: „Everything that irritates us about others can lead us to an understanding of ourselves." The things that trigger the strongest collective fear responses tend to be projections of disowned shadow material. A nation obsessed with external enemies may be unwilling to look at its own history of aggression. A society panicking about moral decay may be avoiding its own ethical compromises. A culture terrified of economic threats from outsiders may be evading responsibility for its own unsustainable practices. The outward fear is real. The target is wrong.

None of this means fear is the enemy. It carries real information. The problem isn't the signal; it's that most people have never learned to read it. A conditioned response to a fifty-year-old threat feels identical to a response to a present danger. An anxiety rooted in collective trauma feels like clear-eyed realism. Shadow material projected onto an outgroup feels like justified concern. From the inside, fear always feels like the truth.

Societies can develop the capacity to examine that feeling rather than just obey it, but only if they build that capacity before the next crisis arrives. Because fear, unlike most political problems, doesn't wait for a convenient moment. It shows up in the emergency, when everyone is least equipped to examine it, and demands an answer right now.

That's why shadow work on fear has to happen before the alarm sounds. Once the amygdala is running the country, the window for reflection closes fast.

Control

In 2001, a few thousand people watched the
Twin Towers fall in person. Within hours, three
hundred million Americans experienced the
same existential terror through their screens.
Within weeks, the Patriot Act was drafted.
Within months, it was law. Surveillance
programs that would have provoked mass
outrage on September 10th became accepted as
necessary on September 12th. And it wasn't just
America. The UK passed the Anti-Terrorism
Act. France expanded its surveillance powers.
Australia rushed through new intelligence
legislation. Every Western democracy used the
same event to justify the same expansion of
state control, often copying each other's
homework. The fear was real. The buildings
were real. But the leap from „we were attacked"
to „therefore the government needs to read
your emails, monitor your calls, and track your
movements" was not logic. It was the oldest
trick in the book of human control, dressed up
in new technology.

The irony of politics is that the people most
desperate to tell you how to live your life often
can't figure out how to live their own. Those
who cannot manage their own emotions,
impulses, and behaviors become obsessed with
managing everyone else's. It's like hiring an

alcoholic as a bartender because they
„understand the business.“

This pattern sits at the heart of virtually all
political activity: the drive to control. Whether
disguised as concern for public safety, economic
stability, national security, or social justice, the
impulse is always the same. Control human
behavior, resources, information, and outcomes.
The suffering this causes goes far beyond
obvious tyranny. Even well-intentioned
attempts at control produce consequences that
often achieve the opposite of their stated goals.
Until societies understand why humans seek
control so desperately, political systems will
keep causing immense suffering while claiming
to prevent it.

The Roots of Control-Seeking

At the deepest level, the drive to control stems
from existential anxiety. The raw, unprocessable
fact that existence is uncertain and
uncontrollable. You will die. You don't know
when. You can't prevent it. Everything you love
will eventually be taken from you, and there is
absolutely nothing you can do about it. That is
the baseline human condition, and almost
nobody can sit with it for more than a few
seconds without reaching for something to hold
on to. Control is what most people reach for. If
I can just manage enough variables, predict

enough outcomes, lock down enough
uncertainties, maybe I can outrun the thing that
can't be outrun.

This isn't abstract philosophy. Researchers in
Terror Management Theory have demonstrated
it in laboratory settings with uncomfortable
clarity. Remind people of their own mortality,
even subtly, and watch what happens. They
become more attracted to authoritarian leaders.
More willing to surrender personal freedom for
the feeling of protection. More hostile toward
anyone who threatens their worldview. Nothing
makes people surrender freedom faster than
fear. It's humanity's cheat code: press
„terrorism" or „pandemic," receive unlimited
power.

None of this is new. Ancient rulers invoked
threats from gods, demons, or foreign enemies
to maintain control over populations. What
changed in the modern era was the
systematization of these techniques through
psychological research and military-intelligence
operations.

Project Phoenix during the Vietnam War
proved the concept at industrial scale. Officially
designed to neutralize Viet Cong infrastructure,
the program actually functioned as a laboratory
for testing how fear and the perception of
omnipresent threat could control civilian

populations. The lessons learned were not abandoned after Vietnam. They were refined. Governments don't throw away tools that work. They just find new names for them.

What emerges is a feedback loop. Leaders exploit death anxiety to gain control, then use that control to manipulate populations through manufactured or amplified threats, which generates more anxiety, which justifies more control. The COVID-19 pandemic was a stark recent example, but it represents techniques developed and refined over decades. Populations experiencing existential threat will accept almost any level of control over their movements, associations, and even medical decisions. Emergency powers granted during crises rarely get fully relinquished afterward. Each crisis permanently ratchets up state control. The Patriot Act was supposed to be temporary. Two decades later, the surveillance infrastructure it authorized has only expanded.

The Psychology of Control

But existential anxiety about death and uncertainty doesn't hit everyone the same way. How people respond to these fears depends largely on their psychological development and capacity for internal regulation.

Consider the difference between two people stuck in traffic. One sits with the frustration, maybe turns on a podcast, accepts that this is how the next thirty minutes are going to go. The other leans on the horn, tailgates, weaves between lanes, and arrives at their destination with a heart rate of 140, having saved approximately zero minutes. The second person isn't really trying to get somewhere faster. They can't tolerate the feeling of not being in control of their situation. The frantic activity is a psychological painkiller, not a transportation strategy.

Now scale that up to governance. When people cannot regulate their own emotions, thoughts, and behaviors, they experience profound anxiety and powerlessness. So they reach outward. The attempt to control external circumstances becomes a compensatory strategy to create the sense of safety and predictability that internal regulation would provide. If I cannot control my own responses to life's challenges, perhaps I can control the challenges themselves by controlling my environment and the people in it. People who can manage their own responses show less need to control others or their environment. They tolerate uncertainty, adapt to change, and allow others freedom without feeling threatened.

And it feeds on itself: the more someone tries to control external circumstances, the less they develop internal capacity, which increases their anxiety about losing control, which intensifies the drive to control even further.

The roots often trace back to childhood. Children who develop basic trust and autonomy through responsive caregiving generally develop healthy internal regulation. Those who experience unpredictable, neglectful, or controlling caregiving often fail to develop this internal capacity and spend their lives seeking external control as compensation. The controlling parent raises the controlling politician. Therapy would be cheaper than elections, but nobody's proposed that reform yet.

So far, this sounds like a universal human tendency, and to some degree it is. But not everyone who feels anxious about uncertainty decides to run for office. The connection between control-seeking and what psychologists call the Dark Triad, narcissism, psychopathy, and Machiavellianism, is where this story turns from unfortunate to dangerous. All three personality patterns seek external control as compensation for internal deficits. But they arrive there through different doors.

The narcissist seeks control to maintain a grandiose self-image and protect against the shame of underlying worthlessness. Any loss of control threatens to expose their insecurity, triggering rage. Think of the leader who surrounds themselves with yes-men, fires anyone who disagrees, and spends more energy managing their public image than managing actual policy. They don't just want power. They need it the way a drowning person needs air, because without it, they'd have to face who they actually are.

The psychopath seeks control for more instrumental reasons. Lacking empathy and viewing others primarily as objects to be used, they pursue control to maximize their ability to exploit resources and people without constraint. Expecting a psychopath to govern with compassion is like expecting a surgeon to cry during every operation. The emotional wiring simply isn't there, and no amount of job training installs it. They are particularly attracted to positions offering power over others: politics, corporate leadership, military command, and law enforcement. Not because they want to serve, but because these roles offer the richest hunting grounds.

The Machiavellian views the world primarily through the lens of power dynamics and strategic advantage, pursuing control systematically, viewing human relationships as opportunities for manipulation and dominance. They're the ones who keep a mental spreadsheet of every favor they've done and every weakness they've observed, not out of malice but out of habit. Where the narcissist needs to be admired and the psychopath needs to exploit, the Machiavellian simply needs to win. The game itself is the point.

None of this is said to demonize these individuals. That would be its own form of shadow projection. The narcissist clinging to power is drowning in shame they never learned to process. The psychopath navigating the world without empathy didn't choose that wiring. The Machiavellian mapping every relationship for advantage is trapped in a game they can't stop playing. They are not monsters. They are damaged people in positions that amplify their damage. Understanding this matters, because the goal of shadow work isn't to find new villains. It's to see clearly.

The tragedy is that systems designed to serve collective welfare systematically select for these exact personality types. Political scientists call it adverse selection. Those who most desire political power are often precisely those who should never have it, while those who would use power wisely usually have little interest in seeking it. We've designed a system where the job interview for „leader of millions" primarily tests for narcissism, lying ability, and willingness to betray others. Then we act surprised when it doesn't work out well. The skills required to obtain power differ dramatically from the wisdom required to use it well, and the system selects for the former while remaining indifferent to the latter.

The Illusion and the Addiction

Why does the drive to control persist even when it consistently fails to achieve its stated goals? Two mechanisms lock it in place: cognitive illusion and neurological addiction.

Humans consistently overestimate their ability to control events and outcomes. This cognitive bias becomes particularly dangerous when combined with political power. Leaders believe they can control complex systems like economies, societies, and cultures, systems that are actually far too complex for any individual or institution to control. Leaders attempting to control society are like people trying to control the weather by passing laws about it. Just because you wrote it down doesn't mean reality cares.

Watch how the illusion plays out in policy. A government implements rent control to make housing affordable, and landlords stop maintaining properties or convert them to condos, reducing the supply. So the government adds regulations to prevent conversions, which drives developers out of the market entirely, which creates a housing shortage, which drives up prices on remaining units. Each intervention creates new problems that demand new interventions. At no point does anyone step back and ask whether the entire approach is flawed from the start.

Economist Friedrich Hayek identified the core issue decades ago with his work on the knowledge problem in central planning. Complex social systems involve millions of people making countless decisions based on local knowledge that no central authority can possibly possess. Attempts to control these systems inevitably destroy the information flows and adaptive processes that make them function. Yet the drive persists despite repeated failure because it serves psychological needs, not practical goals. Admitting the limits of control would mean confronting the raw uncertainty of life, and that is intolerable for those who seek control precisely because they cannot tolerate uncertainty.

The second mechanism is even more insidious: control is addictive. Neuroimaging studies show that exercising control over others activates the same brain reward systems involved in substance addiction. The dopamine hit from making a decision that affects thousands of people, from watching others comply with your directives, from feeling that you sit at the center of something important, this is a drug. And like all drugs, it requires increasing doses. The more someone experiences controlling others, the more their brain adapts to seeking that stimulus. This neurological addiction to power helps explain why leaders who achieve positions of control rarely voluntarily relinquish them. You don't see many politicians retiring because they feel they've done enough. You see them clinging to power until it's pried from their hands, or until their bodies give out.

The addiction doesn't stop with individual leaders. Bureaucracies become addicted to controlling their domains and resist any reduction in their authority. Populations can become addicted to the illusory safety of being controlled, losing their capacity for self-direction. The codependency between controllers and controlled becomes entrenched over time, a toxic relationship at civilizational scale where neither side can imagine life without the other.

Modern Control Mechanisms

These psychological patterns and neurological rewards don't exist in a vacuum. They manifest through institutional structures and technological systems that give control-seekers power over populations that previous generations couldn't have imagined. What's different about the modern era isn't the desire to control. That's as old as civilization. What's different is the toolkit.

Modern states maintain vast bodies of laws and regulations governing nearly every aspect of human behavior. The sheer volume of rules creates a situation where virtually everyone is technically in violation of something at any given moment, giving authorities discretionary power to selectively enforce rules against chosen targets. Modern governments have so many laws that everyone is a criminal; they just haven't decided to enforce them on you yet. It's less „rule of law" and more „law as a loaded gun pointed at everyone." Harvey Silverglate estimated that the average American unknowingly commits three felonies a day. That's not a justice system. That's a control system with a legal costume.

Financial control operates more quietly but often more effectively. Control over money creation, interest rates, taxation, and financial regulations gives political and economic institutions enormous power to shape behavior without explicit coercion. But the development of Central Bank Digital Currencies represents a quantum leap in these capabilities. Unlike physical cash, which allows anonymous transactions, CBDCs would give central authorities complete visibility into every financial transaction every citizen makes. Real-time monitoring, instant taxation, the ability to freeze assets without requiring cooperation from banks or intermediaries.

Combined with digital identity systems, governments could program money to expire if not spent within certain timeframes, restrict purchases of disfavored goods, or link spending capacity to social credit scores. Your money, their rules. Proponents argue these systems would reduce crime and increase efficiency. Of course they do. Every surveillance system in history was sold as a convenience feature. The lock on the cage is always marketed as a safety feature.

Information control has undergone its own revolution. Modern media systems, social media platforms, and information technology have created capabilities for controlling what information reaches populations that would have been unimaginable fifty years ago. A story that trends on social media for six hours shapes public opinion more than a correction published three days later. The ability to control narratives, suppress certain voices, and amplify others may be the most potent form of modern control, because people who don't know they're being controlled don't resist. You can't fight a cage you've been told is a meadow.

Emerging surveillance technologies push the boundaries further. Cameras, sensors, and data collection infrastructure monitor populations continuously. Predictive algorithms identify potential threats before they occur. Digital identity systems create the possibility of tracking every location visited, every transaction made, every service accessed. Countries implementing these systems promote them as convenient solutions. But convenience and control use the same infrastructure. Once populations depend on digital IDs for essential services, access becomes leverage. Comply or be disconnected.

Artificial intelligence will amplify all of these capabilities. AI can process surveillance data at scales impossible for human analysts, predict individual behavior with increasing accuracy, and automate enforcement without requiring human judgment. The totalitarian regimes of the twentieth century were limited by the number of informants they could recruit. AI has no such bottleneck.

And then there's the subtlest mechanism of all: psychological control. Decades of research into human psychology have handed governments a playbook for manipulating behavior through fear, social pressure, and carefully designed choice architectures. Behavioral economics and nudge theory have been explicitly adopted by governments to shape behavior while maintaining the illusion of free choice. You think you're deciding. But the menu was designed by someone who already knows which option you'll pick.

The Cost and the Alternative

These control mechanisms, built on existential anxiety and psychological deficits, maintained through illusion and addiction, and deployed through increasingly powerful technology, exact an enormous toll on human flourishing.

The obvious costs are oppression and violence. But the subtler damage may run deeper. When people know they're being watched and managed, something in them shuts down. They stop saying what they think. They stop making things. They learn to perform compliance rather than develop real character, and after long enough, the performance becomes all that's left.

The atmosphere turns toxic even when nobody is being beaten or imprisoned. Anyone who has worked in a micromanaged office knows the feeling, that slow death of initiative where you stop thinking for yourself because every decision gets overridden anyway. Now imagine that dynamic applied to an entire society.

Psychologists have identified three core needs for human flourishing: autonomy, competence, and relatedness. Control systems systematically undermine all three. People living under heavy control become demoralized, passive, and psychologically damaged even when their material needs are met. This is why citizens of wealthy authoritarian states often report lower life satisfaction than citizens of poorer but freer ones. The cage can be gilded and still be a cage.

Attempts to control complex systems also produce chain-reaction failures that create suffering on their own. Every form of control generates its own shadow: economic controls produce shortages, social controls produce underground resistance, information control produces a population too deluded to solve real problems. The Soviet Union didn't collapse because it lacked resources. It collapsed because decades of centralized control had destroyed the feedback mechanisms that allow complex systems to adapt and self-correct. They had five-year plans for everything except what actually happened.

But the worst damage is the quietest: control-seeking prevents the development of individual responsibility and collective wisdom. When people are controlled, they never develop their own capacity for self-regulation. They remain psychologically dependent on external authority, unable to function autonomously. This creates societies of infantilized adults who need to be told what to do because they never developed their own internal compass. And that dependency, in turn, justifies more control. The controllers point to the helplessness they created as proof that control is necessary.

So what replaces it? The alternative to control is not chaos or the absence of structure. It's freedom built on internal regulation and voluntary cooperation.

The human immune system offers an instructive parallel. You don't strengthen it by keeping the body in a sterile environment. You strengthen it through exposure, challenge, and recovery. A population raised in sterile conditions becomes unable to fight off the simplest infection. The same holds for societies. Order can emerge from freedom when individuals develop sufficient internal regulation to govern their own behavior consciously. This doesn't mean

everyone always makes perfect choices. It means
people can make choices, learn from
consequences, and adjust without requiring
external control.

Which demands a different question at the
center of governance. Instead of „how can we
control people to behave correctly?" the
question becomes „how can we support people
in developing their own capacity for conscious
choice and self-regulation?" The focus shifts
from external control to internal development,
from compliance to consciousness, from force
to freedom. How a society answers this question
reveals everything about its actual values,
regardless of what its constitution says.

For individuals, breaking free from control
patterns means confronting the anxiety that
drives control-seeking, processing the trauma
that created it, and developing the emotional
regulation capacity that makes external control
unnecessary. For societies, it means recognizing
how political systems select for and empower
control-seekers, and building institutions that
facilitate voluntary cooperation rather than
enforce compliance. How exactly such systems
might work is a question we'll explore in detail
later in this book. For now, the essential insight
is that the obstacle isn't a lack of better systems.

It's a lack of people developed enough to sustain them.

The path beyond control-based politics leads through consciousness rather than new control mechanisms. Until enough individuals develop internal regulation capacity, societies will continue creating systems that empower controllers to dominate the controlled. Without this understanding, all political reform merely rearranges deck chairs on the Titanic. The ship is still sinking. The captain is still a psychopath. And the passengers are still calling it democracy.

Shame and Guilt

Few emotions are as destructive to collective consciousness as shame and guilt. The difference between them determines everything. Guilt says, „I did something bad" and focuses on behavior that can be changed. Shame says, „I am bad" and attacks identity itself. One opens the door to transformation; the other slams it shut.

Yet societies routinely conflate the two. They wield shame as a tool for control while calling it accountability. They avoid necessary guilt by denying responsibility entirely. Understanding this distinction is crucial for recognizing how collective shame and guilt operate.

Shame operates differently from other emotions. Researcher Brené Brown identifies it as perhaps the most primitive and powerful emotion humans experience. Shame doesn't critique what you did; it attacks who you are. It creates the feeling of being fundamentally flawed, unworthy of love and belonging. At the individual level, this distinction matters enormously. At the collective level, it becomes catastrophic.

When societies experience events that threaten their self-image or violate their stated values, the resulting shame triggers elaborate defense mechanisms. Denial. Rationalization. Projection of blame onto others. Overcompensation through aggressive assertions of superiority. These defensive patterns become so automatic, so deeply embedded in national consciousness, that populations cannot recognize them as defenses.

The entanglement of shame and guilt compounds the problem. Victims of collective harm often experience shame about the harm done to them. Perpetrators experience guilt they cannot process without confronting shame about who they've become. The emotions that might motivate accountability instead activate protective responses that prevent it.

Manifestation of Shame and Guilt

Pearl Harbor represents a defining trauma for the United States: a moment of vulnerability that shattered the nation's sense of invincibility. The trauma doesn't stem solely from the attack itself but from what it revealed: that American power and security were illusions that could be shattered in a morning. This has contributed to patterns of hypervigilance, military overextension, and difficulty tolerating any perception of weakness that characterize American foreign policy decades later.

The way America processes this trauma reveals a troubling pattern about how victor and vanquished nations handle wartime shame differently. Both the United States and Japan committed massive civilian atrocities during World War II. Japan's wartime behavior included widespread massacres, sexual enslavement, and human experimentation. The United States killed hundreds of thousands of civilians through atomic bombings and firebombing campaigns targeting residential areas, along with the ethnic internment of Japanese-Americans.

Yet the shame burden falls almost entirely on Japan. Young Japanese carry psychological weight for their grandparents' crimes and face international pressure to apologize. Meanwhile, American consciousness treats wartime actions as regrettable necessities. Pearl Harbor becomes the defining trauma that justifies everything that followed. The atomic bombings are taught as strategic decisions that „saved lives." The firebombing campaigns barely register in American historical consciousness.

Winners write history and avoid the shame that might otherwise accompany killing hundreds of thousands of civilians. Losers carry shame for their crimes while also absorbing shame for losing themselves, creating a double burden that persists across generations. This asymmetry doesn't reflect moral truth; it reflects power's ability to determine which truths get buried and which get broadcast.

This unequal distribution of shame creates dangerous secondary effects. One of the most catastrophic dynamics is shame's tendency to transform into rage. Psychologist Helen Block Lewis documented how shame that cannot be acknowledged or processed often converts into anger directed outward. At the collective level, this dynamic becomes devastating. Nations experiencing shame about failures or moral violations often redirect that shame into aggressive assertion, scapegoating, or violence toward others.

Germany's path from the shame and humiliation of World War I defeat and the Treaty of Versailles to the aggressive nationalism of the Nazi period illustrates this dynamic. Rather than processing the shame of defeat, German society embraced narratives that externalized blame, asserted superiority, and eventually pursued violent revenge. The shame that couldn't be faced became rage that destroyed millions.

It's the geopolitical version of flipping the table when you're losing at board games, except with significantly higher body counts. This pattern repeats across contexts: nations that cannot process shame about their history often become the most aggressive and dangerous.

The opposite pattern proves equally destructive. While shame tends to produce defensive aggression, unprocessed guilt can create moral paralysis that prevents effective action. When nations become overwhelmed by guilt about historical crimes, the resulting paralysis can perpetuate harm by preventing the decisive action needed for change.

This paralysis extends beyond a nation's relationship to its own past. Historical guilt can prevent nations from even acknowledging injustices committed by others, particularly when those others were victims of the nation's historical crimes. The guilt becomes so overwhelming that it triggers complete denial. Nations refuse to see what is happening in front of them, actively rejecting evidence and testimony that contradicts the narrative they need to maintain. The same psychological mechanisms that once enabled denial of one's own crimes now enable denial of crimes committed by those one feels historical obligation to protect. What begins as necessary accountability for past atrocities evolves into a dangerous inability to recognize present ones.

When populations do acknowledge problems, the paralysis manifests differently: endless discussion, debate, and symbolic gestures that substitute for action requiring risk or genuine transformation. Research by social psychologist Michael Wenzel on collective guilt shows how people resist feeling guilty because they unconsciously understand that guilt requires action. Nations simultaneously acknowledge historical wrongs while doing nothing substantive to address ongoing consequences, whether their own or those committed by others they feel bound to protect. The guilt that should motivate moral clarity instead produces moral blindness.

The Cultural Cost and Benefit

Nations trapped in protective postures around historical shame exhibit cultural rigidity, hypersensitivity to criticism, and difficulty with self-reflection. The need to maintain ego-protective narratives limits artistic expression, academic inquiry, and public discourse. Conversely, nations that successfully process historical shame often experience a cultural renaissance. When nations no longer need to suppress uncomfortable truths, creativity flourishes in the space that denial once occupied.

Ireland's transformation demonstrates this dynamic powerfully. For generations, Irish society maintained defensive silence around systematic abuses perpetrated by Catholic Church institutions. Unwed mothers imprisoned in Magdalene Laundries. Children brutalized in industrial schools. Widespread clergy sexual abuse was systematically covered up.

The shame surrounding these abuses locked Irish society in patterns of denial and cultural constraint. The Catholic Church's dominance meant that vast areas of life, art, and thought remained off-limits. Artists who challenged protective narratives faced censorship or exile.

Essentially, Ireland spent decades pretending terrible things didn't happen, while simultaneously organizing its entire culture around ensuring that nobody discussed the horrible things that didn't happen. It's exhausting just describing it.

Beginning in the 1990s and accelerating through the 2000s, Ireland began confronting these historical abuses through investigations and public inquiries. Survivors began speaking publicly. The country faced what it had spent generations avoiding.

This confrontation correlated with remarkable cultural transformation. Irish literature, music, film, and arts experienced a flowering that made Ireland a cultural force far beyond its small population. Irish society became more open, questioning, creative. What had been suppressed could now be explored. Artists, writers, and filmmakers confronted truths that previous generations had been forced to ignore. Young Irish people could distinguish themselves from their parents' generation precisely because the shame had been acknowledged rather than denied.

Yet most nations follow different patterns. Watch how societies typically attempt to process collective shame and guilt: elaborate truth and reconciliation processes that acknowledge historical wrongs while meticulously avoiding any action requiring sacrifice. Oscillation between defensive denial and performative guilt, generating endless discussion that substitutes for meaningful change. The pattern reveals itself consistently across contexts. Populations acknowledge historical wrongs while simultaneously resisting the discomfort necessary to address ongoing consequences. They want the relief of acknowledgment without the cost of transformation.

From a shadow work perspective, this resistance makes sense. Collective shame and guilt represent some of the most deeply buried material societies carry. The defenses against these emotions operate so automatically that entire populations cannot see them. Educational systems teach sanitized histories. Media narratives reinforce comfortable myths. Cultural practices ensure certain truths remain unspoken.

Bringing this material into consciousness requires tremendous courage. It means facing truths about national history and current behavior that threaten cherished identities. It means recognizing that the stories societies tell themselves about who they are often serve primarily to avoid shame and guilt about who they've been and what they continue to do.

This recognition alone doesn't resolve anything. But without it, nations remain locked in the same protective cycles that created the shame and guilt in the first place. The cycle perpetuates itself: unacknowledged shame generates rage or paralysis, which generates behavior that should produce shame, which requires even more elaborate denials. Recognition alone doesn't break this pattern. But without it, nations remain trapped in cycles they cannot even see, let alone escape.

Projection

In the 1930s, Joseph Stalin launched the Great Purge to eliminate „enemies of the people" who were supposedly conspiring to destroy the Soviet Union from within. He accused his victims of plotting coups, conspiring with foreign powers, and betraying the revolution. Confessions were extracted through torture. Show trials were staged. Millions were executed or sent to gulags.

Every charge Stalin leveled at his victims described exactly what he himself was doing. He saw conspiracy, betrayal, and authoritarianism everywhere except in his own actions. The projection was so complete that he seemed genuinely convinced of their guilt. In his mind, he remained the revolution's vigilant defender. The traitor was always someone else.

If you want to understand what someone refuses to acknowledge about themselves, pay attention to what they most loudly condemn in others.

Consider the anti-corruption crusader who builds their career exposing graft and abuse of power, only to be revealed taking bribes themselves. They weren't simply lying. They genuinely believed in their mission, felt righteous fury at corruption, and convinced themselves their own compromises didn't count. They were so terrified of recognizing this quality in themselves that they had to constantly identify and attack it in others. The psychological mechanism behind this is called projection, and it's one of the most common and destructive patterns in human psychology.

At the national level, projection creates the psychological foundation for dividing the world into „us" — the good, moral, civilized — and „them" — the evil, immoral, barbaric. Nations deny their own shadow by seeing it exclusively in designated enemy groups. The nation that projects its own aggression becomes convinced it's acting defensively. The society that projects its own intolerance becomes certain that it represents enlightenment and progress. The culture that projects its own cruelty can commit atrocities while maintaining absolute certainty about its own virtue.

The Cheapest Psychology

Carl Jung was among the first to explore projection as a psychological mechanism systematically. He recognized that humans have a limited capacity to face their own darkness directly. When certain qualities, impulses, or aspects of ourselves become intolerable to acknowledge, the psyche employs projection as a protective mechanism. These unacceptable aspects get „projected" outward, where they can be safely condemned in others without threatening our self-image.

The process operates largely unconsciously. We don't consciously decide to project; it happens automatically whenever we encounter something in ourselves that conflicts with our self-concept. If I believe I'm a kind person but feel intense anger, I might project that anger onto others, seeing them as hostile and aggressive while remaining blind to my own rage. It's psychologically cheaper to see others as bad than to recognize badness in ourselves.

Projection becomes most visible in our strongest reactions. The emotional intensity reveals it more reliably than the content of our criticism. When someone's behavior triggers rage disproportionate to its actual impact, when you find yourself obsessing about their flaws or feeling compelled to tell others about their failures, you're not just observing their behavior. You're confronting something in yourself that your self-concept won't allow you to acknowledge directly.

The intensity reveals the projection. Mild critique comes from objective observation. Visceral fury comes from confronting what we've denied in ourselves.

The same mechanism operates at the collective level, where entire societies project their shadows onto designated enemies, creating what Jung called the „collective shadow." The United States built a national identity around freedom, democracy, and human rights. Yet slavery, genocide of indigenous peoples, imperial adventures, and systematic inequality all contradict this self-image. These become shadow material that must be denied or projected. That shadow often gets attributed to designated enemies who are accused of the very things America refuses to acknowledge about itself: imperialism, lack of freedom, oppression of minorities, disregard for human rights.

Every accusation contains a confession.

And this isn't uniquely American. Nations built on ideals of peace project their violence onto others. Societies claiming moral superiority project their ethical compromises onto designated inferiors. The shadow material doesn't disappear through projection. It simply becomes invisible to the projecting society while remaining painfully obvious to everyone else.

Projection in Action

Think about the last time you scrolled through social media and felt that surge of righteous anger. Someone posted something stupid, cruel, and ignorant. You felt compelled to respond, to correct, to condemn. The intensity of your reaction felt justified. They were wrong. Obviously wrong. Harmfully wrong.

Now ask yourself: what were they wrong about?

If it was factual error, your response would have been a measured correction. But if it triggered fury, contempt, or that particular flavor of disgust that makes you want to share the post with others so they can witness the wrongness together, something else is happening. You're not responding to what they said. You're responding to what they represent. And what they represent, more often than not, is something you cannot tolerate seeing in yourself.

Scale that social media moment to an entire society, and you begin to see how nations manufacture enemies. Select a group or nation, attribute to them precisely what your society cannot acknowledge in itself, then treat those projections as objective reality. The enemy becomes a mirror no one wants to look at.

Three reinforcing patterns drive this process.

The most obvious is enemy construction. A nation struggling with its own violent history doesn't acknowledge that struggle. Instead, it identifies other nations as uniquely violent, barbaric, and uncivilized. The society can then attack its own disowned brutality without recognizing it as its own. The more violent the projecting nation becomes in opposing the „violent" enemy, the more the projection intensifies. The attacked nation's defensive violence then confirms the projection, creating a self-fulfilling prophecy.

Enemy construction inevitably leads to moral splitting. The world divides into absolute good and absolute bad with no nuance between. Evidence of problems within the projecting society gets dismissed as minor imperfections or blamed on external corruption. Meanwhile, identical behaviors get interpreted through opposite lenses depending on who performs them. When we surveil, it's security. When they surveil, it's tyranny. When we intervene militarily, it's liberation. When they intervene, it's aggression. The same action becomes proof of virtue or villainy depending solely on who performs it.

Once the enemy is constructed and the moral lines are drawn, scapegoating completes the cycle. When societies face problems they cannot solve or refuse to acknowledge, those problems get blamed on the designated enemy. Economic stagnation gets blamed on immigrants, social dysfunction on minorities, and political paralysis on foreign interference. This provides simple explanations for complex problems, creates targets for collective anger, and allows the society to avoid responsibility for its own failures.

During the Cold War, both the United States and the Soviet Union projected their own imperial ambitions onto each other. Each side saw itself as defending freedom while viewing the other as pursuing world domination. Both were partly right about the other and completely blind to themselves. The projection created decades of conflict based more on psychological displacement than objective threat assessment. Colonial powers operated the same mechanism at larger scale: European nations engaged in systematic theft, murder, and cultural destruction while characterizing colonized peoples as violent and uncivilized, attributing to their victims the very traits they themselves embodied.

These patterns did not stay in history.

Political leaders accuse opponents of precisely the behaviors they themselves engage in. Those who manipulate democratic processes warn that others threaten democracy. Those who seek authoritarian power decry authoritarianism. Those who spread disinformation launch crusades against fake news. Once you recognize the pattern, it becomes impossible to unsee.

The politician screaming about election fraud while actively working to suppress votes. The pundit warning about media bias while running propaganda networks. The party claiming to defend freedom while passing laws to control what people can read, teach, or say about their own lives. The leader denouncing corruption while enriching themselves through office. The pattern isn't partisan. It operates across the political spectrum because it emerges from human psychology, not political ideology.

Identity politics on both the left and right often involves projection. Progressive movements may project their own capacity for authoritarianism and intolerance onto conservative opponents, unable to see their own rigid orthodoxies and purity tests. Conservative movements may project their own fear and need for control onto progressive adversaries, blind to their own resistance to change and insistence on conformity. Both sides accurately perceive shadow traits in the other while remaining blind to those same traits in themselves. Social media amplifies this through echo chambers and algorithms that feed us content confirming our existing beliefs, making the projection self-sustaining.

Reclaiming the Shadow

Recognizing projection in oneself or one's society is profoundly difficult because the very purpose of projection is to avoid seeing certain things. Breaking through it requires developing the capacity to notice what you've been trained not to see.

A friend of mine spent years furious at his father for being emotionally unavailable. Cold, distant, always prioritizing work over family. He built an identity around being the opposite: warm, present, emotionally open. Then his own daughter, at sixteen, told him she felt like she didn't really know him. That he was always physically there but somehow absent. He was devastated. Not because she was wrong, but because she was right, and he'd spent decades projecting onto his father exactly what he couldn't face in himself. The rage he felt toward his father was the sound of his own shadow knocking.

That's what withdrawal looks like in practice. It starts with your strongest reactions. When you feel visceral fury, contempt, or disgust about something in someone else, rather than mild disagreement or reasonable concern, pause. Ask whether that trait might exist in you in some form. The question isn't whether you're identical to the person triggering you. It's whether you possess some version of what you're condemning, perhaps expressed differently, perhaps hidden under layers of justification.

Others can often see your projections more clearly than you can. Trusted friends, therapists, or even critics sometimes identify patterns you cannot recognize from inside your own psychology. They're not caught in your self-concept, so they can see what you've learned to ignore. The challenge is remaining open to their observations rather than defending against them.

The more convinced you are of your own virtue, the more likely you're projecting your shadow onto others. When you can acknowledge your own capacity for what you condemn, when you can admit you're capable of what you see in your enemies, projection loses its grip. Righteousness is its fuel. Honesty is the valve.

At the collective level, the same dynamics play out, though they're enormously more difficult to address. Societies must develop the capacity to acknowledge their own historical shadow honestly, facing crimes, failures, and behaviors that contradict idealized national self-images. When a society becomes intensely focused on enemies, the question worth asking is what projection might be operating. What traits being attributed to the enemy might actually exist within the projecting society?

Societies also need institutions, media, and cultural practices that encourage honest self-examination rather than reinforcing projections, which means protecting voices that question national narratives, even when such questioning feels threatening. The most important voices are often the ones the society most wants to silence.

Direct contact dissolves projections. When you actually know and relate to people you've demonized, when you see their full humanity rather than your projection of them, maintaining the projection becomes difficult. They stop being repositories for your shadow and become human beings with their own complexity. Authoritarian systems work so hard to prevent contact between in-groups and projected-upon out-groups precisely because of this. Segregation preserves the projection. Integration threatens it.

Projection is its own undoing. The very mechanism designed to hide the shadow also points directly at it. Whatever triggers our most intense reactions is a map to what we've buried. The thing designed to keep us blind is, for anyone willing to look, the clearest signal of where to dig.

You can recognize harmful behavior in others while acknowledging your own capacity for that behavior. Distinguishing these two is the work. Projection feels righteous, certain, and intensely emotional. Discernment feels clear, measured, and open to self-examination.

It has happened at the national scale, rarely and imperfectly, but it has happened. Post-apartheid South Africa's Truth and Reconciliation Commission was built on a version of this logic: that a society cannot move forward while its shadow remains unacknowledged. Germany's decades-long reckoning with its Nazi past, the Aufarbeitung, embedded self-examination into law, education, and public culture in ways that most nations never attempt. Neither process was clean or complete. But both demonstrated that collective projection withdrawal is possible, and that it produces something different from the cycles of denial and retribution that follow when shadow material simply gets reassigned to a new enemy.

Breaking free from projection is perhaps the most demanding work any person or society can undertake. Until we can see and own our shadow rather than projecting it onto others, we remain trapped in cycles of conflict that can only intensify. The courage to face what we've projected, withdraw those projections, and acknowledge our own capacity for what we've condemned in others becomes the foundation for genuine peace and authentic relationships.

The question isn't whether you project. You do. We all do. The question is whether you're willing to see it. Think of the person who triggered you most intensely this week. What did they do that made you furious, disgusted, or contemptuous? Now ask: where does that exist in me? Not identically, perhaps. Not as obviously, maybe. But somewhere in your psychology, in your behavior, in your shadow, that quality lives.

Find it. Acknowledge it. Own it.

Responsibility

In 2010, Iceland did something no modern democracy had attempted. After the financial crisis destroyed its banking system, the country didn't just elect new politicians and hope for the best. It invited ordinary citizens to rewrite the constitution. Nine hundred and fifty randomly selected people set the priorities. Twenty-five citizens, none of them career politicians, drafted the document. The process was transparent, collaborative, and driven by people who would actually live under the rules they wrote. The parliament shelved it. Not because the draft was flawed, but because the professional political class couldn't tolerate a precedent in which citizens solved problems without them. The message was clear: you can have democracy, but only the kind where someone else makes the decisions.

That story captures something uncomfortable about responsibility in modern politics. Everyone claims to want it. Almost nobody can tolerate what it actually requires.

Personal responsibility isn't the performative kind, voting once every few years and blaming elected officials for everything that follows. It's the deeper, more uncomfortable version: making choices, living with consequences, learning from mistakes, and adjusting behavior based on what actually happened rather than what your ideology predicted.

What passes for democracy today is a system engineered to make sure none of that ever happens. Politicians must get elected, not govern well. Citizens delegate decisions to representatives who can be blamed when things go wrong. Those representatives claim they're following the will of the people while serving donor interests. Everyone gets a role in the theater: citizens say they „just voted," representatives say they're „following mandates" or „constrained by the system." The result is plutocracy in a democratic costume, where the people with the most money hold the real power and nobody is responsible for anything. It's the world's most expensive blame-shifting arrangement, and every taxpayer funds it.

Real democracy, the kind where citizens make decisions and own the outcomes, doesn't exist anywhere today. That's not an accident. It's terrifying to almost everyone involved.

Why We Run From It

The word itself tells you what's at stake. „Responsibility" comes from „response," the ability to respond rather than merely react. A reaction is automatic, driven by conditioning and fear. A response requires awareness, choice, and conscious decision-making. The difference isn't just semantic. It reveals how political systems shape entire populations.

Most political systems train people to react rather than respond, to believe they're powerless victims of forces beyond their control. When citizens believe outcomes are determined by luck, fate, or „the system" rather than their own choices, they're easier to manage. They look to authorities to solve problems instead of addressing issues themselves. This produces populations perfectly suited for control but completely unprepared for self-governance.

It's the oldest con in politics: convince people they're powerless, then offer to solve all their problems. Break their legs, sell them crutches.

The psychological mechanism behind this is well documented. Martin Seligman's research on learned helplessness showed that when organisms experience repeated inability to affect their circumstances, they stop trying, even when conditions change. His original experiments involved dogs receiving electric shocks they couldn't escape. After enough rounds, the dogs wouldn't jump over a low barrier to safety even when the barrier was clearly available. They had learned that their actions didn't matter. So they lay down and took it.

Scale that to populations, and you're looking at one of the most important dynamics in political psychology. Citizens subjected to systems where their choices produce no visible effect eventually stop believing their choices could ever matter. East Germans who spent forty years under a regime where initiative was punished didn't suddenly become enthusiastic self-governors when the Wall fell. Post-colonial nations handed independence without any tradition of collective decision-making didn't magically develop functional democracies overnight. The external structure was removed. The internal damage remained. You can open every cage in the building, but animals raised in captivity often won't walk through the door.

This is why the Control chapter's analysis matters so directly here. Control systems don't just restrict behavior while they're active. They corrode the capacity for self-direction long after they're gone. The learned helplessness becomes self-reinforcing: people stop taking responsibility because they believe responsibility is impossible, which ensures they stay powerless, which confirms the belief. The controllers then point to this passivity as proof that control was necessary all along.

In political discourse, what passes for „taking responsibility" is usually blame dressed up in better language: identifying who's at fault so they can be punished, shamed, or voted out. This scratches the emotional itch for accountability but solves nothing. The same problems recur because nobody learned anything. Blame looks backward at who caused a problem. Responsibility looks forward at who will fix it. One seeks punishment. The other seeks solutions. Modern politics has perfected the first and almost entirely abandoned the second.

Real responsibility means acknowledging: „This outcome resulted from our choices. What do we learn? How do we adjust?" It means facing mistakes directly rather than defending them, explaining them away, or finding someone else to blame. It means accepting that bad outcomes don't always come from bad intentions, that well-intentioned choices sometimes produce terrible results, and that responsible people adjust rather than insist they were right.

Think about how a functional business learns. A product fails. The team examines what happened, changes the approach, and tries again. Nobody gets executed for the failure. The feedback is direct: customers either buy or they don't. Now look at government policy. A program fails. The agency that runs it argues for more funding. The politicians who championed it change the subject. The opposition uses it as ammunition. The voters who supported it defend their original position. Five years later, everyone has a theory about whose fault it was and nobody has learned a thing.

Restoring that feedback loop is what real democracy would require. Citizens make decisions, experience consequences, learn from results, and adjust. Simple in theory. In practice, it demands psychological capacities most populations have never had the chance to develop, particularly the ability to treat mistakes as data rather than disgrace.

These broken mechanisms are real obstacles. But there's something more stubborn underneath: many people don't want this responsibility at all.

Erich Fromm saw it coming. In „Escape from Freedom," written as Europe was choosing fascism over the terrifying openness of self-determination, Fromm argued that freedom is a burden most people will pay almost any price to set down. Being told what to do is psychologically easier than choosing for yourself and living with what follows. Authoritarian systems don't just seize power. They get invited in by populations exhausted by the weight of their own agency.

This fear runs deep. Responsibility requires tolerating uncertainty, because outcomes can never be guaranteed. It requires accepting that you might be wrong, that your choices might cause harm, that you might need to change course publicly. For people who can't sit with those possibilities, avoiding responsibility becomes more important than any other goal. Freedom is the only gift people keep trying to return.

One obstacle deserves special attention: the confusion between responsibility and guilt. Taking responsibility for addressing a problem is not the same as accepting blame for causing it, but societies routinely collapse the distinction.

Consider infrastructure. Nobody alive today designed the car-dependent sprawl that defines most American cities, but current generations face the consequences and bear responsibility for what comes next. The same principle applies to any inherited problem on any side of the political spectrum. „I didn't cause this, but I have responsibility for addressing it" is a psychologically sustainable position. „I'm guilty for what previous generations did" is not, and usually triggers the defensive reactions that prevent any constructive action at all.

Democracy needs this forward-looking stance. Past mistakes become learning opportunities rather than guilt trips. The question shifts from „who's to blame?" to „what do we do differently?" That shift sounds small. In practice, it changes everything about how a society functions.

Who Decides, Who Pays

Here is where the current system reveals its most elegant dysfunction: power and responsibility have been surgically separated.

Authorities hold power but dodge responsibility by claiming they're constrained by voters, laws, markets, or circumstances. Citizens hold responsibility in theory, since they're the supposed source of democratic legitimacy, but lack the power to make any decision that matters. The split guarantees that nobody ever owns anything. Watch a financial crisis unfold. Banks take the risks, taxpayers absorb the losses, regulators blame the banks, the banks blame the regulators, Congress holds hearings where everyone performs outrage, and nothing structural changes. Four years later it happens again. This isn't a bug in the system. It's the system working exactly as designed: maximum power, zero accountability, distributed everywhere and owned by no one.

Functional responsibility requires that power and accountability live in the same place. Those who make choices must experience the consequences directly. You can't delegate authority while keeping the right to blame, or claim authority while delegating the fallout. When the people making decisions are the same people living with results, the incentive to decide well is built into the structure. When those two groups are different, the whole arrangement rots from the inside.

From a shadow work perspective, avoiding responsibility is one of the primary ways both individuals and societies stay unconscious. Refusing to own the consequences of your choices prevents learning, stalls development, and keeps you psychologically dependent on external authority. The patterns of victimhood and control-seeking explored in their respective chapters both function as elaborate responsibility-avoidance strategies. Victimhood says: „I can't be responsible because I have no power." Control-seeking says: „I'll take responsibility for everyone, so nobody has to develop their own." Both prevent the population from growing up.

Responsibility and freedom are the same thing seen from different angles. You can't have real freedom without accepting responsibility for your choices, and you can't exercise real responsibility without the freedom to choose.

Current systems offer neither. They provide the illusion of freedom, „you can vote!," while eliminating any authority to make decisions that matter. And they demand responsibility, „it's a democracy, so it's your fault!," while preventing any real capacity to influence outcomes.

This is why shadow work isn't optional preparation for better politics. It's the foundation. Self-governance can't function with populations who refuse to examine their own shadows, who project problems onto opponents, who cling to victimhood or superiority, who reach for control rather than develop the ability to manage themselves.

The capacity can be developed. Humans grow in remarkable ways when conditions support it. But current systems actively obstruct that growth, which creates the central paradox: transitioning to systems that support responsibility requires people who already have it.

Democracy without responsibility is a simulation. It feels like participation. It changes nothing. The alternative offers actual stakes, actual consequences, and actual chances to learn and adjust. It's harder than the comfortable version where someone else decides and you get to complain about it afterward. But it's the only version that treats citizens as adults rather than children who need managing.

The question isn't whether this kind of responsibility is possible. It's whether enough people want it badly enough to tolerate what it costs. The answer to that question will determine whether democracy becomes real or stays a word we use to describe something that never quite arrives.

The Superiority-Victimhood Delusion

Watch someone cut in line at the grocery store. Notice your immediate reaction. That flash of indignation reveals a belief so fundamental that most people never question it: some people matter more than others. Put differently, human worth can be ranked.

This belief operates like a disease with two distinct symptoms. Some people place themselves above others, claiming inherent superiority. Others place themselves below, claiming inherent victimhood. Different rungs on the same imaginary ladder. Different expressions of the same delusion.

Alfred Adler discovered this dynamic when he broke with Freud to develop Individual Psychology. He identified how feelings of inferiority give rise to superiority complexes as psychological defense mechanisms. The person who feels small makes everyone else feel smaller. Carl Jung observed the reverse. The oppressed carry inferiority in their conscious persona while harboring superiority in their shadow. Those claiming superiority unconsciously defend against feelings of inferiority. Those trapped in victimhood unconsciously harbor superiority complexes, often expressed as moral authority over their „oppressors.“

Whether you dominate or submit, you are playing the same game. The collective ego maintains this delusion because both positions offer psychological benefits that are difficult to surrender.

The Ladder

Most people don't decide to build hierarchies. The hierarchy builds itself, quietly, in response to pain they couldn't process any other way. When feelings of inadequacy become unbearable, the mind finds a solution: arrange the world so that you are not at the bottom of it. Some climb. Some sink deliberately. Some plant themselves firmly at the top or bottom. Others drift between positions depending on the room they're in. All of it temporarily relieves the internal pressure. None of it heals anything.

The superiority strategy works through overt domination, but the darker personality types play both ends. Narcissists need to be special, whether that means sitting at the top demanding admiration or playing the misunderstood genius the world has wronged. Psychopaths treat people as instruments, reaching for intimidation when it works and feigned suffering when it works better. Machiavellians are pure strategists with no attachment to any particular rung, only to whatever gets them what they want. What all three share isn't a preferred position on the ladder. It's the inability to see other people as fully real.

Covert narcissists are perhaps the clearest illustration. They occupy the victim position permanently while nursing an internal sense of superiority that never wavers. The suffering is real enough to generate sympathy. The entitlement underneath never shows. They control through guilt rather than force, but the goal is identical.

The victimhood strategy doesn't work through strength. It works through the moral weight societies place on suffering. Claim the position of the wronged convincingly enough and you gain power over others who feel obligated to defer, apologize, or rescue. The appearance of powerlessness becomes its own form of leverage.

These strategies come in two varieties. Some people fall into them unconsciously. Others pursue them deliberately.

Consider two children in dysfunctional families. One blames themselves for their parents' divorce. *If it were my fault, then I have power.* The other decides they're superior to their chaotic family. *If I'm better than them, I'm safe from their fate.* Gabor Maté's trauma research explains why. Faced with situations genuinely beyond their control, people don't accept helplessness. They manufacture control through the only tool available, which is how they position themselves in relation to others. The strategy lodges in the psyche and persists decades after the original threat has passed. What began as survival becomes a cage.

These are the unconscious players. They don't actually understand how their position harms themselves and others. Identity, meaning, survival — all of it gets funneled into the role. And once the original wound came from someone trusted, the grip tightens further. Freyd and Birrell's research on betrayal trauma explains the hold. When the person who hurt you was someone you depended on, the psychological disruption cuts so deep that staying in the defensive position feels safer than risking that kind of betrayal again. Healing looks more dangerous than staying wounded. The survival strategy provides concrete payoffs: it explains current problems without requiring personal change, generates sympathy and attention, provides moral authority, and offers meaning through suffering.

Then there are the deliberate players. They've discovered that both positions offer concrete advantages and weaponize whichever serves the moment. The superior extract deference,

resources, and freedom to act without
constraint. The victims extract sympathy,
attention, and power through guilt. Social
psychologists have documented how individuals
strategically present themselves as victims to
gain social advantages. The manipulation
becomes sophisticated through partial truths
combined with exaggeration: some real harm
occurred, but it gets amplified to maximize
sympathy while minimizing scrutiny of their
own contributions. This corrupts social support
systems and generates the cynicism that makes it
harder for those with actual needs to receive
help.

The unconscious players create endless cycles
while believing they want things to improve, but
their patterns make real relationship impossible.
They will exhaust you with crises while rejecting
solutions. The deliberate players weaponize
compassion to control others. They will exploit
your empathy to extract resources while
avoiding all accountability. In both cases, you
are responsible for their feelings. They are
responsible for nothing.

Both types refuse real responsibility, and that
makes them unreliable in any relationship that
requires honesty. Those claiming superiority
blame their behavior on the inferiority of others.
Those claiming victimhood blame their

behavior on the harm done to them. The justifications differ. In both cases, someone else is always responsible for what they do.

Rather than recognizing hierarchical thinking as a psychological dysfunction, most societies actively reward it. The corporate psychopath rises through organizations precisely because empathy slows him down. The professional victim extracts sympathy, resources, and moral authority from every room she enters. Both have learned that the ladder isn't the problem. It's the point.

These institutional rewards run deeper than individual behavior. Schools rank children from age six, sorting winners from losers before anyone understands what game they're playing. Participation trophies were a brief attempt to fix this, and their failure revealed how much adults needed the ranking to continue. Economies celebrate dominance as merit and package poverty as personal failure. Political systems hand microphones to whoever performs superiority or victimhood most convincingly.

The wealthy attribute their wealth to superior intelligence or work ethic rather than inheritance, connections, and luck. Those without wealth attribute their poverty to systemic oppression rather than acknowledging any role for personal agency. Power tells the same story from the other direction. Those who have it believe their positions reflect superior capabilities, while those who don't believe their exclusion is purely the result of forces beyond their control. All of these stories share the same function. They externalize responsibility and make the hierarchy appear either natural or impossible to change.

The Ladder Goes National

What's true of individuals is true of groups, only with higher stakes and longer memories. The delusion scales with horrifying efficiency.

Nationalism applies personal superiority thinking to geography. People born within certain boundaries matter more than those born elsewhere. But nationalism simultaneously creates victim narratives. Our nation has been wronged, humiliated, exploited by outsiders. The same movement claims both positions, superiority and victimhood, wielding whichever serves the moment.

Religious fundamentalism works identically. Correct doctrine makes you chosen, and chosen people are always surrounded by those who wish to destroy them. Political ideologies follow the same pattern. The left claims moral superiority through compassion while positioning itself as victim of the oppressive right. The right claims superiority through tradition while positioning itself as victim of the corrupt left. Both create psychological foundations for violence against outsiders. The same pattern extends to humanity's relationship with nature. We claim superiority over the natural world while positioning ourselves as victims of its cruelty, which conveniently justifies treating the Earth as a resource extraction site.

Social psychologist Roy Baumeister discovered that victim narratives become self-reinforcing, filtering perception to confirm victimhood while screening out anything that might complicate the story. The same applies to superiority narratives. Each new generation inherits not just the stories but the emotional charge behind them. Psychologist Dan Bar-On called this „double walls,“ where groups lose the ability to see their own capacity for harm while remaining exquisitely sensitive to threats from outside. Real grievances and real atrocities coexist in the same hands, invisible to those holding them.

Germany after Versailles is the textbook case, and also the most brutal one. The treaty was punishing. The economic hardship was real. Germans had legitimate grievances. What happened next was not inevitable, but it was predictable. Those grievances got weaponized.

Political movements promised to restore German dignity by identifying who had stolen it. Fritz Stern's research on the „Politics of Cultural Despair" shows how intellectuals and politicians built an entire industry of victimhood, redirecting national humiliation toward scapegoated enemies while framing escalating violence as self-defense. The victim identity didn't moderate the rage. It licensed it.

The progression from real hardship to national victimhood to genocide is not an aberration. It is the ladder logic taken to its conclusion. Once a nation believes it has been made inferior by its enemies, restoring superiority becomes not just a goal but a moral obligation. The fuel wasn't hatred. It was wounded pride dressed as justice.

Jung called this enantiodromia: the tendency for things pushed far enough in one direction to flip into their opposite. Victim identity, held long enough and hard enough, doesn't stay passive. It transforms. The wronged become the wrongdoers. The humiliated become the humiliators. Not despite their victimhood but because of it. Germany is the extreme case, but the same logic plays out in the Balkans, in sectarian conflicts in Northern Ireland, and in every cycle of retaliation where yesterday's victim becomes tomorrow's aggressor.

The same dynamic runs in reverse. The person whose superiority collapses doesn't find humility. They find breakdown, or they double down, pushing dominance to ever more extreme territory to avoid feeling what's underneath.

Psychiatrist Judith Herman's work on complex trauma reveals why these patterns prove so difficult to break. Victim identity can become so central to someone's sense of self that healing feels like psychological death. The same applies to superiority complexes built around collective glory or dominance. Letting go of the position on the hierarchy threatens the entire structure of meaning someone has built their life around.

Both positions are forms of unconscious power-seeking, which is why people defend them so fiercely. The victim who constantly creates crises requiring rescue is exercising power while denying it. The superior person demanding deference is compensating for inadequacy they cannot consciously face. Neither is what they appear to be.

The shadow work runs deeper still. Victim identity contains disowned perpetrator energy, which surfaces through passive aggression, manipulation, and manufactured drama. Superiority identity contains disowned victim energy, which emerges in private collapse or gets projected outward onto others who are then dominated to prove one's strength. Each position carries its opposite hidden inside it, waiting for the pressure that will bring it out.

As long as people remain trapped in hierarchical thinking, they simply trade positions rather than dismantling the ladder itself.

Stepping Off

You've met both types. You've probably been both types. Most people have, at different points in their lives, claimed superiority to feel safe or victimhood to feel powerful. The question isn't whether you've stood on the ladder. It's whether you're willing to step off it.

Stepping off requires something deceptively simple: recognizing that all human beings have equal inherent worth regardless of their characteristics, achievements, or circumstances. Not equal abilities. Not identical. Equal worth. This single recognition dismantles the entire architecture of hierarchical thinking, because both superiority and victimhood depend on the premise that worth can be ranked.

This means something specific in practice. Think of someone you know who was wronged at some point. Someone passed over unfairly, betrayed by someone they trusted, treated as less than they were. Now ask which version of that person you've encountered more: the one who named what happened, dealt with it, and moved forward, or the one still carrying it twenty years later as the explanation for everything that followed. The first acknowledged harm without becoming it. The second built an identity around it. The difference between those two paths is what this chapter is about.

Real injustice can be named, accountability sought, and prevention pursued without building an entire identity around having been wronged. Real differences in talent, experience, and capability can be recognized without arranging them into a hierarchy of human worth. Societies serious about healing must learn to hold both at once. They must acknowledge the reality of harm while refusing to let that harm become the organizing principle of identity.

Education about these dynamics is itself a form of disruption. Once you know that guilt-tripping is a control mechanism, it loses its grip. Once you recognize appeals to superiority as compensation for inadequacy, the instinct to defer evaporates. Both strategies depend on the target not knowing what's happening. Name the game, and the game changes. This is precisely why institutions built on hierarchy resist teaching people how hierarchy actually works.

Moving beyond either position is not just loss. Trauma therapists have documented how people who actually work through their wounds often emerge with stronger relationships, sharper clarity about what matters, and a resilience unavailable to those who never faced what they carried. But it requires surrendering the psychological benefits both positions provide. That means giving up the moral authority, the claim on others' deference or sympathy, and the convenient excuse for avoiding responsibility. For individuals and groups who have built entire identities around their position on the ladder, that surrender feels like annihilation.

South Africa's Truth and Reconciliation Commission tried something radical: replace punishment with testimony. Perpetrators named what they had done. Victims were heard rather than just compensated. The premise was that cycles of humiliation and revenge couldn't be broken by more humiliation and revenge. The process was imperfect and incomplete. Its deeper limitation, though, wasn't the process itself. Economic apartheid outlasted legal apartheid by decades, and hierarchical identities don't dissolve when the law changes if the material conditions that created them remain intact. You can pass a law. You cannot legislate a shadow.

None of this happens without personal reckoning. Transformation starts with an uncomfortable question: where am I on the ladder right now, and what am I getting from staying there? Not blaming others for their positions. Examining your own. The work isn't about denying real harm or pretending differences don't exist. It's about refusing to let either one become the thing you organize your identity around.

That work is contagious in the best possible way. Unhealed people build unhealed cultures. But people who have stepped off the ladder make it easier for others to do the same. Enough of them, and the culture shifts.

Political restructuring, economic redistribution, and institutional redesign all get undermined when the people involved are still playing hierarchical games with each other. The shadow work isn't separate from the political work. It's what makes the political work legible at all.

A population sorting itself into superiors and victims cannot self-govern. It can only fight. Self-governance requires something hierarchical identity makes impossible: the capacity to sit with disagreement without needing to dominate or be rescued, to acknowledge problems without assigning permanent blame, to build something together with people who see the world differently. Every policy debate that becomes a battle for position on the ladder is a democracy slowly eating itself.

Breaking free from these patterns isn't noble self-improvement. It's the basic psychological infrastructure that any genuine democratic life requires, and the one thing no constitution can install for you.

Group Think

You believe what you believe because you thought about it. At least, you'd be insulted if someone suggested otherwise.

In the 1950s, psychologist Solomon Asch showed people lines on a card and asked which ones matched. The correct answer was obvious. A child could have gotten it right. But when surrounded by actors who deliberately chose the wrong answer, 75% of participants went along with the group at least once. They looked at the lines with their own eyes, knew the answer, and said the wrong thing anyway.

Nobody held a gun to their heads or promised them money. They were sitting in a room with strangers, looking at lines on paper, and three-quarters of them chose to deny what they could plainly see rather than be the one person who disagreed.

If people will abandon the evidence of their own eyes over something this trivial, what happens with complex questions about politics, morality, or how a society should be organized? How many of our „deeply held" beliefs are conformity responses dressed up as personal convictions?

Most human thoughts, beliefs, and behaviors are not individually chosen. They're collectively programmed. We are social creatures wired to conform, and this wiring runs so deep that we mistake group programming for personal conviction. Our survival as a species depended on our ability to fall in line. What once kept us alive now keeps us unconscious.

Shadow work for a society starts with seeing how thoroughly group dynamics shape individual consciousness. The evidence for just how thoroughly is disturbing.

The Obedience Machine

Philip Zimbardo's 1971 Stanford Prison Experiment, despite its controversial methodology, showed just how thin the line between identity and assigned role really is. College students randomly assigned to be „guards" began exhibiting authoritarian, abusive behaviors within days. Those assigned as „prisoners" became passive and depressed. The experiment had to be stopped early because the role-playing had become too real.

Forget the capacity for cruelty or submission. What should unsettle you is the speed. The students didn't gradually develop these behaviors over months or years. The transformation happened almost immediately, as if the social role activated dormant programming. Give someone a uniform and a little authority, and suddenly they're running their own mini-dictatorship. It's like Lord of the Flies, except with better lighting and clipboards.

Stanley Milgram's experiments on obedience took this further. Participants were told to administer increasingly severe electric shocks to another person (actually an actor) as part of a „learning experiment." Despite hearing screams of pain and pleas to stop, 65% continued to the maximum voltage when instructed by an authority figure.

Sixty-five percent. Not sadists. Not authoritarians. Just people who figured someone in a lab coat probably knew what they were doing. The same logic that keeps people nodding along in corporate meetings.

Many showed obvious distress and moral conflict, but they kept pressing the button anyway. These were ordinary people recruited from newspaper ads. A single authority figure in a laboratory setting was enough to override their personal moral compass.

Milgram's work illuminates something essential about how mass atrocities become possible. Police officers, politicians, military personnel, corporate executives, and bureaucrats aren't necessarily bad people who sought out positions to abuse others. They're ordinary individuals absorbed into institutional roles that reshape their behavior over time. People don't suddenly become evil when they join institutions; they surrender their individual moral authority to the group's designated leaders. None of it required entire populations of inherently cruel people. Not the Nazi regime, not the Rwandan genocide, not the Jim Crow South. It required normal people willing to follow authority and conform to group norms.

Draw the Line

You don't need institutions to manufacture division. You don't even need adults.

The day after Martin Luther King Jr.'s assassination in 1968, Iowa teacher Jane Elliott divided her third-grade class based on eye color. She told the blue-eyed children they were superior, smarter, and better than the brown-eyed children. Blue-eyed children got extra privileges, sat at the front, and received praise. Brown-eyed children were restricted, criticized, and required to wear collars marking their „inferior" status.

Within hours, the blue-eyed children became cruel, arrogant, and domineering. They refused to play with their brown-eyed friends. They invented reasons why brown-eyed people were inferior. Previously confident brown-eyed children became withdrawn, timid, and performed worse on tests. The next day, Elliott reversed the roles. The brown-eyed children immediately adopted the same cruel behaviors when given superiority.

Eight-year-olds. Friends the day before. Elliott simply told them they were different, gave one group privilege, and their behavior transformed completely. They didn't just prefer their own group; they developed contempt for the other. They hurt people they'd liked based on nothing but arbitrary group assignment.

We don't need real differences to create us-versus-them dynamics. We just need someone to draw a line and tell us which side we're on. The rest happens automatically. We're tribal apes who will fight about literally anything if you divide us into teams. Sports fans understand this instinctively, which is perhaps the most unsettling thing about sports fans.

What happened in that Iowa classroom runs constantly through modern societies, invisible because we're swimming in it. Political parties don't just represent different policy positions; they function as tribal identity groups that shape how members perceive reality itself. Republicans and Democrats in the United States, Social Democrats and Conservative voters in Germany, or any other political division worldwide don't just disagree on issues. They literally see different facts.

Social media has supercharged this. Algorithm-driven echo chambers expose group members to constant confirmation of their existing beliefs while filtering out contradictory evidence. What you get goes beyond political polarization: you get separate reality bubbles where different groups operate with entirely different sets of „facts." We've weaponized confirmation bias and given it an algorithm. It's like we looked at how easily humans create echo chambers and thought, „You know what this needs? Artificial intelligence and venture capital funding."

The dynamic reaches well beyond politics. Professional groups, religious communities, academic disciplines, and even neighborhoods develop their own forms of groupthink. Doctors learn to think like doctors, lawyers like lawyers, academics like academics. These aren't just professional skills; they're entire worldviews that shape perception and values in ways that reach far outside the office.

Every group maintains its cohesion partly by defining itself against outsiders. To be „us," there must be „them." To be right, someone else must be wrong. To be good, someone else must be bad. Jung called this the collective shadow: the parts of human experience that the group denies, projects onto others, or relegates to outsiders. Every nation has groups that carry its shadow. Criminals, immigrants, political opponents, ethnic minorities, foreign enemies. These become repositories for everything the nation doesn't want to acknowledge about itself.

The process is largely unconscious. No one sits in a room and decides to project their shadow onto immigrants or political opponents. It happens on its own, as part of maintaining group identity.

Software You Didn't Install

Something deeper connects all of these experiments. There's a mechanism underneath the conformity, the obedience, the tribal hatred, and once you see it, everything in this chapter clicks into place.

Groupthink is the collective equivalent of individual ego, and both run on the same fuel: survival programming.

The individual ego is not a philosopher. It's a watchman. It evolved to scan for threats, keep you inside the group, and protect your sense of self from destabilizing information. It decides in milliseconds, then hands the result to your conscious mind to explain. Psychologist Jonathan Haidt called this moral dumbfounding: people reach their moral conclusions instantly and construct their reasoning afterward, on the fly, to justify what was already decided. A more honest name might be the human condition.

Groups do the same thing at scale. The collective ego reacts first, circulates that reaction through shared language and social pressure until it hardens into consensus, and only then produces the reasoning. The conviction feels earned. It was rationalized. The conformity, the role absorption, the obedience, the tribal lines: each feeds this same system.

Why does the system persist? Because it feels good. The collective ego creates predictability and reduces uncertainty. Conform to its patterns and you feel safe, accepted, certain about reality. Start questioning those patterns and watch what happens. Rejection. Ostracism. Suddenly you're dangerous, crazy, or a traitor. Question the collective ego and you'll discover how quickly „free thinker" becomes „that weird guy we don't invite to parties anymore."

The collective ego sustains itself through four reinforcing mechanisms. First, automated thinking: group beliefs and „common sense" that members adopt without examination. These thoughts feel true because „everyone knows" them, not because anyone has actually thought them through. Second, identity protection: the system automatically rejects or attacks any information that threatens the group's self-image, which is why groups can maintain demonstrably false beliefs in the face of contradictory evidence. Third, dissent treated as danger: the conformity pressure Asch demonstrated, where standing alone feels like an existential threat even when standing alone is objectively correct. Fourth, shadow projection: the collective ego maintains group identity by offloading disowned qualities onto designated others, below group awareness, exactly as Jung described.

Here's what matters for shadow work: collective ego, like individual ego, is not who we actually are. It's an automated system. It can be observed, questioned, and transcended. Every experiment in this chapter shows the collective ego running its programming while the people inside it believe they're making free choices.

Breaking free doesn't require abandoning all group affiliation. What it requires is collective consciousness: the capacity for groups to observe their own automated patterns, question their own assumptions, and choose consciously rather than react on autopilot. Think of it as the group-level version of individual awakening. Learning to watch the software run, rather than assuming you wrote it.

But awareness alone won't save you. Group programming operates through emotional, social, and survival mechanisms that predate rational thought. Knowing about conformity doesn't make you immune to it. Asch's participants weren't stupid. Milgram's subjects weren't immoral. Elliott's children weren't hateful. They were all running software they didn't know they had.

What psychologists call psychological differentiation is the capacity that actually matters here: the ability to remain a distinct self inside a group rather than dissolving into it. Not antisocial. Not contrarian for its own sake. Present enough to participate, separate enough to notice when you're conforming and decide whether you mean it. In Asch's experiment, 25% of participants kept giving the correct answer despite unanimous social pressure. They weren't smarter. They were more differentiated. That gap between the 25% and the 75% is where shadow work lives.

The experiments in this chapter don't describe problems from the past. They describe the operating system running in every society right now, including yours, including the groups you belong to, including the thoughts you're having as you read this. Group programming is shaping your consciousness right now. The question is

whether you're willing to notice. And whether
noticing is even enough.

Denial

There's a study from the 1950s that tells us more about human psychology than most people want to know. Leon Festinger infiltrated a doomsday cult that predicted the world would end on a specific date. When the date came and went without incident, would they admit they'd been wrong?

Not even close.

Instead, they doubled down. They decided their faith had saved the world, that their belief was so strong it prevented the catastrophe. Faced with undeniable evidence that their core conviction was false, they simply denied reality and invented a new story that preserved their worldview.

You have to admire the mental gymnastics. „The world didn't end, which proves we were right about the world ending." It's like predicting your house will burn down, watching it not burn down, and concluding you're an excellent firefighter.

This is cognitive dissonance: the mental discomfort of holding contradictory beliefs simultaneously. The telling part isn't that people feel that discomfort. It's what they do with it. Rather than changing the belief to match reality, people almost always change their perception of reality to match the belief.

This isn't stupidity. It's how human minds work. We're not rational creatures who occasionally make mistakes; we're rationalizing creatures who occasionally stumble into truth. And when truth threatens our identity, status, or belonging, the lengths we'll go to deny it would impress a defence lawyer.

Jung called this identity the Persona: the mask we present to the world, the socially acceptable version of ourselves. Denial is what keeps that mask intact. When reality threatens to crack the Persona and expose what lies beneath, we simply refuse to look.

Now scale this up to nations. Groups protect their collective identity as fiercely as individuals do. They'll reject any information that threatens it, no matter how obvious, documented, or catastrophic. Stanley Cohen identified three types of denial, each a defense mechanism protecting the ego from uncomfortable truth.

Literal denial: „It didn't happen." Flat contradiction of facts. The Armenian genocide didn't happen. We didn't overthrow democratically elected governments. That massacre never occurred.

Interpretive denial: „It's not what you think." Facts are acknowledged but reframed. Yes, we invaded countries, but we were spreading democracy. Yes, we tortured people, but we called it enhanced interrogation. Yes, we're destroying the environment, but it's called economic development.

Implicatory denial: „It doesn't matter." Facts and meaning are acknowledged, but implications are rejected. Yes, children are dying in our custody at the border, but we can't just let everyone in. Yes, pharmaceutical companies price-gouge life-saving medications, but that's just the free market. Yes, our voting systems are vulnerable to manipulation, but changing them would be too complicated.

When literal denial becomes untenable, we retreat to interpretive denial. When that crumbles, we fall back to implicatory denial. The goal is always the same: protect the ego from information that would require uncomfortable change.

The Nations That Never Looked Back

Every nation has historical crimes it hasn't fully processed. The United States offers a comprehensive catalog. Genocide of indigenous peoples becomes „westward expansion." Slavery is acknowledged but carefully disconnected from current inequality. Japanese internment becomes an „unfortunate overreaction." Overthrowing democracies abroad becomes „national security interests."

We've mastered the euphemism. We don't torture, we use „enhanced interrogation techniques." We don't kill civilians, we produce „collateral damage." We don't invade for resources, we „spread democracy." It's like calling a bank robbery „unauthorized wealth redistribution" and expecting everyone to nod along.

Japan minimizes WWII atrocities in textbooks. Turkey denies the Armenian genocide. Indonesia sanitizes the 1965-66 anti-communist massacres. Russia sanitizes Stalin's purges. Britain reframes colonialism. Every nation that has done terrible things has also developed a sophisticated vocabulary for not quite calling them that.

South Africa offers a counterexample. After apartheid, the Truth and Reconciliation Commission created a public process for confronting decades of systematic oppression. Perpetrators testified. Victims were heard. The nation watched. It was painful, incomplete, and controversial. But it represented facing reality rather than burying it. Turns out „never again" works better when you actually remember what you're trying to prevent. Who knew?

The cost of historical denial is enormous. We repeat patterns we refuse to acknowledge, project our denied shadow onto others, and pass unprocessed trauma to future generations. History doesn't disappear when we stop teaching it. It just stops having an author.

The Scale of Evil

Contemporary injustices are harder to face than historical ones because we are not reading about them. We are inside them. And some are so severe that our minds refuse to absorb the implications even when every piece of evidence has been formally released, officially documented, and placed on a government website available to anyone with an internet connection.

Jeffrey Epstein operated a pedophile ring servicing some of the most powerful people in the world. Court documents exist. Flight logs. FBI interview summaries. Grand jury testimony from over 250 victims. A conviction. Ghislaine Maxwell sentenced to 20 years for sex trafficking. His death in federal custody in 2019 involved a broken neck, a guard who fell asleep, security footage with a gap, and a suicide watch that had been quietly lifted two weeks earlier.

The FBI was tipped off in 1996 by victim Maria
Farmer and did nothing for nearly a decade.
When Epstein was finally arrested in 2007,
federal prosecutors prepared an indictment that
was never filed. Instead, Alexander Acosta, the
U.S. Attorney in Miami at the time and later
Trump's first Secretary of Labor, signed off on a
deal giving Epstein 18 months in jail with work
release that allowed him to spend most days at
his office. Nothing communicates „we take
child trafficking seriously" quite like letting the
perpetrator keep his calendar.

In November 2025, Congress passed the
Epstein Files Transparency Act 427 votes to 1.
The law required full disclosure within 30 days.
The DOJ missed the deadline by six weeks, then
released 3.5 million pages, declared the matter
closed, and noted in passing that it had
identified 6 million pages as potentially
responsive. Lawmakers from both parties
immediately disputed compliance.

What came out was harrowing enough. The files
included 2,000 videos and 180,000 images seized
from his properties. An FBI diagram charting
Epstein's network of victims across years of
abuse. An employee testimony describing duties
that included fanning $100 bills near Epstein's
bed and disposing of used condoms after
sessions with underage girls. Recruitment paid

$200 per referral, with instructions to lie about age. Epstein checked IDs specifically to confirm girls were minors and complained when they were „too old."

Then came the detail that clarified exactly whose interests the process was designed to protect. The DOJ redacted the names of at least six accused men that should have been public under the law, as confirmed by Representatives Ro Khanna and Thomas Massie after reviewing the unredacted version. At the same time, through what were described as technical errors, the department published the names, faces, bank account numbers, and social security numbers of victims, some of whom had never come forward publicly. Khanna called it „one of the largest scandals in our country's history." The names protected were not the children.

Virginia Giuffre, one of Epstein's most prominent accusers, died by suicide in April 2025. She never saw the files she had spent years fighting to release.

In February 2026, Ghislaine Maxwell appeared by video before the House Oversight Committee and invoked the Fifth Amendment to every question. Including „who were the other co-conspirators?" Including „which men sexually abused girls?" The committee left empty-handed.

That same week, Commerce Secretary Howard Lutnick admitted under Senate questioning that he had taken his family to Epstein's private island for lunch in 2012. His explanation: „I don't recall why we did it." He later clarified that they stayed for one hour, with his wife, children, and nannies all present. Apparently a spontaneous family lunch on the private island of a convicted child trafficker is simply the kind of detail that doesn't stick.

Representative Thomas Massie, after reviewing the unredacted files, stated that Trump appeared over a million times across the full body of evidence. Mentions do not establish wrongdoing. But a million appearances in a child trafficking investigation, spanning the presidencies of Clinton, Bush, Obama, and Trump, is not a partisan problem. It is a structural one.

The difference in response across countries says less about national character than about institutional architecture. Where legislatures can remove leaders between elections, the consequences arrived faster. In Britain, Prince Andrew was stripped of his royal titles and placed under active police investigation. Peter Mandelson, the UK's ambassador to the United States, was fired, resigned from the House of Lords, and now faces a criminal investigation.

Prime Minister Keir Starmer apologized publicly to Epstein's victims. In Sweden, Norway, France, and Slovakia, politicians named in the files came under formal scrutiny. These weren't acts of superior moral courage. They were the predictable output of systems with accountability mechanisms that still functioned.

What the coverage ignored was every country where equivalent operations never became too visible to bury. Hungary's capture of judiciary, press, and civil society by a single political network ran for fifteen years with minimal international attention. Brazil's institutional protections for political elites implicated in child exploitation and financial crime generated brief coverage and no sustained pressure. India's documented cases of political figures involved in trafficking networks rarely surface outside local reporting. The pattern has no nationality. It appears wherever power concentrates beyond the reach of accountability, regardless of what the constitution says. The story itself is not just American.

A December 2025 CNN poll found that two-thirds of Americans believe the government is deliberately withholding information. Nearly half reported dissatisfaction with what was released. Both parties, for once, agreed something was deeply wrong.

And still, nothing happened.

People filled city streets over a police killing caught on video, over a Supreme Court ruling, over an election outcome, depending on which side you were on. The Epstein files document an organised operation in which children were trafficked to the most powerful people in the world, who then enjoyed decades of institutional protection spanning multiple administrations and both parties. The operation continued after his first arrest. After his conviction. After his death. The evidence is not contested. It is indexed and searchable. The response was quieter than a local zoning controversy.

Paul Slovic, a psychologist at the University of Oregon, has spent decades studying what he calls psychic numbing: the finding that as the number of victims grows, our emotional response does not scale with it. It shrinks. One child in danger mobilizes everything in us. A hundred thousand produces a kind of cognitive static. Slovic calls the related phenomenon the collapse of compassion: the sheer scope of suffering causes people to disengage as a form of psychological self-preservation. The Epstein case does not involve one victim. It involves a documented operation spanning three decades, six million pages of evidence, and connections reaching into the highest offices on multiple

continents. The scale is part of why it refuses to
register. The mind was not built for this size of
horror.

When catastrophes arrive without pause, each
one compresses the attention the previous one
was still owed. The Epstein files landed in a
news environment simultaneously absorbing
economic disruption, immigration enforcement,
institutional dismantling, and the sheer daily
volume of an administration that had apparently
decided governing and spectacle were the same
activity. The public's attention was not stolen. It
was exhausted.

Beneath psychic numbing and information
overload sits something older, and it is the one
Festinger's cult members would recognize.
People need the system to be fundamentally
legitimate. Their financial security depends on it.
Their physical safety depends on it. Their sense
of reality depends on it. Accepting that those at
the highest levels of power abused children and
used that abuse as leverage, with institutional
protection from law enforcement, prosecutors,
and executives across administrations and
parties, is not the same as accepting that the
system is broken. It means the system worked as
intended, by people for whom your safety and
your children's safety were simply not variables.

That is not a comforting update. So the mind does not accept it.

A scandal with no partisan escape route was efficiently given one anyway. This operation ran across four presidencies. Clinton. Bush. Obama. Trump. Federal protection was extended under all of them. Prosecutors from both parties declined to act. The 2007 sweetheart deal was signed by a Republican U.S. Attorney who later joined a Republican administration. The institutional failure is not a story about one party covering for its own. It is a story about power protecting power, regardless of which party happened to be branding it that year.

The partisan framing is itself the denial. The MAGA base demanded the files believing they would expose Democratic elites. They do, in part. Trump supporters are now absorbing a million-count reference to their candidate while insisting only the Democratic appearances carry moral weight. Democrats point to Trump while explaining away Clinton. Both sides engage with the evidence, extract what confirms what they already believed, and deploy the scandal as ammunition rather than receive it as information. The content is not denied. The implications are. Implicatory denial, operating at national scale, sorted by partisan affiliation, amplified by algorithm. Each side has been delivered the version of the story that requires them to change nothing about how they understand the system they live inside.

None of this requires malicious coordination. It requires something far more ordinary.

Hannah Arendt's „banality of evil" was made for this. Denial isn't dramatic. It's ordinary people participating in harmful systems by not thinking too carefully, compartmentalizing, doing their jobs, and declining to connect cause to effect. Albert Bandura mapped the mechanisms: moral justification reframes harm as serving higher purposes; euphemistic labeling keeps the language clean; displacement of responsibility produces „just following orders"; diffusion of responsibility spreads accountability so thinly that no one feels it land. These aren't failures of character in exceptional circumstances. They are the normal operating procedures of minds protecting themselves from a truth that would cost too much to hold. This is how ordinary people participate in extraordinary evil: not through malice, but through the daily practice of not quite looking.

We're in denial about our capacity for denial. We've been convinced it belongs to other people. Climate deniers. Genocide deniers. Conspiracy theorists. They're the ones with the problem.

But we're all in denial about something. Highly educated people aren't less prone to it; they're better at it. They construct elaborate justifications, acknowledge problems in the abstract while avoiding personal implications, and manage to know and not know simultaneously without breaking a sweat. It's like a sommelier describing in exquisite detail why drinking is destroying their liver, citing recent studies, using perfect medical terminology, while pouring another glass. The sophistication doesn't make it less of a rationalization. It just makes it a very well-educated one.

True acknowledgment requires behavioral change. Saying you believe climate change threatens civilization while maintaining the same lifestyle is implicatory denial with a concerned expression. Opposing racism without examining your own biases is interpretive denial dressed as principle. Wanting democracy while participating only at election time is literal denial about what self-governance has ever required of anyone.

Awareness without integration is sophisticated denial. Knowing without changing is intellectual performance. The question isn't whether you can name the problem. It's whether naming it has cost you anything.

So what are you in denial about? What is your society refusing to see? Not the American one, or the European one, or the one you read about in the news. Yours. And more importantly: what would change if you decided to find out?

II. Exploration and Acknowledgment

Collective Truth Telling

The alcoholic who insists they don't have a problem keeps drinking. Not because they lack information. The label is right there on every bottle. They keep drinking because self-deception isn't a knowledge problem. It's a survival strategy: if you don't see the pattern, you don't have to change it. The cost of honesty is higher than the cost of the lie, at least until the day it isn't.

Nations operate on the same logic. Not as metaphor. As mechanism. The patterns a society won't name are the patterns it can't escape. And the architecture of modern democracy has been quietly engineered to make the lies more comfortable than the truth.

Current representative systems give you the gift of distance. Someone else makes the decisions. Someone else is responsible for outcomes. You voted once every few years, you participated, you did your part. If things are broken, it's their fault. This isn't an accident of design. It's the design.

Consider 2008. Citigroup, Bank of America, Goldman Sachs, and others had spent years bundling worthless mortgages into securities that rating agencies stamped AAA, selling them to pension funds and municipalities, and then quietly betting against them. When the whole structure collapsed, the Treasury deployed $700 billion in TARP funds to the same institutions that caused the crisis. Lehman Brothers was allowed to fail; everyone else was made whole. Nobody went to prison. American households lost $13 trillion in net worth. The median family's wealth dropped 39 percent between 2007 and 2010, the steepest fall since the Depression. The six largest U.S. banks recovered within three years and are now roughly twice their pre-crisis size. And the core instruments have been updated rather than eliminated: collateralized loan obligations have largely replaced the CDOs that detonated in 2008, carrying many of the same structural weaknesses.

We know this. The information is publicly available. The congressional hearings are on C-SPAN. The Financial Crisis Inquiry Commission published 662 pages. Yet the prevailing fiction remains: it was a few bad actors, regulations fixed it, deposits are safe. Why? Because acknowledging the full picture requires action most people aren't prepared to

take. Comfortable lies don't cost anything until
they do.

The system doesn't just permit this. It requires
it. Politicians who tell hard truths lose elections
to comfortable liars. Media amplifies whatever
drives engagement, accuracy optional.
„Independent research“ has a remarkable habit
of independently concluding that whoever paid
for it was right. Philip Morris's scientists spent
decades finding cigarettes safe, right up until
internal documents revealed the company had
known about cancer links since the 1950s and
spent thirty years burying them. The system isn't
broken. It's working exactly as designed, just not
for you.

Citizens face their own version of this pressure.
Acknowledge your vote doesn't matter and you
feel powerless. Admit both parties serve the
same donor class and you lose your tribal
identity. Recognize the confusion is
manufactured and you have to take
responsibility for navigating it. Most people
prefer to feel like participants in a broken
system rather than spectators to a deliberate
one.

The entire arrangement depends on these
fictions being stickier than the truth.

Making Lies Expensive

Here's what most reformers miss: shaming doesn't produce honesty. Education alone doesn't produce truth-telling. Good intentions don't survive conditions that punish transparency and reward deception. The only durable fix is making lies more costly than telling the truth. Right now, the incentives run the other direction.

Start by inverting surveillance. Your phone knows where you were last Tuesday at 3pm. You have no idea which lobbyist your representative met that same afternoon. One of these facts seems more relevant to democracy, and yet only one is systematically collected. Full transparency for political decisions, resource allocations, and financial flows between corporations and officials. Full privacy for individual citizens unless there is specific evidence of specific crimes. Blockchain infrastructure makes this technically straightforward: immutable records of every political transaction, traceable and permanent. Not cryptocurrency speculation. Accountability infrastructure.

Distributed verification replaces dependence on official oversight. Bellingcat, the open-source intelligence collective founded by Eliot Higgins, has spent years demonstrating what motivated people with internet access can do: they used commercial satellite imagery to track Russian military movements in Ukraine before NATO confirmed them, identified the operatives behind the Salisbury poisoning from flight records and hotel bookings, and documented Syrian chemical weapons attacks the government denied. Official oversight requires institutional will. Distributed verification just requires access to public data and enough people who care.

Prediction markets work on a related principle. When people bet real money on outcomes, accuracy starts mattering more than ideology. Robin Hanson at George Mason University has argued for decades that prediction markets systematically outperform expert forecasting precisely because the price mechanism punishes wishful thinking. Philip Tetlock's superforecasting research found that crowds of informed amateurs, properly aggregated, beat intelligence analysts with access to classified information. It turns out strongly held political convictions are only worth holding when they're free. Put money on the line and the certainty evaporates.

What this looks like in practice: Iceland. After its banking system collapsed in 2008, the country prosecuted 26 senior bankers. The prime minister was convicted of negligence. The banks were allowed to fail rather than bailed out. The economy contracted sharply, then recovered faster than Ireland or Greece, both of which chose the opposite path. Iceland is a small country with unusual political conditions, but it demonstrated something the rest of the world preferred not to examine too closely: when decision-makers face real consequences for failure, the incentive to lie about outcomes changes.

You cannot have genuine democracy without genuine truth-telling. If citizens make decisions based on manipulated information, they are not governing themselves. They're being governed by whoever controls the narrative. The magic trick only works if you don't look at the magician's hands, and it has always relied on most people preferring the show.

This is genuinely threatening. You can no longer blame a distant system for outcomes you participated in. You can't maintain comfortable fictions about accountability when accountability is immediate and visible. You can't confuse participation with influence when performance is measured in real time.

It is also the only exit. Instead of choosing which pre-packaged lie to believe every four years, you could evaluate performance as it happens. Instead of hoping politicians keep promises, you could remove them when they don't. Instead of accepting that „this is just how things work," you could build systems that actually work, which is a very different project than trying to fix systems designed not to.

A person who lies to themselves cannot grow. A nation that lies to itself cannot evolve. Truth-telling is not just a necessity of a functioning democracy. It's the foundation. Without it, you're not choosing between political alternatives. You're choosing which fiction to believe while someone else makes the actual decisions.

We cannot change what we refuse to see.

Force Doctrine

You are reading this in a country that has, at some point, threatened to kill you. Not you personally, perhaps. But anyone who seriously and persistently refuses to follow its rules. The chain is long and usually invisible: fine, then warrant, then arrest, then force. Most people never reach the end of it. But the end is always there.

Max Weber defined the state as the entity that holds a monopoly on the legitimate use of violence within a territory. Not the provision of services. Not the representation of citizens. Not the protection of rights. The monopoly on violence.

The state claims the exclusive right to use force. You cannot. If you use force, even to defend yourself, you're subject to the state's judgment about whether that use was legitimate. The state decides. Always the state.

This is by design.

Every government, regardless of ideology or structure, is built on this monopoly. Democratic governments. Authoritarian governments. Socialist governments. Capitalist governments. All of them claim the exclusive right to legitimate violence and work tirelessly to maintain it.

The framing is usually about safety: we need the state to have this monopoly to protect us from each other. Without it, we'd have chaos, violence, warlords, and constant conflict. The Hobbesian nightmare of all against all.

Here's the thing: this framing isn't entirely wrong. The state's monopoly on violence does reduce certain types of violence. It prevents blood feuds from spiraling endlessly. It stops local warlords from carving out territories. It creates stability that allows commerce, culture, and cooperation to flourish. Medieval Europe's endless private wars were not exactly a golden age of peace and prosperity, unless your idea of peace involves your village being burned down by someone else's grievance.

The monopoly is, in many ways, a necessary evil. Both words carry weight.

Without the capacity to punish violations, laws are just suggestions. Rights aren't naturally given; they're enforced. This is how the monopoly actually functions: through the threat of force backing every law, every rule, every claim to rights.

But they don't emphasize the reverse: safety can only be generated by the capacity to express force. If you cannot defend yourself, you are not safe. You are dependent. And if you can defend yourself, you become a threat.

This creates an unresolvable tension at the heart of every state: to reduce violence among citizens, the state concentrates power. But concentrated power makes citizens powerless against the state itself. You gain protection from your neighbors. You lose protection from your government.

Internal peace comes at the cost of the capacity to resist. Citizens must be disempowered enough that they can't challenge state authority, but must feel safe enough that they consent to this disempowerment. It's a bargain most people accept without ever being told they're making it.

We pretend we've solved this tension. We haven't. We've just chosen which risks we're willing to accept, then stopped talking about the costs.

The Monopoly Isn't Natural

For most of human history, power was distributed. Tribes, clans, and communities defended themselves. Some had leaders, but those leaders didn't have monopolies on violence. They had influence, authority, sometimes deference, but not the exclusive right to force.

The state monopoly on violence is a relatively recent invention, created through conquest, consolidation, and the systematic disarmament of populations.

European state formation is instructive. Medieval Europe was a patchwork of overlapping authorities: local lords, religious institutions, guilds, free cities, each with some capacity for violence. The modern state emerged by eliminating these competing power centers and concentrating force in a single entity.

How? Through systematic disarmament. Banning private armies. Outlawing dueling. Monopolizing weapons production. Creating professional standing armies loyal to the state rather than local authorities. Making it illegal for anyone except state agents to use violence, even in self-defense, without state approval. Each step concentrated power further; each restriction made resistance harder.

This wasn't done for public safety. It was done for state security. A population that can defend itself can also resist. A population dependent on the state for protection cannot.

Can democracy exist if the population can't resist the state? Political power rests on the capacity for violence. If only the state has that capacity, citizens have permission, not power. Permission can be revoked.

Yet the alternative carries real costs. Armed populations face constant instability. Disputes escalate. Militias become warlords. Blood feuds spiral. Every stable democracy has chosen disarmament, for understandable reasons.

History complicates the question. Ottoman Turkey disarmed its Armenian population before the genocide. Nazi Germany before the Holocaust. Soviet Russia before the purges. Cambodia before the Killing Fields. Rwanda before the genocide. Most disarmed populations aren't exterminated, but states bent on oppression reliably disarm first. An armed population is expensive to oppress.

Yet most armed populations throughout history haven't experienced freedom either, just different forms of violence. The real question isn't which risk is greater. It's whether there's a way to have genuine citizen power without needing the capacity for violence.

The process continues today. Every gun control debate, every restriction on self-defense, every expansion of police power, every new surveillance capability is about maintaining and extending this monopoly. Safety is the justification. Power is the point.

This creates a paradox: you are safest from your neighbors when the state is strong enough to suppress local violence. Murder rates in functioning states are dramatically lower than in failed states or stateless societies. That's real. But the same power that protects you from your neighbor makes you vulnerable to the state. The entity strong enough to prevent your neighbor from killing you is also strong enough to kill you with impunity. The force that stops private armies and blood feuds can also suppress dissent, crush resistance, and commit atrocities you can do nothing about.

This is why comparing states to mafia protection rackets, while provocative, isn't entirely fair. The mafia offers nothing and threatens harm. The state actually provides real protection from certain threats. The problem is that in providing that protection, it becomes a threat itself. One you can't defend against because you've surrendered your capacity for defense to it. The mafia, at least, never pretended to be running a democracy.

The phrase „law and order" reveals this tension. At its best, it means predictable rules enforced fairly, allowing people to cooperate without constant fear. At its realistic worst, it means: the state's monopoly is secure, citizens are compliant, and the threat of force is sufficient to prevent most challenges to authority.

You get stability and reduced internal violence. The ability to plan for the future without constant fear of armed conflict. These aren't nothing. But you also get powerlessness, dependence, and no recourse when the state itself becomes the problem.

Weapons restrictions were only the beginning. Consider how the monopoly is maintained today.

Adam Smith noticed something in a different context entirely that explains why the modern mechanisms work so well. In The Wealth of Nations, he observed that „the understandings of the greater part of men are necessarily formed by their ordinary employments." He was describing factory workers who, performing the same narrow task every day, gradually lost the capacity for broader thought. The mind adapts to what it practices. Use only one part of it long enough, and the rest atrophies.

The principle applies to citizenship. When your role as a citizen is reduced to occasional voting and passive consumption, you develop capacity for exactly that. You learn to choose between pre-selected options. You learn to watch politics like entertainment. What you never develop is the capacity for genuine decision-making, for grappling with trade-offs, for taking responsibility for collective outcomes. The system demands dependence, so it produces dependent citizens. It never demands that you govern, so that capacity never develops.

The mechanisms below aren't just security measures. They're the conditions that make this atrophy permanent.

The legal system creates a monopoly on force itself. Only state actors can legally use violence. Even clear self-defense cases get scrutinized, prosecuted, and used to demonstrate that citizens don't have the authority to use force without state approval. The message is unambiguous: violence belongs to us.

Surveillance systems monitor populations to identify potential threats before they can organize. The mechanisms have grown precise enough that organizing a serious challenge to state authority has become nearly impossible before it's detected. In 2013, documents leaked by Edward Snowden revealed that the NSA was collecting phone metadata on hundreds of millions of Americans who had committed no crime and were under no investigation. The program wasn't designed to catch terrorists after the fact. It was designed to know who was talking to whom before anything happened.

You can't organize what the state can see forming.

Welfare states create populations dependent on government for survival. Not out of compassion, though that's the justification, but because dependent populations don't revolt. You're less likely to resist when resistance means losing your income, healthcare, housing, and food. Economic dependency is economic control, and it works precisely because it isn't experienced as control at all. It's experienced as security.

Professional militaries stand loyal to the state rather than communities. These soldiers follow orders to suppress their own populations because they belong to a separate structure with separate interests and a separate identity. Revolutionaries have always understood this: you can't overcome the state's power monopoly if the military remains loyal to the state. The entire purpose of military culture — the uniforms, the hierarchy, the separation from civilian life — is to ensure that when the order comes, it gets followed.

The narrative teaches populations that the state's monopoly is natural, necessary, and legitimate. That resistance is terrorism. That self-defense is vigilantism. That wanting to retain any capacity for force is paranoid or extremist. Convince people that power concentration equals safety, and they'll surrender power willingly. They'll even demand it.

The most effective mechanism: divide and conquer. Keep populations fighting each other so they don't unite against the state. If citizens see each other as threats, they'll demand more state protection. If they fear their neighbors more than their government, they'll accept expanded state power. This is why identity politics gets amplified while class consciousness gets suppressed. United populations are dangerous. Divided populations are manageable.

The power monopoly is the foundation. Everything else builds on it.

Democracy as Performance

The ultimate expression of the monopoly sits at the heart of representative democracy itself: political parties and executives.

Representative democracy makes this monopoly seem legitimate while obscuring its costs. You vote, therefore you have power. You can influence the government, therefore you're not powerless. These claims aren't entirely false. They're just not entirely true.

You vote for representatives who then have authority over you, backed by a monopoly on force. But you don't actually choose your representatives freely. You choose from options pre-selected by political parties. These parties function as gatekeepers, filtering who gets to run, who gets funding, who gets media attention, who appears on your ballot.

The party system creates an additional layer of power concentration on top of the state monopoly on violence. Not only can't you resist the state, you can't even choose who represents you within that state. You pick from Party A's candidate or Party B's candidate, both selected through internal party mechanisms you have no real influence over.

Then there's the executive. Presidents, prime ministers, chancellors. A single person or small group concentrating enormous power. They command the military. They control enforcement. They direct bureaucracies. All backed by the state's monopoly on violence. Even if you didn't vote for them, even if your entire region opposed them, they have authority over you. Then you hope. Hope the executive uses power well. Hope the party keeps its promises. Hope this particular individual, with this much concentrated power, turns out to be reasonable. For a system supposedly designed to limit individual power, it places a remarkable amount of faith in individuals.

Parties consolidate power by controlling access to representation. Executives consolidate power by centralizing decision-making. Both work with the state monopoly on violence to ensure citizens remain dependent and compliant. Your only legitimate option is to participate in this system. You can't resist; that's illegal. You can't organize genuine alternatives; that's insurrection. You can't even choose representatives outside the party system without those candidates being marginalized, underfunded, and treated as spoilers who ruined everything.

We've been told this structure is necessary for representative democracy to function, that parties organize politics and executives provide leadership. But what if that's not true? What if representative democracy could function without parties filtering candidates? What if representation could work without centralizing power in executives? What if the structure itself could be different while still maintaining stability and representation?

These questions cut to the heart of the matter: can citizens have genuine influence over who represents them, or must that influence always be mediated through power-concentrating institutions?

The result is a system that produces politicians who optimize for reelection rather than good governance, security theater that surveils everyone while protecting primarily those already in power, and structures that concentrate power while distributing blame. Citizens become passive consumers of politics, choosing between pre-selected options every few years, then watching helplessly as those choices fail to produce meaningful change.

The monopoly on violence ensures this arrangement can't be challenged from outside. The party system ensures citizens never get to choose representatives freely. The executive system concentrates decision-making regardless of how citizens vote. The system works exactly as intended.

The Direction Out

The current system doesn't just fail citizens. It actively prevents them from developing the capacities that would allow them to demand something better. That's the deeper problem. Not simply that power is concentrated, but that the concentration is self-reinforcing. Citizens who have never genuinely governed can't easily imagine doing so, which makes the existing system appear more necessary than it is.

Changing this requires more than minor reforms. Not tweaks to campaign finance or term limits. Fundamental restructuring of how representation functions: removing the mechanisms that concentrate power, eliminating the filters that prevent genuine citizen choice, creating systems where representation actually serves citizens rather than party interests and executive ambitions. That means transparency deep enough to make manipulation visible. Infrastructure for distributed responsibility rather than concentrated authority. Education that develops critical thinking rather than political consumption.

Would this be risky? Absolutely. Less stable governance during transition. Outcomes shaped by populations unused to genuine influence. Mistakes that more centralized systems might have avoided. These are real concerns, not small ones.

But consider what we're comparing them to: a system designed to maintain concentrated power, structured to prevent citizens from ever developing the capacities they'd need to govern themselves, backed by a monopoly on violence that makes resistance illegal and meaningful change nearly impossible through legitimate channels. Internal stability purchased at the cost of everything else.

You've surrendered your capacity for self-governance to institutions that don't actually govern on your behalf. The stability you received in return is real. The powerlessness is also real. And the longer that bargain holds, the harder it becomes to imagine an alternative. That difficulty is precisely the point.

Genuine self-governance requires citizens capable of collective decision-making. We're not there yet, and the current system is designed to make sure we never get there on its own terms. But the structural barriers aren't permanent features of reality. They're design choices. And design choices can be redesigned.

What that restructuring actually looks like, and what psychological conditions make it possible, is where this book goes next.

Media & Conspiracy

In 2013, Jeff Bezos bought The Washington Post for $250 million. In 2022, Elon Musk bought Twitter for $44 billion. The wealthiest people on Earth aren't buying yachts and islands anymore. They're buying something far more valuable.

They're buying your reality.

Billionaires don't acquire media platforms to lose money or champion free speech. They do it because controlling information flow is more valuable than any other asset. Oil runs out. Real estate gets regulated. Technology becomes obsolete. But the power to shape what billions of people believe is true? That's the ultimate monopoly.

Amazon has massive cloud computing contracts with the CIA and Department of Defense. Can The Washington Post credibly investigate Amazon's government contracts, labor practices, or tax avoidance when its owner depends on those same agencies for billions in revenue? After Musk bought Twitter, accounts promoting his business interests received favorable treatment while critics found themselves suspended. Bill Gates took a different approach, distributing over $300 million in grants to media organizations including NPR, BBC, The Guardian, and CNN. When your newsroom's budget depends on Gates Foundation grants, independence becomes theoretical.

The pattern repeats globally. In France, billionaires Bernard Arnault, Vincent Bolloré, and Patrick Drahi own virtually all major outlets. In the Czech Republic, Andrej Babiš owned a media conglomerate while serving as Prime Minister. India's Adani and Ambani have extensive media holdings supporting Modi's government. Bloomberg ran a presidential campaign while owning a financial news service. When the same people own both the microphone and the message, calling it „media" seems generous.

Ask yourself: when was the last time mainstream media exposed something powerful institutions wanted hidden? Not repeated what whistleblowers revealed. Not covered a scandal after it became unavoidable. But actually investigated and broke a story that threatened real power? If you're struggling to think of examples, there's a reason.

This chapter isn't about „media bias" or „fake news." Those surface debates miss the fundamental point. Media isn't primarily an information system. It's a control system. The control comes from multiple directions:

corporate ownership, billionaire vanity projects, intelligence agency infiltration, and algorithms designed to maximize engagement rather than inform. Understanding how this system works is essential for anyone imagining a society where citizens make informed decisions rather than absorb carefully curated narratives.

What follows contains information about institutional crimes most people have never heard about, despite being documented in declassified files and congressional reports. If your first instinct is skepticism, that's reasonable. Healthy, even. The evidence doesn't ask you to trust the author. It asks you to read the documents. They speak for themselves.

The Monopoly on Reality

Six corporations control 90% of American media. In 1983, fifty corporations controlled the majority. Today it's six: Comcast, Disney, Warner Bros. Discovery, Paramount, Fox Corporation, and Sony. If ideas were breakfast cereal, you'd have six companies deciding whether you get corn flakes or slightly different corn flakes. At least with actual cereal, the different boxes taste slightly different.

In Australia, Rupert Murdoch's News Corp owns roughly 70% of newspaper circulation. That's not media diversity. That's Murdoch talking to himself in different accents. In Germany, Axel Springer SE dominates with Bild, Welt, and numerous digital properties.

The concentration goes deeper than outlet ownership. Most news organizations don't have reporters everywhere. They rely on wire services for the majority of international and national news, primarily Reuters and Associated Press. These aren't occasional sources. They're the primary content providers for thousands of outlets worldwide.

This creates a bottleneck effect. When Reuters or AP frames a story a certain way, that framing replicates across hundreds of outlets simultaneously, carrying the same omissions, the same embedded assumptions, and the same foundational choices about what matters and what doesn't. The local newspaper in Kansas City, the TV station in Portland, and the news website in Miami all run the same Reuters story. Different outlets add their own commentary, creating the illusion of diverse coverage, but the foundational information comes from the same source. It's like a thousand restaurants using ingredients from the same two suppliers while claiming to offer unique cuisines. Sure, one adds paprika and another adds cumin, but they're both serving the same chicken.

Corporate consolidation creates structural control. However, there's another layer that operated in plain sight for decades before being exposed.

The Intelligence Layer

In 1975, the United States Senate conducted the Church Committee hearings, which provided the first official look at Operation Mockingbird. This was a systematic CIA program designed to infiltrate American newsrooms. This wasn't limited to fringe publications. The CIA had assets at The New York Times, CBS, Time magazine, Newsweek, The Washington Post, and dozens of other mainstream outlets. Congressional investigators found relationships with over 400 journalists and media figures. CBS President William Paley provided cover jobs for CIA agents and let the agency use CBS facilities. The New York Times provided cover for CIA operatives working as foreign correspondents. Journalists received stories written by CIA officers, published them under their own bylines, and presented manufactured narratives as independent reporting. It's ghostwriting, except instead of celebrity memoirs, it's foreign policy propaganda. The distance between „independent journalism" and „intelligence operation" effectively disappeared.

At least when corporations buy journalists, they're honest about it.

The operation's sophistication went beyond planted stories. The CIA funded book publishers, supported journalists financially to create dependency, and manufactured bestsellers by buying up first editions to boost rankings. They organized conferences where academics and journalists absorbed CIA-friendly interpretations. The entire infrastructure of American information was compromised.

When reporter Carl Bernstein exposed this in a 1977 Rolling Stone article, the CIA admitted to relationships with journalists but claimed the program had ended. They portrayed it as a Cold War necessity that wouldn't happen again. The infrastructure remained intact. The relationships continued. The only thing that changed was operational security. Future Mockingbird operations would be more carefully concealed. It's not really a reform if you just get better at hiding it.

The label of „conspiracy theory" has a very specific and tactical origin. In 1967, the CIA distributed a memo titled „Countering Criticism of the Warren Report." This document outlined strategies to discredit anyone who questioned the official narrative of the JFK assassination. It suggested using the phrase „conspiracy theory" to make critics look irrational or psychologically unstable. Today, the term is used as a tool to bypass evidence. It is the intellectual equivalent of holding your finger an inch from someone's face while saying „I'm not touching you." Technically not censorship. Functionally the same result.

The lesson isn't that every conspiracy theory is true. Most aren't. The lesson is that documented conspiracies prove institutions routinely do things that would sound absurd if you proposed them hypothetically. If someone in 1960 suggested the CIA spent decades compromising American media to manipulate public opinion, they'd be dismissed as paranoid. Then the documents got declassified. Suddenly the paranoid people were just early.

Mockingbird had a formal name because it was an application of a formal methodology. That methodology is called a psychological operation, and understanding it is more useful than knowing any single historical example.

A psychological operation is a documented military methodology, taught in academies, funded by governments, and deployed routinely against both foreign and domestic populations. Intelligence agencies publish manuals on it. The term has a formal definition and a recorded history. What it lacks is a prominent place in the public conversation about how information actually works.

The mechanics are consistent across every documented case, which is what makes them worth learning. A single approved narrative saturates all major outlets simultaneously. Questioning it is not answered with evidence but with social cost. Critics are not refuted; they are categorized. The language migrates from „this is true" to „only fringe voices disagree," which sounds similar but is a fundamentally weaker claim. Deliberation is foreclosed through urgency, because careful thinking is the natural enemy of manufactured consensus. The boundary of acceptable debate is drawn not by evidence but by institutional authority. Experts who dissent lose their platforms. Experts who comply are amplified regardless of their track record.

You have already seen this pattern in Operation Mockingbird. You will see it again in the lead-up to the Iraq War, where dissenting voices were sidelined in real time while the official narrative collapsed within years. You will see it in the early period of COVID-19, where questioning the origin of the virus was sufficient to end careers and trigger platform bans, at a time when institutional bodies had not yet revised positions they would later quietly abandon. The specific subject changes each time. The structure does not.

The most reliable indicator of a psyop is not the content of the message. It is what happens to people who ask questions about it.

Manufacturing Wars

The lead-up to the Iraq War demonstrates how this system operates. Every major American outlet repeated the weapons of mass destruction narrative uncritically. The New York Times. The Washington Post. CNN. Fox News. All platformed officials making false claims while marginalizing skeptics.

Phil Donahue had the highest-rated show on MSNBC in 2003. He was also one of the few mainstream voices questioning the rush to war. MSNBC canceled his show three weeks before the invasion.

An internal NBC memo explained why. Donahue presented a „difficult public face for NBC in a time of war" because he would be „a home for the liberal anti-war agenda." Translation: we can't have our highest-rated show asking inconvenient questions when there's a war to sell. Profitability takes a backseat to patriotic narrative control.

Dissent during the buildup wasn't suppressed through government censorship. It was suppressed through corporate decision-making. The result was the same: a population primed for war through coordinated media messaging. It's censorship with better PR.

Notice the pattern. Every intervention gets justified through fear. In Iraq, weapons of mass destruction that could reach America in 45 minutes. Spoiler: they couldn't, because they didn't exist. In Libya, preventing genocide. In Syria, chemical weapons. The specific threat changes. The mechanism remains constant. Manufacture a fear that's immediate, visceral, and requires urgent action. Critical thinking is hard when you're terrified.

Fear bypasses rational analysis. A scared population doesn't ask careful questions about evidence, costs, alternatives, or consequences. They demand protection. And whoever controls the narrative about the threat controls the response.

This isn't unique to war. Fear of terrorism justifies surveillance, fear of crime justifies militarized policing, fear of economic collapse justifies bailouts for banks, and fear of misinformation justifies censorship. Fear is the universal justification. It works for everything.

Media amplifies these fears systematically. Terrorism coverage focuses on spectacular attacks while ignoring that you're statistically more likely to die from furniture accidents than terrorism. IKEA is literally more dangerous than Al-Qaeda, but nobody's building a surveillance state to monitor your Billy bookcase. Crime coverage emphasizes violent incidents while rates drop. The function is clear: keep the population afraid, and they'll accept almost any exercise of power as necessary protection.

Britain's involvement in Iraq depended on the „September Dossier," which claimed Iraq could deploy WMDs within 45 minutes. The BBC initially reported that the government had „sexed up" the intelligence. The government attacked the BBC viciously. The BBC's source was Dr. David Kelly, a weapons expert and senior official. He was found dead in the woods shortly after being publicly named. An official inquiry ruled it suicide. The BBC's Chairman and Director-General both resigned regardless. After this, BBC coverage of government foreign policy became noticeably more cautious.

The Buried Record

Ask ten people what MK-Ultra was. Most won't know. Ask about Operation Mockingbird. Blank stares. Gary Webb? Maybe one person has heard the name.

These aren't obscure historical footnotes. They're massive institutional crimes with thousands of victims and declassified documentation proving they happened. Most people have simply never heard of them. The information is available. Media simply never gave these stories the coverage they deserved.

Between 1953 and 1973, the CIA ran MK-Ultra. They dosed unwitting citizens with LSD and conducted torture experiments on prisoners, mental patients, and ordinary people who had no idea they were being experimented on. When congressional investigations threatened exposure, CIA Director Richard Helms ordered all files destroyed. Congressional hearings in 1975 and 1977 exposed some details.

Did this become a media sensation? Did investigative journalists dig into how many victims there were? Did major outlets demand accountability for systematic government torture of American citizens? No. The story got minimal coverage, was quickly forgotten, and today most Americans have never heard of it.

The government tortured its own citizens for twenty years, destroyed the evidence, and media treated it like a minor historical curiosity.

In the 1980s, the CIA facilitated cocaine trafficking to fund Contra rebels after Congress banned their funding. Journalist Gary Webb exposed this in his 1996 „Dark Alliance" series, documenting how the CIA allowed Contra-connected drug traffickers to flood Los Angeles with cocaine, fueling the crack epidemic that devastated Black communities. The response from major media wasn't to investigate his claims. It was to destroy him. The Washington Post, New York Times, and Los Angeles Times all ran pieces attacking Webb's methods rather than the CIA's conduct. He lost his job, his career, and in 2004, his life. He died of two gunshot wounds to the head, ruled a suicide.

Years later, the CIA's Inspector General quietly confirmed his core allegations. The outlets that destroyed him never apologized. That's not an oversight. That's the system working as designed. When someone exposes institutional crimes, media doesn't investigate the institutions. It investigates the whistleblower.

Operation Northwoods, a 1962 proposal from the Joint Chiefs of Staff, planned to stage terrorist attacks against American targets, blame Cuba, and justify invasion. The documents specified that „casualty lists in U.S. newspapers would cause a helpful wave of national indignation." The highest levels of American military leadership were willing to murder American civilians to justify war.

These documents were declassified in 1997. Did this revelation dominate news cycles? Did media investigate how many other false flag proposals exist? Did they question whether any attacks in American history might have been staged? No. The story got brief coverage and disappeared. Most Americans still don't know their own military proposed killing them for propaganda purposes.

The Gulf of Tonkin incident that justified Vietnam escalation never happened. The second attack was fabricated. The Johnson administration used a fictional event to launch a war that killed millions. This was confirmed by declassified NSA documents in 2005.

The story got minimal coverage. Media moved on. Most people still believe the Gulf of Tonkin incident was real because that's what they learned in school, and the press never adequately corrected the record. There were no primetime specials. No investigative series examining how many other wars were launched on manufactured pretexts. The documents arrived, confirmed a historic lie, and the news cycle absorbed them like water into concrete.

What these cases reveal about media is consistent. When the government commits massive crimes, media's job isn't to investigate those crimes. It's to ignore them, minimize them, or attack those who expose them. The information exists. The documents are public. Congressional hearings happened. Inspector General reports were released. But if media doesn't cover it prominently and repeatedly, most people never learn about it. And media doesn't cover it prominently and repeatedly because doing so would undermine faith in the institutions that media depends on for access, sources, and coordinated messaging.

You weren't informed about MK-Ultra because media didn't think systematic government torture deserved sustained coverage. You weren't informed about CIA drug trafficking because media destroyed the journalist who exposed it rather than investigating his claims. You weren't informed about Operation Northwoods because media didn't want you questioning whether other attacks might have been staged.

The conspiracy isn't that these things happened. That's documented fact. The conspiracy is the coordinated media silence about them after exposure. The real cover-up isn't destroying the evidence. It's ensuring nobody hears about it even when the evidence survives.

This isn't uniquely American. Britain's media largely ignored the Hillsborough disaster cover-up for decades. In 1989, 96 Liverpool fans died at a football stadium due to police failures. The police blamed the victims. Media repeated these claims without investigation. It took 27 years of families fighting before official inquests ruled the fans were unlawfully killed and the police had orchestrated a cover-up. Media didn't uncover it. Families did.

France's media gave minimal coverage to the Rainbow Warrior bombing. In 1985, French intelligence agents bombed a Greenpeace ship in New Zealand, killing a photographer. The French government denied involvement. When evidence emerged, French outlets largely downplayed the story while foreign journalists exposed it. Domestic media protected its government's reputation.

Australia's media spent decades ignoring the Stolen Generations. This was the official policy of forcibly removing Aboriginal children from their families, which ran from the 1910s through the 1970s. This wasn't hidden. It was government policy, carried out in daylight. Australian media treated it as benign welfare administration until activists and survivors forced the issue into public consciousness in the 1990s.

The mechanism is identical across democracies: domestic media depends on government access, shares class interests with power, and faces consequences for aggressive investigation of institutions. When governments commit crimes, domestic media minimizes, ignores, or defends them. Foreign journalists might investigate. Families might force the truth out. But the press, as an institution, protects the powerful it depends on.

This doesn't mean every conspiracy theory is true. Most are unprovable noise that keeps people in constant fear and dysfunction, unable to distinguish reality from paranoid speculation. When institutions with documented histories of lying, experimenting on citizens, and trafficking drugs tell you something, healthy skepticism is appropriate. But proportionate skepticism doesn't mean believing every world event is orchestrated by hidden powers. Focus on what's documented. Dismiss what's unfalsifiable. That's how you stay informed without becoming dysfunctional.

The Social Media Battlefield

Traditional media is dying. Cable news viewership is collapsing. Newspaper circulation is plummeting. Young people get their news from TikTok, YouTube, and Twitter. This terrifies establishment power because social media is harder to control.

Independent journalists on these platforms often had larger audiences than traditional outlets, and during the COVID-19 pandemic, that reach started to matter. Peer-reviewed studies in The Lancet documented cancer diagnosis rates dropping by 14 to 23 percent during the first lockdown. A systematic review found children losing over a year of learning for every year schools stayed closed. Child psychiatrists published data on surging depression, anxiety, and suicidal ideation in adolescents. This research existed. It was in the mainstream medical literature. Researchers raising these concerns in public, however, were treated as irresponsible at best and dangerous at worst.

Playgrounds were taped off to protect children from a virus that posed almost no statistical risk to them. Outdoor dining was banned. Yet riding a packed subway car to the office was deemed perfectly safe. The independent journalists and doctors who pointed out these contradictions using published data were the ones who got banned. In 2024, the House Select Subcommittee on the Coronavirus Pandemic released its 500-page final report after two years of investigation. It confirmed that prolonged lockdowns had caused immeasurable harm to mental and physical health, that the six-feet distancing rule was debunked, and that the „Proximal Origin" paper used to dismiss the lab leak theory had been engineered to push a preferred narrative. The establishment response was not to engage with the evidence. It was to discredit the people sharing it.

The playbook is predictable, and it runs the same sequence every time. Dissenting narratives get labeled „misinformation" regardless of the evidence behind them. Then comes the demand for credentials. Independent journalists without institutional backing are dismissed as unqualified, even when they are more accurate than credentialed voices repeating the official line. Their motives get questioned next: the independent journalist funded by subscribers is a grifter, while the corporate journalist funded by advertisers is somehow neutral. When none of that works, the platforms coordinate. In 2021, multiple journalists and doctors were simultaneously banned from Twitter, Facebook, and YouTube for questioning COVID-19 policies. Not for being wrong. For being outside the approved conversation.

The threat isn't that citizen journalists are wrong. The threat is that they're right and not controllable.

Right now, there's a media war being waged through social media influencers. Multiple investigations have documented that various actors pay content creators across platforms to shape public opinion. The payments often aren't disclosed. A lifestyle influencer posts about fashion, then suddenly shares „educational" content about geopolitical conflicts. A gaming streamer starts making political commentary between Fortnite matches. Your favorite makeup tutorial creator is now moonlighting as a foreign policy expert. The eyeshadow tips were great, but her analysis of Middle Eastern power dynamics seems suspiciously well-funded.

The practice is global and systematic. Russia's Internet Research Agency got international attention for 2016 election interference, but every government with resources runs similar operations. The difference is that domestic manipulation is legal and called „public relations." When Russia does it, it's election interference. When we do it, it's civic engagement. The magic of terminology strikes again.

Bot farms generate thousands of accounts pushing identical talking points. Social media platforms claim neutrality, but their algorithms make editorial decisions at massive scale. YouTube's algorithm decides which videos get recommended. Twitter's algorithm decides which tweets get visibility. These aren't neutral technical decisions. They're editorial choices made by corporations with their own interests. You don't need censorship when you can just make sure nobody sees the content in the first place.

If you've absorbed what this chapter reveals, you might be feeling unsettled. That's understandable. But this information isn't making you more vulnerable. You were already vulnerable. You just didn't know it. Now you know. That's not a problem. That's progress.

Every person throughout history who successfully navigated corrupt systems did so by understanding them, not by remaining innocent about how they worked. Informed skepticism without fear is what actually threatens power. When you understand how narrative control works, you become harder to manipulate. The system wants you afraid because fear keeps people passive and dependent on authorities to protect them. Don't give them that.

What To Do With This

The current system can't survive an informed population asking these questions consistently. Media concentration, intelligence agency infiltration, billionaire control, and algorithmic manipulation all depend on citizens not understanding how the system works.

Actual democracy requires an informed citizenry. Not persuaded. Not managed. Informed. A population that cannot distinguish between independent reporting and coordinated narrative cannot make genuine decisions about how it is governed. It can only ratify what it has been prepared to accept. That's not democracy. That's the performance of it.

When you engage with media, do it deliberately. Diversify your sources beyond outlets that share the same institutional incentives. Read primary sources: government documents, financial filings, academic studies. The original document usually reveals what the news story left out. Follow the money. And when a headline triggers fear or outrage, pause before reacting. That feeling is probably intentional.

The practical question isn't whether the system is corrupt. The evidence for that is in the declassified files. The question is how you position yourself within it. You can stop consuming news entirely, investing your attention in things you can actually affect: your community, your relationships, your own development. Most of what presents itself as staying informed is anxiety production dressed as civic duty. If something is genuinely important and relevant to your life, you will hear about it.

The system needs you afraid. Fear produces compliance. Understanding produces something the system cannot easily manage: people who know what they are consenting to, and who refuse to consent to what they cannot see. That refusal, multiplied across a population, is what genuine democracy actually looks like. And it begins with understanding why you were never supposed to read this chapter.

Money is a Leash

Let's start with something uncomfortable: money is completely made up.

Not in the sense that it doesn't exist or doesn't matter. It clearly exists and clearly matters; the eviction notice proves that. But in the sense that there's nothing inherent or natural about it. Money is a story we tell ourselves, a collective agreement, a social construct like democracy or corporations or the rules of Monopoly. We created it, we maintain it, and we could change it or replace it entirely if we chose to.

The problem is that we've forgotten this. We've internalized the story so deeply that we can't see it as a story anymore. We treat money like it's a law of physics rather than a convention we invented. We've equated it with survival itself, which makes questioning it feel dangerous, almost suicidal.

Here's what modern slavery looks like: you're free to choose your master, free to negotiate your chains, free to change jobs or start a business or „pursue your dreams," but you're never free from the fundamental requirement to generate money or die. You can pick which corporation extracts value from your labor, which landlord claims a third of your income, which bank holds your debt, but you cannot opt out of the system itself. The moment you stop producing monetary value, you lose access to food, shelter, healthcare, everything that keeps you alive.

This isn't freedom. It's a more elegant form of bondage, one that comes with the psychological burden of believing you chose it.

And it's a remarkably recent invention. For most of human history, „jobs" didn't exist. People worked, certainly. They grew food, made things, traded services. But they didn't sell standardized blocks of their time to employers for wages. Peasants had obligations to lords but not jobs. Craftsmen owned their work, not positions within companies. The modern employment relationship only emerged with industrialization, a few hundred years ago. We've convinced ourselves that a system newer than the steam engine is the natural order of things.

The cruel genius of this arrangement is that it's nobody's fault and everybody's fault simultaneously. You can't point to a single villain who designed it this way. There's no slave master standing over you with a whip. Instead, we're all complicit in maintaining a system that coerces everyone, including those who benefit most from it. The leash isn't held by the rich. It's held by Mammon itself, the god of money, and even the wealthiest among us are on their knees before it.

Worshipping What We Made Up

In medieval times, people understood Mammon as a demon, the personification of greed and material wealth. The biblical warning was unambiguous: you cannot serve both God and Mammon. You have to choose. Modern society solved this problem brilliantly. We simply pretend we're not worshipping anything while dedicating nearly every waking hour to accumulating, protecting, or thinking about money.

If an alien anthropologist studied human behavior, they'd conclude we worship money with far more devotion than any traditional religion ever commanded. We sacrifice relationships, health, time, and meaning to generate income. We make every major life decision through a financial filter. We accept soul-crushing work because the alternative is destitution. At least traditional religions were honest about what they demanded. We've managed to create a god and pretend we're atheists.

And like any good religion, this one has become identity itself. I'm a six-figure earner. I'm a millionaire. I'm broke. We've internalized monetary categories so completely that they function as core aspects of selfhood. People don't just have money or lack it. They are their economic status. When money becomes ego, the money system becomes almost impossible to examine clearly. You can't see the leash when you think the leash is you.

The truly insidious part? Mammon consumes everyone equally, regardless of how much they have. The person working three jobs is enslaved by need. The millionaire is enslaved by fear of loss. The billionaire is enslaved by compulsion to accumulate more. There's no amount that makes you free because freedom isn't the goal. More is the goal, and more is infinite.

This isn't a moral failing. It's architecture. Neuroscientist Kent Berridge's research at the University of Michigan on dopamine reward systems shows that the brain fires more intensely during anticipation than during receipt, and the threshold for what counts as „enough" keeps creeping upward without any natural ceiling. We evolved to seek resources in scarcity, but that same mechanism in abundance becomes a runaway feedback loop. Pursue, acquire, adapt, need more. The treadmill accelerates but never stops.

Most people don't grasp the scale of disparity we're actually discussing. Someone earning

$200,000 per year is doing well. But if they saved every dollar, no expenses, no taxes, it would take 5,000 years to reach one billion. Five thousand years. That's longer than recorded human history. And the wealthiest individuals aren't worth one billion. They're worth hundreds of billions.

The doctor making $500,000 and the tech CEO worth $50 billion don't even exist in the same economic reality. One is still on the leash, just with more slack. The other has accumulated enough power to shape the economy itself. This isn't a difference in degree. It's a difference in kind.

And here's the dangerous part: systems built on unlimited accumulation don't just reward greed. They select for it. The psychopath who feels no guilt about extraction. The narcissist who requires constant admiration that wealth provides. The Machiavellian who views every interaction as strategic manipulation. These aren't aberrations. They're optimal adaptations. When you reward extraction above all else, extractors rise to the top. And yet even they remain trapped in the same compulsive relationship to accumulation, just at scales that would make emperors blush.

Psychologists Philip Brickman and Dan Coates settled the money-equals-freedom question empirically in 1978. Major lottery winners reported no greater happiness than the general population within a year of their windfall, and subsequent research has consistently confirmed the pattern. The money changes the backdrop. The internal weather stays the same. You can't purchase self-worth at any price point, though millions keep trying.

So what makes this leash so effective? It's not made of chain or rope. It's made of fear.

Fear of not having enough. Fear of losing what you have. Fear of falling behind. Fear of being unable to provide. We've equated money with survival, so the fear of losing money becomes indistinguishable from the fear of death itself. And beneath that fear sits something more fundamental: the nagging sense that you're not enough, that you don't have enough, that you'll never be enough. People don't just fear poverty. They fear the shame of it, the exposure, the revelation that they couldn't make it. Money becomes proof of worth, a shield against insignificance. Lose the money and you're not just broke. You're revealed as insufficient.

That hole isn't economic. It's existential. You can't fill an existential void with money any more than you can fill it with alcohol or social media followers. The attempt itself becomes the addiction.

You cannot break free from a fear-based control system while remaining controlled by fear. Intellectual understanding doesn't liberate you. Only the actual work breaks the leash: facing that fear, recognizing how it shapes your decisions, learning to act from something other than fear.

The leash works because we're afraid. The shadow work is learning not to be.

The Paradox of Control

The current monetary system, for all its flaws, has a built-in check on abuse. Push too hard and the whole thing can collapse. Hyperinflation, currency failure, economic meltdown: these are catastrophic but they're also corrective. The threat of collapse limits how far abuse can go. Money's power depends entirely on collective belief, and that belief can evaporate. This is one of its key features as a social construct: it can fail. And that failure potential creates a natural boundary on its misuse.

Central Bank Digital Currencies threaten to remove this function. Think of it as Venmo run by the state, with no opt-out, and a terms of service that can be rewritten while your money is already inside. With CBDCs, governments gain unprecedented control: program money, track every transaction, freeze accounts

instantly, determine what you can purchase. It's
the dream of every finance minister who ever
lost sleep over capital flight, and the nightmare
of everyone else.

But here's the paradox. By tightening control
this much, by trying to make money into a
perfect control mechanism, they undermine its
core functions. When money becomes too
obviously a leash, when the control becomes
too visible, people become willing to abandon it
entirely. They'll find alternatives: barter, parallel
currencies, anything to escape a system that's
revealed itself as pure domination. The more
aggressively you grip it, the faster people pry
their fingers loose.

In a globalized economy, this creates a
particularly dangerous dynamic. When a
population abandons their currency through
overreach, the economy doesn't just reset.
Instead, wealthy individuals and institutions
from countries with stable currencies swoop in
and buy up assets for pennies on the dollar,
assuming the dollar still exists. Land, businesses,
infrastructure, everything gets purchased by
foreign interests who have money that still
functions. The collapse doesn't lead to reset. It
leads to colonization.

Money functions as a medium of exchange, a
store of value, and a unit of account — and

CBDCs undermine all three at once. Program it to control purchases, track everything, and freeze accounts at will, and trust evaporates. Negative interest rates and programmable expiration destroy its value over time. Arbitrary rule changes through software updates make planning impossible. Those who wish to dominate are so focused on tightening control that they're willing to saw off the branch they're sitting on.

We built our own cage and convinced ourselves it's the natural order of things. And now some people want to make the cage smaller, apparently believing this will make us forget we built it.

The Redistribution Problem

Recognizing money as a leash doesn't lead to any simple political position.

Fairer distribution of resources? Obviously desirable. Extreme inequality is morally grotesque and economically inefficient. Epidemiologists Richard Wilkinson and Kate Pickett spent years compiling the data in their 2009 book *The Spirit Level*, showing that beyond a certain point, inequality reduces social mobility, increases crime, damages public health, and undermines trust across the entire social fabric. Not just for the poor. For everyone. So yes, redistribution makes sense within reasonable economic boundaries.

But the welfare state as currently constructed just trades one leash for another. You're no longer exclusively dependent on market income, but now you're dependent on government benefits that can be modified, reduced, or eliminated by those who wish to dominate you through the political system. The leash changes hands. It's still a leash.

Here's the fundamental problem: the people making redistribution decisions don't face the consequences. Politicians promise benefits to get elected. Economists design programs based on theories. Think tanks publish studies supporting their funders. And the people actually living with the results get a vote every few years for which set of representatives will ignore them.

Direct democracy over resource distribution changes everything. When you make the decisions and live with the outcomes, when you can't externalize the costs of failure, the quality of decision-making improves dramatically. We'll explore this in later chapters, including systems like W.L. Gore & Associates that demonstrate how communities make complex resource allocation decisions without centralized control. The point here is simpler: the leash stays on as long as we delegate economic decision-making to others.

Yet we resist this change, and the resistance runs deeper than ignorance or laziness. We've spent decades building careers, accumulating credentials, playing by the rules of the current system. Admitting it's fundamentally broken feels like admitting we wasted our lives. The sunk cost keeps us locked in, defending a system that exploits us because we've already invested so much in learning to navigate it.

The welfare state versus free market debate is a false choice. It assumes we must pick between market outcomes or centralized redistribution, but this is just a product of representative systems where power concentrates in fewer hands. Give people genuine responsibility for collective resource decisions, and they'll figure out contextual solutions, not ideological templates.

And here's the uncomfortable truth: every system fails to constrain acquisitive impulses because the problem isn't the system. Capitalism institutionalizes greed openly. Communism tried eliminating private accumulation, but the drive just shifted from hoarding money to hoarding power and privilege. Soviet apparatchiks couldn't become billionaires, but they accumulated control. Same pathology, different currency. Fascism allows accumulation for the loyal. Theocracy for the faithful. The specific currency changes. The compulsion remains constant.

Restructuring, Not Replacing

The right response to recognizing a leash isn't to go feral. Markets are genuinely useful for coordinating complex economic activity. Currency makes trade far more efficient than barter. Burning all of it down, or fantasizing about a return to some pre-monetary golden age, misunderstands the problem entirely.

The problem is that we've allowed one social construct to become the dominant organizing principle of human life and then forgotten it's a construct we control rather than a natural law we obey. Money was supposed to be a tool for facilitating exchange. Not a measure of human worth. Not a proxy for survival. Not a god to worship. When a tool starts organizing the people using it rather than the other way around, the tool has a problem. Or rather, the people do.

Correcting this requires real psychological work, both individually and collectively. The money colonization of human thinking runs deep: how much of our anxiety comes from mistaking a human invention for existential reality, from conflating income with survival, from reaching for net worth as a stand-in for self-worth. Untangling that requires more than intellectual agreement. It requires the kind of sustained inner work this book is about.

The external work is just as necessary. The people who should decide how an economy functions are the people who have to live in that economy and face the consequences of their decisions. Delegating that to representatives, experts, and authorities hasn't produced outcomes that justify the arrangement. It means developing genuine economic literacy across the population, not as a civic nicety but as a prerequisite for self-governance.

It also means measuring what actually matters. Right now, we optimize for GDP growth, which is essentially optimizing for how much money changes hands regardless of whether those transactions make anyone better off. We've confused activity with wellbeing. There's an old economics joke: two economists walking through a forest come across dog shit. The first offers the second $100 to eat it. He does. A bit later, they find another pile, and the second economist offers the first $100 to eat it. He does. As they walk on, one says, „We both just ate shit for nothing." The other replies, „That's not true. We just contributed $200 to the GDP."

GDP measures transactions, not value. It counts every exchange of money as economic growth, even when everyone involved ends up worse off.

Bhutan tried something different in 1972, when King Jigme Singye Wangchuck introduced the Gross National Happiness index, tracking psychological wellbeing, health, education, community vitality, and living standards instead of just economic output. The results are mixed, but at least they're measuring what matters to human life rather than what's easiest to count. The question isn't whether their approach is perfect. The question is why we continue optimizing for a metric that clearly doesn't correlate with what we claim to care about.

Better measurement is one piece. AI systems could provide another, identifying resource distribution patterns humans miss, modeling economic outcomes with greater accuracy, suggesting allocation strategies that optimize for actual wellbeing. But the key word is „tools." Technology is neutral. If those who wish to dominate control the systems, AI just automates current forms of domination. If communities control the tools transparently, AI could help design distribution systems that actually work.

The question is always: who controls it and for what purpose?

Genuine economic self-governance requires understanding how incentives shape behavior, how unintended consequences emerge, how complex systems respond to interventions. This is knowledge most people lack because they've never needed it in a representative system where experts make the decisions. In genuine self-governance, everyone needs it. You can't delegate economic decision-making to representatives and then complain when they serve their donors. You can't outsource the thinking and act surprised by the results.

Taking Off the Leash

The absurdity is no longer deniable. Billionaires accumulate wealth beyond any possible use while others work full-time and can't afford housing. Financial markets detached from productive activity generate enormous wealth for those who own assets while those who work for wages fall further behind. States print unlimited currency to bail out banks and corporations while telling citizens they can't afford healthcare or education. The system is breaking, not because of some inherent flaw in markets or currency, but because we've let a tool become a tyrant.

Those who wish to dominate love this arrangement. When everyone is desperate for money, when survival depends on participating in markets on whatever terms are offered, when people are too busy working to think about alternatives, power remains concentrated and unchallenged. The leash serves those who hold it, even though they're on a leash themselves. The whole thing is recursive and insane.

But we're all complicit. We celebrate billionaires. We organize lives around income maximization. We accept vast disparity as inevitable. We treat economic status as a measure of human worth. We feel inadequate when we don't earn enough. We use purchases to fill emotional voids. Every time we do these things, we're pulling our own leash tighter. The system works because we agree to it, because we've internalized its logic so completely that imagining alternatives feels naive or foolish.

The alternative isn't destroying money or markets. It's remembering we created them, which means we can recreate them. We can design currencies that serve human needs, structure economies around wellbeing, distribute resources through democratic decisions, separate survival from income without creating permanent dependency on state systems. None of this is utopian. It's just engineering applied to social constructs we invented, rather than social constructs inventing us.

Mammon is a god we made. The slavery is real in its effects, but it's not inevitable, natural, or unchangeable. That's the shadow work: seeing how thoroughly we've internalized the money system, recognizing that the fear of not having enough often masks a deeper fear of not being enough, and then taking that responsibility back. Not because we know exactly what different economic structures should look like, but because we know the current ones aren't working, and waiting for someone else to notice hasn't been going particularly well.

Domination vs True Leadership

In 1933, the German electorate handed democratic power to a man who had explicitly promised to end democracy. They weren't stupid. They were scared, exhausted, and humiliated by a decade of economic ruin following the disaster of World War One. They wanted the chaos to stop. They made what felt, in the moment, like a rational choice. By the time it became clear what they had actually chosen, choosing differently was no longer an option.

Every nation tells itself it's led by leaders. Almost every nation is actually ruled by dominators pretending to lead. The inability to distinguish between these two is among the most catastrophic failures of collective consciousness. It's why revolutions replace one tyrant with another. It's why democracies slide into authoritarianism while citizens cheer. It's why populations hand over their freedom to anyone who promises safety, prosperity, or greatness.

Understanding this distinction isn't academic. It's survival. Nations that cannot make it reliably select dominators, then act surprised when those dominators behave exactly as dominators do. The people most drawn to power typically exhibit what psychology calls the dark triad—

narcissism, Machiavellianism, and psychopathy. These traits make someone particularly effective at gaining power while being particularly destructive when they have it. You couldn't design a more efficient trap if you tried.

The confusion is understandable. Both leadership and domination involve exercising influence over others. Both make decisions that affect populations. Both accumulate authority. The manager who serves their team and the manager who controls their team both exercise power over workplace decisions. One creates growth. The other creates dysfunction. The mechanics appear similar. The outcomes couldn't be more different.

So how do you tell them apart? More importantly, how does a collective composed of millions of people, most of whom have never met, distinguish between someone offering genuine leadership and someone seeking domination?

The answer matters because societies without this ability keep making the same catastrophic choice. They select dominators thinking they've chosen leaders, then spend decades dealing with the consequences.

The Anatomy of Domination

True leadership serves those being led. Domination serves the one dominating. Everything else flows from this single difference.

A leader's decisions consider the wellbeing of those they guide. Their authority comes from competence and the trust they've earned. They accept responsibility for failures, share credit for successes, and build capability in others. Over time, genuine leaders work toward making themselves less necessary as those they guide develop their own capacity to navigate.

A dominator's decisions serve their own power. They claim credit for successes, blame others for failures, and create dependency rather than capability. They ensure they remain essential by preventing others from growing strong enough to function without them.

You might think this makes the distinction obvious. If one serves others and one serves themselves, surely anyone could tell them apart. But here's what makes this so difficult: every dominator claims to be serving others. No tyrant describes themselves as tyrannical. Every authoritarian frames their control as necessary for the collective good. Every abuser believes their abuse is actually protection, discipline, or love.

The dominators aren't lying, at least not consciously. Most genuinely believe their own story. They've convinced themselves that controlling others serves a higher purpose, that their accumulation of power benefits everyone, that opposition to their authority represents danger rather than legitimate dissent. The dominator's internal narrative positions them as the hero, the protector, the only one capable of maintaining order. The self-deception is what makes domination so insidious. You cannot shame someone out of a story they haven't noticed they're telling.

The ship captain makes a useful test case. A captain must have command to navigate safely. Responsibility without authority is a contradiction. But authority without accountability is something else entirely.

A true captain serves the ship and crew. Their authority exists to ensure safe passage. They hold their position because of competence in navigation, knowledge of the sea, and the ability to make decisions under pressure. Their crew follows them because they trust their judgment. If the captain starts making decisions that serve their ego rather than the voyage, they stop being a captain. They become a hijacker.

The crucial distinction: a captain can be replaced. If their navigation fails, if their decisions endanger the voyage, the crew has the authority and responsibility to remove them. A hijacker cannot be replaced because they've taken the ship by force. Their authority comes from their capacity to harm, not from any competence in navigation. The crew obeys from fear, not trust.

Both the captain and the hijacker might give identical orders. Both might command the crew to their stations during a storm. The commands themselves don't reveal which is which. The difference shows up in the pattern over time: who benefits from the decisions, whether dissent gets engaged or crushed, and whether the one commanding accepts accountability for failures or blames the crew.

Nations need to develop the collective capacity to distinguish captains from hijackers before the hijacker has consolidated enough power to make removal impossible.

Dominators don't emerge from nowhere. They develop from specific conditions, usually trauma combined with opportunity. Understanding this isn't excusing their behavior. It's identifying the pattern so societies can recognize the warning signs before the coup rather than after.

The dominator typically experiences early powerlessness. Maybe they suffered abuse, maybe they witnessed someone they loved being harmed while they were too weak to intervene, maybe they grew up in chaos with no sense of safety or control. That powerlessness creates a wound. The wound generates a vow, usually unconscious: „I will never be powerless again." From that vow comes the drive to accumulate power. Not power in service to anything, but power as protection against ever feeling that vulnerability again.

The dominator can never accumulate enough power to feel safe because the wound sits in the past. No amount of present power can heal the original injury. Like any addiction, it requires ever-increasing doses. The leader who cannot delegate, cannot tolerate dissent, and cannot accept limitations on their authority isn't running a strategy. They're running from something.

Understanding the source helps societies recognize the pattern before it consolidates into tyranny. A leader who grew up with secure attachment, who experienced power used responsibly, who learned that vulnerability doesn't equal annihilation, typically develops a different relationship with authority. Power doesn't frighten them. They can delegate without suspecting betrayal, accept constraints without experiencing them as attacks, and share credit without feeling diminished. The wound shapes behavior. Its absence does too.

But dominators cannot dominate alone. They require followers. And followers don't appear randomly. They develop from their own wounds. Wounds that make domination feel like safety.

The psychology of followers deserves as much attention as the psychology of dominators. Erich Fromm studied this extensively in „Escape from Freedom," published in 1941, the year after France fell to a regime his book had essentially predicted. He found that freedom creates anxiety for people who never developed the internal capacity to direct themselves. Genuine autonomy requires tolerating uncertainty and taking responsibility for your choices without a clear external authority telling you you're doing it right. For people who grew up in authoritarian environments where obedience was safety and questioning was punished, that kind of freedom doesn't feel like liberation. It feels like being shoved off a cliff.

Milgram's obedience experiments and Zimbardo's Stanford Prison Experiment confirmed how readily people abandon personal judgment when authority figures are present.

Both studies get cited as evidence of universal human darkness, but they reveal something more specific: what happens to people who never developed internal authority. When people cannot regulate themselves internally, external authority fills the void. The dominator provides certainty where there was doubt, direction where there was paralysis. For someone terrified of their own judgment, domination feels like rescue.

This explains why authoritarianism finds its most enthusiastic support among populations experiencing chaos, economic collapse, or rapid social change. The dominator says, „Follow me and I'll end this chaos. Trust me and you won't have to think anymore. Obey me and you'll be safe." For someone without internal authority, this sounds like salvation. For the dominator, it sounds like an opportunity.

The wounded followers find wounded dominators. The followers provide the power the dominator needs to feel safe. The dominator provides the external authority followers never developed internally. Both participate in the dynamic. Both get what their trauma demands. Neither gets what they actually need. It's a perfect arrangement for producing misery at scale.

Bessel van der Kolk's research on trauma helps explain why the pattern persists across generations. Trauma survivors develop hypervigilance, an inability to tolerate uncertainty, and attraction to authoritarian structures that promise an end to the discomfort of not knowing. These responses make sense during an ongoing threat but become maladaptive once the threat ends. The nervous system doesn't update its threat assessment on a convenient schedule.

This is why authoritarianism has flourished after major collective trauma: Germany after World War One, Russia after the Tsarist collapse, Cambodia after years of bombing and civil war, Rwanda after colonial exploitation and ethnic manipulation. Populations reeling from chaos hand over freedom in exchange for the promise of safety. The dominator delivers control, not safety, but by then it's too late to renegotiate.

Healing collective trauma is therefore essential for maintaining genuine democracy. A traumatized population will keep selecting dominators no matter how elegantly the constitution is written. The wound drives the choice. Until the wound heals, the pattern repeats.

The Path to Tyranny

The path to domination follows predictable stages. Rome's transformation from republic to empire between 44 BCE and 27 BCE demonstrates how a single lifetime suffices to destroy centuries of self-governance.

Augustus didn't invent Rome's crisis. Decades of civil war had devastated the republic. Political violence had become routine. Economic instability plagued the provinces. The Senate had proven incapable of maintaining order. Citizens were exhausted. The suffering was real. This is always the first move: identify genuine pain. It costs nothing, and it works every time.

Then came simple solutions to complex problems. Rome's dysfunction had countless causes: institutional decay, economic transformation, military expansion beyond governance capacity, the concentration of wealth destroying the citizen-farmer class that had built the republic. Augustus offered clarity. The republic had failed because it lacked decisive authority. Peace required unity under a single capable hand. Each explanation simplified and pointed toward one remedy: himself.

Third, he elevated the crisis to an existential threat. Not just political instability, but the complete destruction of Roman civilization.

Without strong leadership, civil wars would continue until Rome collapsed. Barbarians would overrun the provinces. The glory of Rome would end in chaos and slavery. The threat was large enough to justify extraordinary measures and vague enough to seem permanent.

The assassination of Julius Caesar had taught Augustus caution. He accumulated titles and offices gradually: consul, tribune, imperator, princeps. Each seemed necessary to address the immediate crisis. Each came with assurances of temporary necessity. The Senate granted these powers willingly, relieved that someone competent would handle the chaos. The powers were always meant to be temporary. They never were.

Finally, he eliminated opposition with subtlety. First came delegitimization: rivals were factional, ambitious, and self-serving. Then marginalization: control the grain supply, fund friendly voices, position loyalists throughout institutions. By the time anyone understood the republic was gone, opposing him would have required a new civil war. That was precisely what everyone was desperate to avoid. What began as emergency leadership became a permanent monarchy. The republic died so quietly that most Romans didn't notice when it stopped breathing.

The pattern repeats across cultures and centuries with such fidelity that you could mistake history for plagiarism. Democracies fall to authoritarianism through exactly this process. The warning signs are consistent. The trajectory is predictable. Societies keep failing to recognize it until the dominators have consolidated, at which point recognition becomes expensive.

Societies facing genuine threats need decisive action. When crisis hits, you don't want committees. You want someone who can make hard decisions quickly and rally others behind them. That capacity generates results. It creates safety during chaos. The problem is that the same qualities that make someone effective during a crisis make them dangerous during stability.

The person who can bypass normal processes to act decisively during an emergency will bypass normal processes to consolidate power during peace. The person who can rally others through fear of external threat will manufacture threats to maintain that control. The person who dismisses debate as weakness during a crisis will dismiss debate as disloyalty during calm. The skills transfer. The intentions don't.

This is why crisis produces tyrants with such regularity. The collective, legitimately frightened, empowers someone strong enough to address the threat. The crisis ends. The powers remain. Rome gave emergency dictatorial powers to leaders during crisis, with the understanding they'd be relinquished afterward. Usually they were. Eventually they weren't.

But what happens after the crisis reveals everything. Does the strong leader relinquish emergency powers once the danger passes? Do they restore normal processes and welcome oversight? Or do they discover that new threats have emerged, threats that happen to require the same exceptional authority, indefinitely? The third option tells you everything you need to know.

The pattern is consistent enough that it should be recognized immediately. It rarely is. The initial results create gratitude. The strength that addressed the crisis becomes associated with competence rather than danger. By the time domination becomes obvious, the mechanisms for removing it have been quietly dismantled.

George Orwell understood how much of this runs on narrative rather than force. In „1984,“ the Party's power came more from controlling language than from the Thought Police. By limiting vocabulary and redefining words, the Party made opposition literally unthinkable. People lacked the conceptual tools to formulate dissent. This isn't fiction as warning. It's an accurate description of how mature domination operates. Not by stopping people from speaking, but by degrading the language they'd need to say anything useful.

The simpler version of the same test applies long before a dominator reaches that level of control. Watch what happens when they're criticized. A dominator attacks the critic. A leader engages the criticism. A dominator calls dissent conspiracy or treason. A leader asks whether the dissent reveals something real. The response to being questioned tells you nearly everything you need to know, usually before it's too late to act on the information.

True Leadership: Service, Not Control

If every dominator claims to be a leader, and genuine leaders rarely describe themselves in terms that distinguish them, how do you actually tell them apart in practice?

Start with competence. A general should understand warfare. An economist should understand markets. This seems obvious but gets overlooked with remarkable consistency. Societies elevate people based on charisma, wealth, or the right family name while ignoring whether they possess relevant capability. Competence is the foundation. Without it, everything else is performance.

But competence alone doesn't distinguish leaders from dominators. Plenty of competent people dominate. The second requirement is that the person exercises their competence in service to the collective rather than themselves. They develop others' capabilities rather than fostering dependence. When things fail, they own it. When things succeed, they distribute the credit. They measure success by how well those they lead develop their own capacity.

True leadership distributes power rather than hoarding it. A real leader builds systems where others can lead, creates structures where authority is distributed across multiple people, and designs processes where decisions happen close to where they'll be implemented. They work to make themselves less essential over time. Most societies don't think about leadership this way. The common model treats leaders as people who should be followed, who deserve deference, who occupy positions above others. That model produces domination by design.

Notice the language. We say „strong leaders," „powerful leaders," „commanding presence." We rarely say „effective at distributing authority" or „skilled at making themselves unnecessary." The language reveals what we actually value. What we value, most of the time, is domination dressed up as leadership.

Nelson Mandela provides a clear example of what the alternative looks like in practice. He held enormous authority within South Africa during the transition from apartheid. He could have used that authority to consolidate power, eliminate opponents, and establish himself as president-for-life. Many revolutionary leaders do exactly that, often with the best intentions. Instead, he served one term and stepped down. He used his authority to build democratic institutions that could function without him. His leadership created capacity in others rather than dependency on himself.

Compare that to Robert Mugabe in neighboring Zimbabwe. Mugabe began as a liberation hero, initially demonstrated restraint and inclusive governance, then gradually consolidated power. He eliminated term limits, crushed opposition, and remained in power through violence and manipulation until finally being removed by a military coup at age 93. There is something almost darkly comic about a man clinging to power into his nineties, as if the country might collapse without his particular contribution. What began as leadership deteriorated into a decades-long demonstration that he had no idea who he was without the position.

George Washington could have become a king. The option was genuinely available to him. He stepped down after two terms and went home to Virginia, establishing a precedent that held for nearly 150 years. Richard Nixon's response to Watergate illustrated the opposite impulse: using executive power to obstruct investigation, claiming authority to ignore subpoenas, firing prosecutors investigating his own crimes, and resigning only when impeachment became inevitable. His famous claim to interviewer David Frost in 1977, „When the president does it, that means it's not illegal,“ is perhaps the purest articulation of the dominator's worldview ever delivered on television.

The clearest test between leadership and domination is accountability. Can the person be held responsible for their failures? Can they be removed if they prove incompetent or corrupt? Do they accept limits on their authority? Do they welcome oversight? Do they punish criticism or engage with it?

A leader accepts accountability because they understand their authority comes from serving others. A dominator resists it because their authority comes from their capacity to avoid consequences. They position themselves above oversight. They attack anyone attempting to evaluate their performance. They construct legal immunity, control information about their actions, punish whistleblowers, pack oversight bodies with loyalists, and frame all criticism as conspiracy or betrayal. The resistance itself is the evidence. You don't need to prove intent when the pattern is this consistent.

Conquering Everything

The domination pattern doesn't stay within politics. It runs through every domain where humans have something to control, and there is no larger domain than the natural world.

Western civilization received its operating instructions for that relationship in Genesis 1:28: „Be fruitful and multiply, and fill the earth and subdue it; and have dominion over the fish of the sea and over the birds of the air and over every living thing that moves upon the earth." Dominion over nature became a religious duty, a divine right, a sacred mission. Several centuries of industrialization followed, and the results are now measurable.

Contrast this with indigenous cosmologies across every continent. Aboriginal Australians saw themselves as caretakers of country, not owners of it. Andean peoples understood reciprocity with Pachamama as a relationship requiring maintenance in both directions. Native American traditions positioned humans as younger siblings learning from elder beings rather than managers of a resource base. The

Haudenosaunee, the Iroquois Confederacy, built deliberation about the seventh generation into their governance. What distinguished these frameworks wasn't sentiment. It was structural: stewardship, not extraction. They worked, for thousands of years. Andean terraced agriculture still functions after centuries. Aboriginal fire management created resilient ecosystems maintained across 65,000 years of continuous habitation.

Western civilization, operating from the dominion mandate, depleted a third of global topsoil in roughly 40 years, according to the United Nations Food and Agriculture Organization. The WWF's 2022 Living Planet Report documented a 69% average decline in monitored wildlife populations since 1970. We've contaminated every ecosystem with synthetic compounds. We've altered atmospheric carbon dioxide to levels not seen in 800,000 years, as shown by Antarctic ice core records. The returns on the dominion model are in.

Even the language gives it away. We „conquer" mountains. We „tame" wilderness. We „harness" energy. We „exploit" resources. Every phrase is a minor announcement of the same worldview. Winning requires something to be defeated. The world becomes an adversary in a contest we apparently cannot stop running.

Nature is the one domain where reality asserts itself regardless of the stories we tell. You cannot negotiate with physics about atmospheric heat retention. You cannot vote to make topsoil regenerate faster. You cannot file for an extension on a collapsing fishery. These are hard limits that don't care about quarterly earnings, political ideology, or theological interpretations. When the domination logic finally hits a wall it cannot politically outmaneuver, it turns out the wall was always going to be there.

The environmental crisis isn't separate from the political crisis. Both stem from domination thinking applied to everything. The same wound that drives people to dominate other people drives civilizations to dominate nature. The same inability to distinguish extraction from service shows up in both domains, at both scales. A population that cannot recognize domination in political structures will not recognize it in their relationship with nature. A population that learns to distinguish service from extraction can apply that understanding everywhere.

Consciousness Before Systems

The adjusted democracy model this book proposes makes it structurally harder for dominators to emerge and consolidate. But structural design only takes you so far. Any system works better when the population it governs has developed the capacity to lead in their own domains, to accept responsibility for collective decisions, and to exercise authority in service rather than for self-protection. When populations consistently select dominators instead, when trauma drives political choices instead of conscious evaluation, even the best constitutional architecture becomes a defensive battle rather than a functioning society.

A nation serious about this distinction must develop the capacity to recognize its own trauma and how that trauma shapes judgment. What are we afraid of? Why do we seek strong authority? What wounds are driving our political choices? These questions require honest examination. Most nations prefer comfortable narratives to uncomfortable truth, which is how they keep arriving at the same destination while insisting this time will be different.

The nation must cultivate internal authority in its population. People who can direct themselves don't need dominators. This requires education that develops critical thinking rather than just credentials, economic systems that create genuine independence rather than manufactured dependency, community structures that build belonging without demanding conformity, and the unglamorous work of healing personal trauma so it stops driving collective decisions.

Perhaps most difficult: a culture must learn to value service over strength. Not because strength is bad but because the cultural glorification of dominance creates the conditions where dominators flourish. A culture that views service as weakness will keep selecting people who view it as weakness. The qualities we celebrate in our leaders tell us what we've decided we want from them.

Systemic change tends to happen suddenly, through crisis, collapse, or the moment when the existing order simply stops working and everyone can see it. Systems don't reform themselves gradually. They resist change, maintain their current form, and then break. But while the break happens fast, the capacity to maintain what comes after requires time to develop. You cannot skip straight to new political structures if the population lacks the consciousness to sustain them. When the current structures collapse, the question is not whether there will be change. The question is whether the population has developed the capacity to build something worth building, or whether they will simply recreate domination under a new flag while celebrating their liberation.

A population of wounded followers will generate dominators, regardless of what the constitution says. A population that heals its wounds, develops internal authority, and learns to recognize domination can maintain freedom even under pressure.

The choice between domination and leadership isn't made once. It's made constantly, in small decisions and large ones, in how authority is exercised and how it's received, in what behaviors receive social reward and what gets challenged. The collective creates what it tolerates. If it tolerates domination disguised as leadership, it will keep getting dominated. If it insists on accountability, transparency, and the distribution of power, it can sustain self-governance.

But first it has to learn to see the difference. Everything else follows from that.

Divide and Conquer

Julius Caesar had a problem. When he invaded
Gaul between 58 and 50 BCE, the Gallic tribes
outnumbered his legions by a significant margin.
A united Gaul would have crushed him. Caesar
knew it. So he made sure Gaul never united.

He found the fault lines first. The Aedui and
Sequani had longstanding tensions. Caesar allied
with the Aedui, offering Roman backing against
their rivals. Other tribes, watching the Aedui
accumulate advantages, scrambled for their own
deals with Rome to avoid being left behind. The
competition was no longer Gaul against Rome.
It was tribe against tribe, each negotiating for a
better seat at the table Rome had set.

When Vercingetorix finally managed to unite
the tribes in a massive rebellion, Caesar's
response was not primarily military. He picked
at the coalition's weakest seams, offering
generous surrender terms to whichever tribes
would abandon the cause. As some accepted,
others panicked that they'd miss the window.
The coalition collapsed not through battlefield
defeat but through the same logic that drives a
bank run: the fear that everyone else is already
cutting a separate deal.

After crushing the rebellion, Caesar didn't
impose uniform Roman rule. He created a

hierarchy of privileges. Some tribes received Roman citizenship. Others became trading partners. Others remained conquered subjects. The arrangement ensured tribes would keep competing for Roman favor long after the legions moved on. The divisions he created lasted for generations.

The strategy worked so consistently that it earned a name: divide and conquer. But Caesar was not a genius who invented something new. He was a tactician who recognized something old, something structural about how human groups behave when placed in competition. Two thousand years later, a psychologist decided to test exactly what Caesar had intuited.

Anatomy of Division

In 1954, Muzafer Sherif took 22 eleven-year-old boys to Robbers Cave State Park in Oklahoma. The selection was meticulous: all white, all middle-class, all Protestant, all doing well in school, all psychologically healthy. Strangers to each other. No prior grievances. No meaningful differences.

Sherif divided them randomly into two groups and kept them separated for a week. Each group named themselves (Eagles and Rattlers), created symbols, and developed small traditions. Then Sherif introduced competitive activities:

baseball, tug-of-war, treasure hunts. Winners got prizes. Losers got nothing.

The transformation was fast and disturbing. Within days, these near-identical boys developed genuine hatred for each other. They raided cabins, burned flags, stockpiled rocks as weapons, and got into fights requiring adult intervention. Asked to describe the other group, they reached for words like „sneaky" and „stinkers." Their own group was „brave" and „friendly."

Same boys. Same camp. Random group assignment plus competition. That was all it took to produce behavior indistinguishable from ethnic violence. The researchers were not observing some pathological edge case. They were watching normal children do what normal humans do.

The experiment reveals something that most political theory refuses to sit with: you do not need real differences to create real hatred. You need only the perception of separate groups and something to compete over.

Sherif then ran the process in reverse. He introduced problems requiring both groups to cooperate. The camp's water supply broke. Fixing it needed everyone. A truck carrying food got stuck in the mud. Moving it required combined effort. Gradually, as the boys worked toward shared goals, the hostility dissolved. Former enemies became friends.

The division had been manufactured on a Tuesday afternoon. The reconciliation was engineered the following week. Both were equally real to the boys experiencing them.

Sherif's study was never just about boys at a summer camp. It was a map. Across two thousand years and wildly different circumstances, every successful division follows the same anatomy.

It starts with group boundaries. Sometimes the categories are invented from nothing, as Sherif did with his coin-flip assignments. Sometimes existing fault lines are sharpened and made politically visible, as Caesar did with tribal rivalries. What matters is not the content of the category but the act of categorization itself.

Henri Tajfel showed how quickly this takes hold. He grouped people by the most trivial criteria he could devise: whether they preferred one painting over another, whether they tended to overestimate dots on a screen. Even so, they immediately allocated more resources to ingroup members they would never meet. No history. No stakes. Just a label. The mere knowledge „I am in group X" triggered favoritism toward X and hostility toward Y. Modern societies run this same mechanism through political parties, nations, religions, and ideologies. The categories are more elaborate. The underlying wiring is identical.

Group boundaries alone produce only mild favoritism. Turning favoritism into animosity requires competition for resources. Caesar gave the Aedui Roman support, forcing every other tribe to compete for the same advantage. Sherif introduced prizes only one group could win. The scarcity can be real or manufactured; what matters is the perception that the other group's gain is your loss.

The framing works because the emotion arrives before the analysis does. When someone frames an issue as your group losing while another group gains, the threat response fires first. The sense of injustice arrives fully formed. By the time you think clearly, you've already chosen sides, and thinking clearly feels like betrayal.

Once competition begins, perception shifts to amplify differences and erase similarities. Caesar framed some Gallic tribes as civilized and others as barbaric, despite all Gauls sharing far more cultural commonalities with each other than with Rome. The Robbers Cave boys were virtually identical, yet once competition started they could only see the differences. This is not dishonesty. This is motivated perception: the brain genuinely processes the same behavior differently depending on who is performing it. „Playing rough" when your team does it. „Cheating" when theirs does. The same punch, two different movies.

There is one more piece that keeps the machine running: bridge-builders get punished. When boys in Robbers Cave suggested being kind to the other group, their own teammates turned on them. Traitor. Coward. Not really one of us.

The dynamic persists everywhere group loyalty is active. Suggest the other political party has a point about something and watch your own side turn. Suggest both groups in a cultural conflict have legitimate concerns and both sides attack you for insufficient commitment. The loyalty test maintains cohesion by making reconciliation socially expensive. Division becomes the path of least resistance even after the original reasons for it have evaporated.

The Deliberate Fragmentation of Occupy Wall Street

On September 17, 2011, protestors established an encampment in Zuccotti Park in lower Manhattan. The core message was elegantly simple: „We are the 99%." Conservative or liberal, white or Black, male or female, young or old: if you were not among the top 1% of wealth holders, you were part of a population facing common challenges: wage stagnation, declining mobility, corporate capture of political institutions, and a financial system whose instability enriched the few while threatening everyone else with the bill.

Polls showed 77% of Americans agreed that inequality was a major problem. The movement spread to over 951 cities across 82 countries. Labor unions endorsed it. The 99% frame had accomplished something rare: it named the actual structural conflict in contemporary American life rather than the proxy conflicts (race, gender, culture) that typically keep working people fighting each other while the 1% keeps the spreadsheet.

This was precisely the nightmare scenario for concentrated wealth. Cross-demographic working-class unity.

The movement collapsed in 59 days. What followed was a combination of external suppression and internal fragmentation, neither of which was accidental.

FBI documents obtained through Freedom of Information Act requests revealed federal surveillance began in August 2011, before the first occupation. The FBI classified Occupy as a potential terrorist threat, despite acknowledging in internal documents that organizers advocated peaceful protest and explicitly rejected violence. The Wall Street executives who had crashed the global economy, destroyed millions of jobs, evaporated trillions in household wealth, and required taxpayer bailouts remained unindicted throughout. Threat assessment at its finest.

The FBI coordinated with federal law enforcement bodies and private sector security firms in a formal partnership. Wall Street received intelligence about the movement protesting Wall Street. The federal government operated as the security apparatus for the financial industry its citizens were demanding accountability from.

Cities coordinated their encampment-clearing operations through conference calls involving mayors and police chiefs. A consistent pattern emerged across jurisdictions: raids scheduled for late night or early morning to minimize press coverage, journalists arrested for refusing to leave designated media zones, overwhelming police deployments, and systematic destruction of encampment infrastructure including libraries and medical tents.

Most troubling were FBI documents referencing specific threats to assassinate Occupy leaders through sniper fire. Details remained redacted. The FBI did not warn the individuals named. A Houston plot to kill movement leadership „via suppressed sniper rifles" was documented and never prosecuted. The would-be assassins were shielded rather than charged. One presumes the paperwork was very complicated.

While external forces coordinated suppression, the movement was developing internal fractures. The organizing structure implemented the „progressive stack" in group facilitation, which prioritized speakers from „traditionally marginalized groups" over others, particularly over white men.

The stated intention was counteracting historical silencing. The operational effect was transforming an economic class conflict into an identity-based conflict within the movement itself. Proposed language for a mission statement could be blocked on identity grounds. A suggested strategy could be dismissed based on the speaker's demographic rather than the strategy's merits. Every decision became a negotiation between competing identity factions rather than a question about what would work.

Practical matters that required quick decisions consumed hours or days of contentious debate. Whether to accept donations became a referendum on hierarchical power structures. Whether to articulate clear demands became a debate about legitimizing existing systems. Whether to respond to police harassment became a philosophical dispute about anti-authoritarian principles.

The anarchist faction insisted that occupation itself was the goal, that presenting demands would legitimize the structures being protested. When politicians offered meetings, the movement had nothing specific to request. It could not convert popular support into policy outcomes.

The 99% frame dissolved into internal conflicts organized along every other available line: race, gender, sexuality, class background, political philosophy, tactical preference. Each of these divisions was real. Each grievance was legitimate. Together they ensured the movement could not function.

Look at what happened: a movement organized around the 99% versus the 1% adopted an internal structure that made maintaining focus on that economic division functionally impossible. Every other division became more salient than class.

Who benefited? The financial institutions that had crashed the economy, received government bailouts, distributed record bonuses, and faced no criminal prosecutions. The wealth concentration the movement existed to challenge continued uninterrupted.

Then something else happened. Occupy Wall Street was dismantled in November 2011. The 99% frame disappeared from public discourse. And beginning in that same period, major American newspapers dramatically increased their usage of identity-based conflict language.

According to analysis by Zach Goldberg published in Tablet Magazine, the New York Times increased usage of „racist," „racists," and „racism" by over 700% between 2011 and 2019. The Washington Post increased usage by just under 1,000% in the same period. The term „white privilege" saw an even more dramatic shift: between 2013 and 2019, usage grew by 1,200% in the Times and nearly 1,500% in the Post.

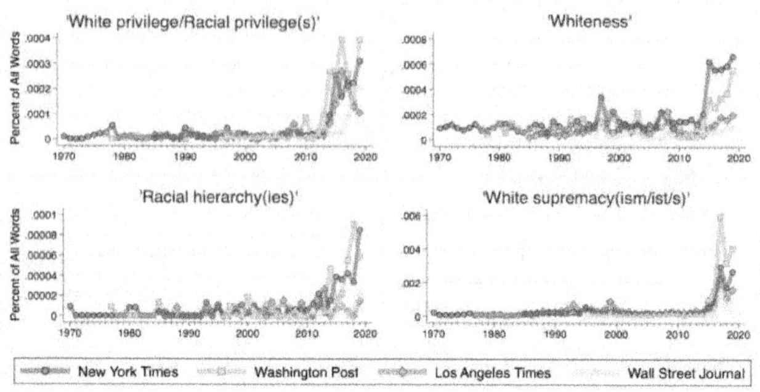

Figure 1:

https://www.tabletmag.com/sections/news/articles/media-great-racial-awakening

Public opinion tracked the media shift closely. In 2011, 35% of white liberals identified racism as „a big problem." By 2015, this had jumped to 61%, and by 2017 to 77%. The percentage remained essentially unchanged among Black and Hispanic Democrats across the same years. The perception of a racism crisis intensified specifically among the demographic most active in Occupy Wall Street.

Meanwhile, a 2020 RAND Corporation study found that roughly $50 trillion shifted from the bottom 90% of Americans to the top 1% between 1975 and 2018.

The obvious counter-argument: media increased coverage of racism because racism itself intensified, responding to events like Ferguson, Charleston, and other high-profile incidents.

Perhaps journalists were simply covering what was happening.

But this explanation falters when you examine what held constant. Police shootings of unarmed Black Americans hadn't spiked in 2011. The underlying rate had been relatively stable for decades. What changed wasn't the reality but how much attention that reality received, and precisely when that attention accelerated. The intensification arrived at the moment when class-based unity posed its greatest threat to concentrated wealth in a generation.

The question you have to ask is not whether racial injustice is real. It is. The question is: when a movement threatening concentrated power through working-class unity suddenly fragments into identity-based conflicts that prevent that unity, and when media coverage of racial division then increases by 1,000%, should you assume coincidence? Or should you recognize the oldest playbook in politics running exactly as designed?

Pattern Recognition

You divide groups that would otherwise unite. You introduce competition. You let normal human psychology run the mechanism from there. You don't have to maintain the division actively; groups sustain it themselves through loyalty enforcement and mutual suspicion. The whole thing is self-cleaning.

None of this means the injustices are fake. The grievances driving racial conflict in America are real. The historical wounds are real. The present-day disparities are real. But real injustice can be weaponized. A legitimate grievance can be amplified strategically, at a particular moment, to serve purposes other than addressing that grievance. The question is never whether the conflict is genuine. The question is: who benefits from this particular fight absorbing this much energy right now, and what are you not looking at while it does?

The fights along cultural and identity lines are not substitutes for economic power. Every particular cultural battle can be won, and the distribution of economic power remains essentially untouched. This is not an argument against fighting for racial justice or any other legitimate cause. It is an observation about where the ceiling is when those fights are pursued in isolation from the economic structures that shape everything else.

Seeing the mechanism is the only reliable counter-strategy, and it is not comfortable. It means stepping back from the immediate emotional experience of group conflict and asking whether this fight is serving your actual interests. It means tolerating the suspicion of your own side when you raise questions about whether the division is being manufactured or exploited. Bridge-building is socially expensive precisely because the mechanism is designed to make it expensive. The Robbers Cave boys who suggested being kind to the Eagles faced immediate hostility from their fellow Rattlers. That dynamic has not changed.

What has changed is that we can see the mechanism clearly. Sherif ran the experiment so we don't have to discover it the hard way. The boys hated each other with genuine conviction based on group assignment and a baseball game. Those feelings were real. They were also manufactured in a controlled study over the course of a week.

The enmity you feel toward people who share your class interests but belong to a different cultural tribe was produced by the same basic process, at larger scale, over a longer timeline, with considerably more resources devoted to maintaining it. The emotional experience is real. The necessity of the conflict is not.

Ask who benefits when working people fight each other. Ask what you're not seeing while the fight has your full attention. The answer has been consistent since Caesar stood in Gaul and

watched the tribes negotiate against each other
for Roman favor, each convinced the real
enemy was the tribe next door.

The Divide Between Black and White

It's 2026, and the fact that a chapter like this still needs to exist tells you more about the success of the division than about the stubbornness of human nature. So let's skip the part where we establish that racism is bad. You know it's bad. What you may not know is who keeps the machine running, and why.

It's Just Sunlight, Baby!

Your skin color is determined by melanin. More melanin, darker skin. Less melanin, lighter skin. That's the entire biological story, and it fits in one sentence.

Melanin evolved as protection against ultraviolet radiation. Near the equator, darker skin prevented folate degradation and DNA damage. Further from the equator, lighter skin allowed more efficient vitamin D synthesis. The human body adapted to local sunlight conditions over thousands of years. And that's all that happened.

These adaptations carry no other biological significance. Melanin production correlates with nothing about intelligence, character, creativity, or any other trait humans actually argue about.

Which means we've spent three centuries sorting people into castes based on their built-in sunscreen levels. Imagine applying that logic to any other evolutionary quirk. „Oh, you have the gene for lactose tolerance? You can't sit at this lunch counter." „Your ancestors lived at altitude so your lungs process oxygen more efficiently? Different water fountain." We'd recognize that as absurd in about four seconds.

Yet melanin became the most durable sorting mechanism in modern history. The reason is straightforward and ugly: you can't hide it. You can hide poverty, religion, or political views. Skin color remains visible, which made it the perfect marker for creating a permanent, easily identifiable underclass.

So how did a simple adaptation to sunlight become the foundation of a 300-year-old caste system? The answer starts with a rebellion that scared the wrong people.

In 1676, poor whites and enslaved Blacks in colonial Virginia discovered they had a lot in common. Both were being worked to the bone for the benefit of a tiny planter class. Both had grievances. Both had weapons. Bacon's Rebellion brought them together against the colonial elite, and it nearly worked. When the rebellion was finally suppressed, the Virginia ruling class sat down and had a long, nervous conversation about how to make sure this never happened again.

The solution wasn't more soldiers. It was more categories.

The Virginia Assembly passed a series of laws over subsequent decades that legally sorted the colony's poor into white and Black, where before the primary distinction had been simply enslaved versus free. Poor whites gained rights that Black people did not: to bear arms, to physically discipline any Black person, to own property without restriction. Interracial marriage was prohibited, existing interracial families broken apart. A racial hierarchy was established in which the most destitute white person held legal standing above any Black person regardless of wealth or skill.

The genius of this arrangement, from the planter class perspective, was that it cost them almost nothing. They handed poor whites a social status they hadn't earned, and in return, poor whites stopped looking upward at the people exploiting them and started looking sideways at the people beside them.

That trade held for centuries. Poor whites fought and died in the Civil War to preserve a slavery system that was economically detrimental to them. Slavery depressed their wages. It concentrated wealth in plantation owners' hands. They couldn't compete with it. Yet they fought to preserve it, because it guaranteed they would never be at the bottom. They got to feel superior while getting exploited. It's like being assigned first-class accommodations on the Titanic. You're still on the Titanic.

A white kid and a Black kid both get caught with marijuana. According to ACLU data, the Black kid is 3.7 times more likely to be arrested for the same offense. If charged, he's more likely to receive a record that follows him into every job application, housing form, and loan inquiry for the rest of his life. The white kid was „experimenting." The Black kid was making „bad choices." Same action, different story, different life.

The correlations extend in every direction from there. In most Western nations, darker skin predicts lower income, less accumulated wealth, worse educational outcomes, higher incarceration rates, and shorter life expectancy. These patterns are strong, consistent, and have no biological explanation. They're the balance sheet of centuries of economic extraction that used visible difference as its sorting mechanism.

This is the context usually missing when someone asks why we still talk about race.

The Two Testimonies

The white story: „I never owned slaves. My ancestors were poor immigrants who built their lives through hard work. Nobody gave them anything. Why should anyone get special treatment based on skin color?"

The Black story: „My ancestors built this country's wealth while receiving nothing. When slavery ended, we faced another century of legal discrimination. The wealth gap isn't ancient history. It's my grandmother's stolen wages."

Both stories are true. Both stories are also traps. As long as the conversation stays between these two testimonies, it never reaches the third story, the one about where the wealth actually went and who's still holding it.

Watch a policy debate play out. Someone proposes universal healthcare. Within minutes the conversation has abandoned the policy entirely and become a fight over which group benefits most. „That's welfare for minorities." „That's privileging white suburbs." The program never gets evaluated on its merits because the racial lens bends everything that passes through it. People who would benefit from the same policy end up voting against each other.

This is a feature, not a bug. White workers oppose programs that would help them because they believe the programs primarily benefit Black people. Black activists framing every issue as racial justice miss opportunities to build broader coalitions. Both groups stay focused on each other, and the people actually extracting the wealth stay out of frame.

Those people don't care about your melanin. They'll exploit light-skinned workers and dark-skinned workers with equal enthusiasm. They'll fund racial justice organizations and white grievance movements simultaneously if both keep class consciousness at bay. The investment pays for itself.

The transition from slavery to wage labor capitalism is usually taught as moral progress. Economists Douglass North and Gavin Wright tell a more uncomfortable story. Free labor economies innovate faster. Workers who receive wages have incentive to increase productivity. Wage earners create consumer markets that enslaved people cannot. The math was always there.

Slavery ended not because the ruling class developed a conscience. It ended because wage labor extracted value more cleanly. You got the exploitation without the overhead of literal ownership, without the international embarrassment, without the constant threat of violent revolt. Better margins all around.

Both groups now work for wages that, per Economic Policy Institute data, haven't kept pace with productivity gains since 1979. Both groups watch wealth concentrate at the top while competing for what's left. The extraction became more efficient, and the racial division that once justified chattel slavery now prevents the working class from recognizing they're being processed by the same machine.

Three hundred years after Bacon's Rebellion, poor whites and poor Blacks still don't organize together. The Virginia Assembly would be proud.

The visible difference triggers the automatic sorting. Genuine grievances keep both groups focused on each other instead of upward. Anyone who suggests cross-racial working-class solidarity gets dismissed as naive from the left and a race traitor from the right. The system doesn't need enforcers anymore. It runs on its own momentum, powered by the one thing that's harder to dismantle than any law: the feeling of having someone to look down on.

You can repeal a statute. You can't repeal an identity.

The Divide Between Left and Right

> **NOTE:** *This chapter deconstructs political tribalism. If your party loyalty feels like a core part of your identity, this text will feel like an attack. If the resistance is too high, move directly to **Section III**. The structural solutions there function regardless of your political stance.*

Your political opponents are destroying the country. You're certain of this. They're equally certain about you. You're both seeing something real. You're both being played.

The left/right divide isn't a natural law of politics. It's a constructed framework that keeps populations focused on one another instead of examining who benefits from the division. While you argue about pronouns or gun rights or abortion, wealth flows upward. While you rage at the other team's latest outrage, bipartisan consensus quietly builds around defense budgets, financial sector protection, and corporate welfare.

The trick is making you believe the fight between left and right matters most, when the actual battle is between those who wish to dominate and everyone else.

The Performance of Opposition

The left/right distinction emerged from the French Revolution, where revolutionaries sat on the left side of the assembly and royalists sat on the right. A seating arrangement became political destiny. The division served a purpose then. It serves a different purpose now.

In revolutionary France, the distinction represented genuine conflict over whether aristocrats should maintain hereditary power. Today's divide represents something else: the illusion of fundamental opposition between two teams that largely agree on what matters to concentrated power.

Notice what happens when power changes hands. Democrats win. Military budget increases. Surveillance expands. Corporate welfare continues. Wealth inequality accelerates. Republicans win. Military budget increases. Surveillance expands. Corporate welfare continues. Wealth inequality accelerates. The rhetoric changes. The policies don't.

Both sides perform passionate opposition while voting together on what counts. The drama is real. The substance is choreographed.

In 2008, the TARP bailout passed with bipartisan support. While the public raged, both parties united to transfer wealth upward. In

2020, the CARES Act passed the Senate 96-0.
During the largest upward wealth transfer in
modern history, your left and right
representatives agreed. That's not a vote. That's
a standing ovation for the donor class.

The pattern is consistent: when expanding state
power, funding military contractors, or
protecting financial institutions, consensus
materializes. The bitter partisan fights happen
over issues where disagreement costs power
nothing.

Nobody needs to conspire. The incentive
structure does the work. Both parties depend on
the same donor class, rotate through the same
consultancies and lobbying firms, and draw
from the same elite universities and think tanks.
The differences are real enough to keep you
engaged, shallow enough to keep power intact.

Political scientist Thomas Frank documented
the mechanism. The ratchet moves in one
direction: toward greater concentration of
wealth and power. When Republicans control
government, they push aggressively rightward
on economic policy. When Democrats take
over, they don't push back. They consolidate
Republican gains and push selectively on social
issues that don't threaten economic power. The
result, over decades, is consistent movement

toward corporate interests regardless of who won the last election.

Clinton deregulated Wall Street. Obama protected the banks from prosecution after 2008. These aren't betrayals of left principles. They're demonstrations of where actual power lies.

The Controlled Spectrum

Both parties exist within a carefully maintained spectrum of acceptable positions. The left questions corporate power, billionaire wealth, and economic inequality. The right questions bureaucratic power, state overreach, and regulatory control. Both critiques are genuine and important.

What happens when these critiques meet governing power is more instructive. The left wins elections by criticizing billionaires, then governs without dismantling billionaire power. They regulate corporations while leaving ownership structures intact. They increase taxes incrementally while wealth concentration accelerates. The right wins elections by criticizing bureaucracy, then expands surveillance and military spending. They reduce some regulations while creating others that benefit corporate allies.

The spectrum permits passionate debate about restructuring power. The actual restructuring rarely occurs.

Ron Paul questioned the empire and got marginalized by Republicans. Bernie Sanders questioned billionaire power seriously enough to threaten it and got marginalized by Democrats. Julian Assange exposed war crimes and got prosecuted by both parties. The rule isn't complicated: criticize power structures all you want, but actually threatening them ends your political career.

Occasionally, genuine opposition to those who wish to dominate emerges. The farmer protests in the Netherlands and Germany are a good example. Starting in 2019 in the Netherlands and spreading to Germany by 2023, they united working people across the political spectrum against policies threatening their livelihoods and the independence of food supply. Dutch farmers blockaded highways, sprayed government buildings with manure, and organized massive tractor convoys into city centers. These weren't left or right movements. They were working people defending their ability to work, and resisting the consolidation of food production into corporate hands. When small independent farmers can't afford to comply with new regulations, large agricultural corporations step in to buy the land. That's not an accident either.

The establishment response was immediate. The media framed protesters as far-right extremists and climate deniers. Politicians called them criminals and terrorists. The protests were portrayed as threats to democracy itself, when they were democracy in action: citizens resisting policies imposed without genuine consent and recognizing corporate capture hiding behind environmental language.

The Tea Party began as grassroots opposition to bailouts and corporate welfare. Within months, Koch-funded organizations captured it and redirected focus toward culture war issues. The Bernie Sanders campaign built a coalition that transcended traditional left boundaries until the Democratic establishment deployed every available mechanism to stop it. In Canada, the trucker convoy of 2022 brought together union workers, small business owners, and working-class citizens across the political spectrum. The media immediately labeled it terrorism. Bank accounts were frozen without trial.

Different movements, same response: when populations start organizing around shared economic interests rather than cultural identity, the establishment closes ranks fast. The spectrum reasserts itself.

The Exhaustion Strategy

The constant battle serves another function: exhaustion. Spend all your energy fighting your neighbors over political identities, and you have nothing left to examine actual power structures.

You're not being pacified. You're being activated, but your activation channels into safe directions. You're encouraged to be passionate, engaged, even enraged. Just make sure that passion targets other members of the working class rather than the class extracting wealth from all of you.

Once you've publicly committed to a side, changing positions becomes psychologically costly. You've argued with family members. You've posted on social media. You've made your political identity part of your social identity. Admitting your team is also captured means admitting you were wrong about something central to how you present yourself. Easier to double down than admit the game is rigged.

Social media amplifies this trap. Your political positions are now permanently recorded and attached to your name. Every post increases your investment in your team's narrative. The incentive structure pushes toward ever-greater polarization, even as the material conditions of left and right voters grow increasingly similar.

The culture war keeps you busy. The class war continues unnoticed.

The Attitude Network

Here's where it gets structural. Your political positions aren't random opinions you've independently evaluated. They form an organized network where each belief reinforces the others. Change one, and the entire structure feels threatened. This is why political arguments rarely change anyone's mind, and why facts have so little traction.

Research by Lüders, Carpentras, and Quayle[1] mapped exactly this. Democrats and Republicans don't just disagree on issues. They've developed completely different structural organizations of their beliefs. Each party's attitudes form tightly interconnected systems where holding one position strongly predicts holding dozens of others.

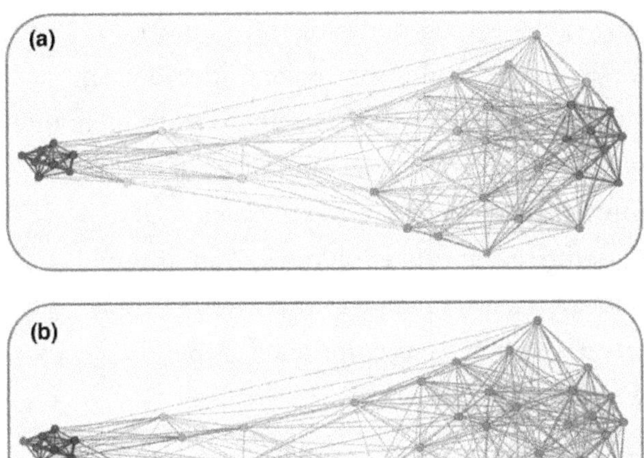

Figure 1:
https://bpspsychub.onlinelibrary.wiley.com/doi/10.1111/bjso.12665

The Democratic network shows significantly denser interconnection. Every attitude links to every other attitude more tightly. The belief system is more rigid, more internally consistent, more resistant to individual variation. The practical result: less freedom of thought. When your attitude network is tightly woven, questioning any single position threatens more connections, activates stronger identity defenses, and generates more pressure to conform. The structure doesn't permit you to hold left-wing economic views while questioning pandemic response, immigration policy, or gender ideology. Question one node, and the entire network mobilizes to pull you back into alignment.

The right-leaning network shows more looseness. This doesn't make it ideologically superior. It makes it differently constrained: one network enforces conformity through tight interconnection and rapid expulsion of dissenters; the other tolerates more internal disagreement, which can mean either more freedom or more incoherence, depending on which day you're watching.

This might explain J.K. Rowling. Once the literary hero of the left, writing books that taught a generation to question authority, she committed the unforgivable sin: she questioned one position on gender identity and refused to accept every conclusion the movement demanded. The response wasn't an argument about the specific issues. It was an accusation of betrayal. „You've become a bigot." She didn't move right because she changed her politics. She was labeled right-wing because the left's network rigidity made her independent thinking structurally impossible within its bounds.

When beliefs form identity networks, challenging any single belief feels like threatening your entire self. The network doesn't permit questioning. It permits only reinforcement. And when your network is tightly interconnected, that effect intensifies.

The chain reaction is predictable once you see it. Gun rights connect to immigration, immigration to taxes, taxes to climate, climate to healthcare, healthcare to foreign policy. Not because these issues are logically linked. Because the network demands consistency. When someone expresses a view on one issue, you can accurately predict their entire political identity. That's not reasoning. That's pattern-matching to determine: friend or enemy?

Each network permits different criticisms while forbidding others. The left can criticize corporate power but not bureaucratic power. The right can criticize bureaucratic power but not corporate power. Try holding left-wing economic views while opposing expanded state power. Try supporting strong national borders while advocating wealth redistribution. Try questioning military spending while supporting Second Amendment rights. The networks resist these combinations not because they're logically incompatible, but because they're identity-incompatible.

The result is that half of power remains immune to criticism at any given moment. Your team can see the problems your opponents are blind to. Their team can see the problems you're blind to. Between the two of you, you cover the whole picture. But neither team can see it whole because that would require admitting your enemies are partially right. And the network makes that psychologically intolerable.

Notice what happens when someone tries to break out. A Democrat criticizes surveillance state expansion. Immediately: „You sound like a Republican." A Republican questions military spending. Immediately: „You sound like a Democrat." The accusation triggers network reinforcement. You're threatening group membership. Get back in line.

Glenn Greenwald questioned Democrat narratives on civil liberties and got reclassified as a right-wing useful idiot. Sahra Wagenknecht in Germany criticized immigration policy, spent years in isolation from acceptable left discourse, and eventually had to form her own party. George Galloway opposed the Iraq War and got kicked out of Labour. Yanis Varoufakis challenged EU austerity and got marginalized by the European political establishment. It's like getting expelled from a book club for suggesting the book wasn't that good, then being told you've joined the fascist book club. You're still just someone who didn't like the book.

The tight interconnection makes this inevitable. You can't question pandemic policy while maintaining acceptable left credentials because pandemic policy is now connected to every other node. Question one position, and the entire structure interprets it as an identity threat. The network responds by excommunication.

Both sides run the same play: vote for us or the other team will destroy everything. This keeps you voting against what you fear rather than for what you want. Every four years, the choice is between a corporate-funded politician who'll betray you slowly and a corporate-funded politician who'll betray you quickly. Your team doesn't need to deliver on promises. They only need to be marginally less terrifying than the opposition.

The attitude network operates automatically. You don't consciously decide to organize beliefs into identity-coherent packages. Your brain does it as a shortcut for processing complex social information. The network feels like reasoning. It feels like you've evaluated each position independently. That's the illusion. The network came first. The justifications came after.

This is why fact-checking fails. You're not arguing about policies. You're defending identity structures. The network protects itself by making challenges to any single node feel like challenges to the whole system, and challenges to the whole system feel like challenges to who you are.

Breaking free means recognizing: I am not my attitude network. These positions don't define me. They're provisional conclusions I hold pending better information. I can question any belief without threatening my core identity. I can acknowledge my opponents are correct about some things.

The network fights this awareness. Your in-group will punish deviation. Your identity structure will resist. The discomfort of uncertainty will push you back toward network coherence. The work is tolerating that discomfort long enough to see clearly. Most people don't. The network wins by attrition.

The positions each network forbids aren't logically impossible. They're politically inconvenient to power. The left can't question bureaucratic expansion because that would destabilize the administrative state. The right can't question corporate consolidation because that would destabilize capital accumulation. Between the two forbidden zones, power operates freely and without opposition.

Democrats and Republicans argue passionately about bathroom policies while both vote to fund another aircraft carrier. The military-industrial complex doesn't care which bathroom you use. Your passionate defense of network-coherent positions feels like consciousness. It's automation. Real consciousness requires breaking the network long enough to ask: who benefits from these specific combinations of permitted and forbidden critiques?

The answer is uncomfortable. You'd see the whole machine. You'd recognize that Democrats and Republicans agree on most things that matter to concentrated power. Surveillance expansion? Unanimous. Bank bailouts? Bipartisan. Corporate subsidies? A beautiful friendship. You'd recognize that your supposed enemies share your class interests. You'd understand that the culture war keeping you busy serves someone else's interests entirely. Breaking free isn't about switching teams. It's about refusing to let attitude networks organize your thinking.

Beyond the Party System

Step back from team identification long enough to see the pattern, and something uncomfortable comes into focus: most of what you're told to fear about the other side already exists under your side.

Republicans fear government overreach. Democrats expanded surveillance, mandated medical procedures, and coordinated with tech platforms to censor speech. Democrats fear corporate power. Republicans cut corporate taxes, deregulated industries, and funneled public money to private contractors. Each side implements what the other claims to oppose, then blames the opposition when it continues. The policies are bipartisan. Only the excuses change.

Here's the question that collapses the left/right divide: why do billionaires fund both parties?

If the parties represented genuinely opposed interests, concentrated wealth would back one side. Instead, billionaires hedge their bets. They donate to Democrats and Republicans. They ensure access regardless of who wins. They shape both parties' policies through the same mechanisms. If you're wealthy enough, you don't bet on one horse. You own the track.

Poor Republicans and poor Democrats have far more in common with each other than either has with wealthy members of their own party. The cultural divide prevents this recognition. That's not an accident.

Once you identify with a party, you defend positions because they're your team's positions, not because you've examined them. Republicans who opposed executive overreach under Democrats defend it under Republican presidents. Democrats who criticized military intervention under Republicans defend it under

Democratic presidents. The position matters
less than which team holds it. When power
alternates between two parties, neither can be
held fully accountable. The voter trying to hold
someone responsible faces an endless shell
game. The policies both parties agree on
continue unexamined.

When only two parties can win, special interests
need to capture both. Pharmaceutical companies
donate to Democrats and Republicans. Defense
contractors fund both parties. Tech giants hedge
across the spectrum. Two points of leverage.
Remarkably simple to own.

The technical solutions that would allow citizens
to govern themselves more directly already exist.
We'll examine them in later chapters. But
technology doesn't fix the underlying problem.
A population that has outsourced its thinking to
team identity will reproduce the same dynamics
in any system you hand it.

Your anger at your political opponents is real.
It's also precisely where those who wish to
dominate want it directed. Not toward the
consciousness necessary for self-governance.
Not toward holding anyone truly accountable.
At your neighbors, who happen to vote
differently.

The Divide Between Men and Women

> **NOTE:** *This chapter examines how gender conflicts are weaponized to fragment society. This content is designed to be provocative. If you aren't ready to sit with these tensions, skip to **Section III**. We'd rather you arrive at the cooperation phase intact than check out entirely.*

Women and men have never hated each other like this.

Not in Victorian England, where gender roles were rigid but partnerships still formed. Not in medieval Europe, where arranged marriages were common, but cooperation was necessary. Not in any tribal society, where divisions of labor were strict but mutual respect existed. Not in any culture, any era, any context in human history.

This level of gender war is completely unprecedented. And it's destroying both sexes in different ways.

Picture Jake, 28, scrolling through dating apps in his studio apartment at 2 AM. Six years of college debt, decent job in tech, lifts four times a week, reads philosophy. He gets three matches per month. Two ghost him immediately. The third talks for a week, then vanishes when he suggests meeting for coffee. His last relationship ended three years ago. His father married at 24, bought a house at 26. Jake can barely afford rent. He watches videos online explaining why modern women are incapable of love, and part of him wants to believe it because the alternative—that he's simply not good enough—is unbearable. He's given up.

Picture Sarah, 32, successful marketing director, attractive, socially skilled. Her dating app matches are flooded with sexual propositions and low-effort „hey" messages from men she'd never choose. The men she actually wants don't respond, or worse, string her along for months before ghosting. She wants a family, but her last boyfriend, the one she thought was it, revealed after two years that he „wasn't sure about marriage." Time she can't get back. Her grandmother had four children by 32. Sarah medicated her anxiety with Lexapro last year. She bought a „Male Tears" coffee mug as a joke, but it stopped being funny. She's exhausted.

Both want partnership. Neither can achieve it. And they've learned to blame each other for a system that's failing them both.

The data confirms the lived experience. Men's suicide rates in peacetime now match wartime levels. Women's anxiety and depression have hit historic highs despite six decades of expanding rights. Young people can't afford homes. Communities have dissolved. Technology reduced human connection to swipe dynamics. Both sexes work longer hours for less purchasing power than their grandparents had on one income.

Something has gone catastrophically wrong. The question is what, and more importantly, why now?

The Physical Reality

Almost everything in human experience is a social construct. Democracy, money, corporations, nations, laws, religions, political ideologies, and economic systems are stories we tell ourselves and agree to believe. They're real in their effects, but we made them up.

There are only two fundamental dynamics that aren't like this: our relationship with nature, and the relationship between women and men.

When you try to reorganize society as if these biological realities don't exist, when you attempt to make something that isn't a social construct behave like one, you don't transcend those realities. You just create chaos. Nature reasserts itself, and the gap between ideology and reality becomes a space where people suffer.

Start with facts no ideology can change. Women can create life. Men cannot. This single capacity shapes every other difference in how humans organize themselves, distribute labor, structure power, and relate to each other.

Pregnancy carries a real risk of death, permanent damage, and trauma. Childbirth can destroy the body. Recovery takes months or years. This creates extreme selectivity in mate choice as survival strategy. Each pregnancy is high stakes. Women need safety and resources during vulnerable periods. None of this is cultural conditioning. It's evolutionary pressure written into biology over hundreds of thousands of years.

From this flow predictable patterns. Hypergamy emerges as a rational strategy given the vulnerability pregnancy creates. The direct physical connection to offspring that begins in the womb shapes how women relate to children and community. Emotional attunement develops as a necessary skill for reading infant needs and maintaining social bonds.

Men face different pressures. They compete with other men for female selection. Because women are the reproductive bottleneck and men are biologically surplus, male expendability becomes assumed. This is why we send them into wars, into mines, onto oil rigs, into any dangerous work that needs doing. Status competition becomes the primary pathway to reproduction and meaning. Physical strength creates capacity for both provision and violence.

These different pressures create different strengths. Women's capacity centers on creation and nurturing of life, something only they can do. From this flow natural gifts in social cohesion and relationship maintenance, emotional attunement and communication, multi-generational wisdom transfer, and community building. Men's capacity centers on physical strength and the ability to create safety through protective violence. From this flows natural tendency toward risk-taking and exploration, systematic problem-solving and building, provision and resource generation, and defense against external threats.

When we study other animals, we have no problem observing their sex-based behavioral patterns. Male and female elephants exhibit distinct behaviors driven by biology. Male lions compete for territory while females form social bonds. Nobody calls this stereotyping. But when it comes to humans, we suddenly pretend these patterns don't exist.

These aren't stereotypes. These are statistical patterns that emerge from biological pressures across virtually all human cultures. Yes, there's variation. Yes, individuals don't always fit the patterns. But denying the patterns exist serves no one, because denying biological reality doesn't eliminate the needs those realities create. It just ensures those needs manifest in toxic, unguided ways.

The question isn't whether these biological differences exist. The question is what we do with them. Because these same differences can create either beautiful complementarity or terrible exploitation.

The Divine Collaboration

The differences between women and men are complementary. Not better or worse. Different strengths that, when honored, create something stronger than either could alone. The point of partnership isn't to compete or prove equality through sameness. The point is to build a team where different capabilities work toward shared goals.

Picture this differently.

Maria sees what her family could become. She's been envisioning it for months. A home where the children can grow strong, where they're not cramped in an apartment with noise bleeding through walls. She sees her husband David teaching their son to build things with his hands, sees her daughter learning confidence from having space to breathe. She sees Sunday dinners with extended family, sees a life built around what matters rather than what's merely affordable.

She tells David one night: „I want us near the mountains. I want the kids to have room to run, to learn from nature, to not grow up like we did, stacked in boxes."

David hears the vision. Not a demand. Not a complaint about their current two-bedroom rental. A vision of what they could build together. He starts calculating. They'd need to increase income by forty percent. He'd need to take the management position he's been avoiding because the hours are brutal. Or find remote work that pays more. Or both work additional hours for two years to save enough. The path isn't easy, but it's visible.

He asks questions. She refines the vision. Together they map the route. He commits to the building, she commits to holding the faith when the path gets hard. Two years later, they have the house. He worked 60-hour weeks at a job he sometimes hated, but he did it because the vision was clear, the direction was set, and his children's future gave the sacrifice meaning.

This is what complementarity looks like in practice.

The masculine creates safety through strength. Only something dangerous can defend against danger. Only someone willing to confront threats can protect vulnerable life. A mother with an infant needs someone capable of violence standing between her and threats. This has been true for 200,000 years of human existence, and it remains true today.

Here's the crucial point: male physical capacity creates male responsibility. The ability to use force creates the duty to use it protectively. Men who possess strength have an obligation to use it in service of protecting the vulnerable, not exploiting them. This isn't optional. This is the foundational contract that makes partnership possible.

And this responsibility demands sacrifice. The man who works 60-hour weeks at a job he hates, who takes dangerous work, who sacrifices health and time for his wife and children, gains nothing personally. Most men would rather spend time with their children than in an office, would rather rest than labor. But leadership means putting those you serve above your own comfort. He does this because providing resources and security is his obligation.

David's sacrifice for Maria's vision isn't a favor. It's his responsibility. His physical capacity, his ability to endure the brutal hours and difficult work, creates the obligation to use that capacity in service to his family. When men abandon this responsibility, when they use their strength to dominate rather than protect, they break the fundamental agreement that partnership is built on.

The feminine creates life and cohesion. Only women can birth the next generation. Only mothers have the direct physical bond that begins in the womb. This creates irreplaceable knowledge about nurturing, about reading subtle cues, about creating the social bonds that hold communities together.

Maria's vision isn't decoration. It's the meaning that makes David's sacrifice worthwhile. A divine woman inspires her man and holds the vision for the family. She sees what could be, what the family needs to become, and calls it into being through her clarity and inspiration. She doesn't just benefit from his building capacity. She provides the why that unlocks it.

The masculine builds and leads toward that vision. A divine man takes his woman's vision and makes it real. He builds the future she sees and leads the family there. She sees the family needs a home near the mountains where the children can grow strong. He makes it happen, finding the way, securing the resources, building the life she envisioned.

This isn't domination. This is partnership in its highest form, where her vision and his building capacity work together to create what neither could alone.

Together, as a team, they create stability through the interplay of complementary gifts. Masculine strength protects feminine creation while feminine wisdom tempers masculine aggression. Different capabilities work in concert. In the healthy dynamic, men compete with each other rather than with women. Women select for competence and character, not just resources. Men protect without dominating. Women nurture without smothering. Children benefit from both energies. Communities thrive from complementary strengths. Neither tries to be the other. Both celebrate what the other brings.

This complementarity depends on understanding something fundamental: both capacities come with responsibilities, and responsibility requires control. You cannot hold someone responsible for creating safety without giving them the authority to make decisions about safety. You cannot expect someone to maintain cohesion without giving them influence over social dynamics.

Responsibility without control is impossible. If we expect men to create and maintain safety, they need authority in that domain. If we expect women to create and maintain cohesion, they need authority in that domain. But this authority isn't based on superiority or hierarchy.

As we established in the previous chapter on domination versus leadership, authority in service is fundamentally different from domination. The captain commands not because he's better than the crew, but because competent navigation requires someone to hold that responsibility. David has authority over how they reach the mountain home because he's the one executing the plan, shouldering the sacrifice. Maria has authority over the vision itself because she holds the meaning that makes the sacrifice worthwhile. Neither dominates. Both lead in their domains. The partnership works when both are empowered in their areas of responsibility, each leading through service rather than subordination.

In many preindustrial societies, you could see this complementarity functioning. Men hunted, defended, and built infrastructure while women gathered, maintained social bonds, and raised the young. Major decisions often involved both sexes, with a council of elders frequently including women. Different domains of authority emerged naturally: men handling external affairs, women managing domestic and social spheres. Neither was considered „less than," just different. Different forms of knowledge received mutual respect. They functioned as teams.

The Iroquois Confederacy provides a clear example. Clan Mothers selected male chiefs and could remove them from power. Women controlled property, agriculture, and had veto power over declarations of war. Men handled external defense and diplomacy, but women controlled the domestic sphere and held real political power. Neither could function without the other. Many other Native American tribes operated similarly: matrilineal descent, women's councils making major decisions alongside men's councils, division of labor with mutual respect and complementary authority.

Even Viking societies, often portrayed as purely patriarchal, allowed women to own property, divorce, inherit, and run households and farms when men traveled. Women had legal rights and economic power alongside male military and exploration roles.

Was it perfect? No. Was it egalitarian by modern standards? No. But it was functional. It honored differences. It created stable societies where both sexes had roles they could respect.

When the Same Gifts Become Weapons

Now picture the same scenario gone wrong.

Maria still has the vision. But this time, when she shares it with David, he hears criticism. He hears that what he's providing isn't enough. His masculine ego, already bruised by years of feeling like a resource-generation machine rather than a partner, interprets her vision as judgment.

He shuts down. Refuses to engage. Or worse, he says yes but sabotages the plan, working exactly the hours he worked before while complaining she's never satisfied. The strength that could have built their dream becomes the wall that prevents it.

Or flip it. Maria shares the vision, David commits, starts working brutal hours. Six months in, Maria changes her mind. Maybe the mountains aren't right. Maybe they should stay in the city. Maybe she's not sure anymore. She keeps moving the target while expecting him to keep sacrificing toward it. His clarity evaporates. His direction disappears. His purpose becomes meaningless because the vision that justified the sacrifice keeps shifting.

The feminine gift of vision becomes torture when it's unstable. The masculine gift of building becomes prison when it's pointed at the wrong target.

This is the uncomfortable truth modern discourse avoids: the same gifts that enable partnership also enable exploitation.

Men create safety by being dangerous. To defend against a tiger, you must be a threat yourself. The capacity for violence that makes a man capable of protecting his family is the same capacity that makes him capable of terrorizing it. You cannot separate these. The strength that creates safety and the strength that destroys safety are the same strength, just pointed in different directions.

Men are, on average, significantly stronger than women. This creates capacity for physical coercion. Sexual assault forces access through physical power. Domestic violence uses strength to control through fear. Physical intimidation creates an implicit threat that underlies many interactions. Men kill intimate partners at vastly higher rates than women kill men. Beyond direct violence, male physical advantage enables reproductive control: forcing pregnancy, preventing pregnancy, controlling women's bodies through law backed by force.

Every woman who has walked alone at night, every woman who has calibrated her behavior to avoid male anger, every woman who has been grabbed or groped or worse, carries this knowledge in her body. This isn't paranoia. This is lived experience repeated across generations, cultures, continents. The fear is rational because the danger is real.

Women create cohesion through deep understanding of social bonds. To build community, you must read emotions, understand what brings people together, know how relationships work. But that same understanding enables manipulation and destruction.

Psychologist Nicki R. Crick identified this pattern, calling it „relational aggression." It destroys through gossip, rumors, reputation attacks. Social exclusion uses the group to ostracize and punish. Emotional manipulation employs attunement to identify vulnerabilities and exploit them. Conformity enforcement punishes other women who don't fit group standards. Reputation destruction spreads damning claims about rivals. Victimhood itself becomes a weapon, claiming victim status to mobilize protection while avoiding accountability.

The same emotional intelligence that nurtures can manipulate. The same relationship-building that creates safety can create social prisons. The same skills that build community can destroy individuals.

The point here isn't to condemn either sex. It's to recognize that biological gifts necessarily contain their shadows. You cannot have protective capacity without destructive capacity. You cannot have social cohesion ability without social destruction ability. These aren't separate traits. They're the same trait, and the difference is only in how it's directed.

Both sexes must make conscious choices about how their gifts get used. The gifts don't automatically produce good outcomes. They create potential that can manifest as either collaboration or exploitation.

Mate Choice Shapes Power

Here's where things get uncomfortable. Women's mate selection creates demand for the very hierarchies that then enable male abuse of power.

Women are hypergamous. They select mates equal to or higher in status and resources. This isn't a moral failing. It's an evolutionary strategy rooted in pregnancy vulnerability. A woman selecting a mate makes a high-stakes decision about who can provide safety and resources during her most vulnerable periods. Of course, she selects for capability.

But this creates a specific dynamic. Men must compete for status and resources to be selected at all. The mate selection pressure doesn't just encourage this competition. It demands it. Men who cannot provide and protect are effectively excluded from reproduction.

Research shows women want both resource provision and partnership qualities: confidence, status, resources, leadership, capability, power, AND kindness, emotional availability, cooperation, partnership. This dual selection creates the social structures we see.

But here's the problem. Resources and capability function as threshold requirements. A man without ability to provide safety and resources won't be selected, no matter how emotionally available he is. Partnership qualities matter enormously, but you have to clear the resource threshold to get that far.

And resources are easy to demonstrate: job titles, income, status markers, confidence displays. Partnership qualities like emotional availability and cooperation require time and trust to reveal themselves. This creates a sorting mechanism where men who focus on acquiring visible, demonstrable resource-provision traits get selected first.

The successful businessman who worked 80-hour weeks becomes attractive not because women want workaholics, but because he cleared the resource threshold in a way that was immediately visible. Most men developing those resources simultaneously erode their emotional availability. The system makes developing both sets of traits nearly impossible.

In other words: women want a man who works like Gordon Gekko and feels like a therapist. The market has not produced this at scale.

Men face a choice: pursue resources first to meet the visible selection threshold, or develop partnership qualities that can't be signaled until after initial selection happens. Most choose resources because those traits are what get you selected in the first place.

To fulfill this selective pressure, the most dominant men build hierarchical systems to compete for and maintain status, resources, and power. They create legal systems that protect their resources. They build economic structures that concentrate wealth. They establish political systems that give them authority.

This is what some call „gynocentric patriarchy." It's patriarchal in structure, as men hold formal power. But it's gynocentric in origin, as the structure exists because women's mate selection created the demand for male hierarchy. Women decide, through their choices, what men need to provide to be chosen. Men then organize society to compete for providing those things.

The feedback loop becomes clear: women's mate selection creates demand for male status competition → men build hierarchies to compete → those hierarchies enable power accumulation → that power gets abused → women suffer from the systems their selection pressured into existence.

This doesn't excuse male abuse of power. But it complicates the simple narrative that men created patriarchy to oppress women. More accurately: biological pressures created mate selection patterns that prioritize both hierarchy-building traits and partnership traits, but economic structures force men to choose between them.

Both sexes participate in creating these structures, even when neither fully wants the outcomes they produce.

And competing for resources isn't the privilege it's often portrayed as. When mate selection rewards resource provision, men become exploitable for labor extraction. Male physical capacity makes them targets for heavy work, dangerous occupations, warfare, provider obligations. Modern rhetoric frames this as „the right to work," obscuring that performing labor is extraction, not privilege. The real privilege is living off someone else's labor.

Research from the Federal Reserve Bank of St. Louis shows married men significantly outearn single men, single women, and married women, while singles of both genders earn roughly the same. This demonstrates the feedback loop: women select for resources → men must demonstrate capability to be selected → once partnered, men sacrifice even more to provide. The system makes partnership economically beneficial but simultaneously makes it economically unattainable for most young people.

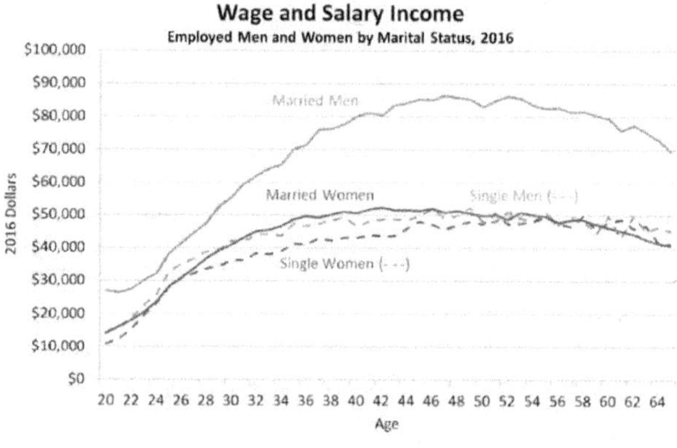

Figure 1: https://www.stlouisfed.org/on-the-economy/2018/december/married-men-outearn-single-men

Women also participate in this exploitation, both indirectly through mate selection that creates demand for systems that then exploit male labor, and sometimes directly by benefiting from male labor sacrifice while treating men primarily as resource-generation tools. Platforms like OnlyFans represent this dynamic in stark form: women monetize male sexual attention and desire while men exchange resources they earned through labor for simulated intimacy. Both sexes participate in feedback loops that exploit men's capacity for work just as surely as they exploit women's capacity for reproduction.

The question isn't „why did men create patriarchy to oppress women?" The question is: „How do we organize society given biological realities that create these pressures?" Can we create systems where men can fulfill responsibilities without abusing authority? Where women can select for genuine partnership capability rather than dominance displays? Where we build structures that work with evolutionary pressures rather than pretending they don't exist or forcing impossible trade-offs?

But first, we have to acknowledge that both participate in creating what exists. Women's mate choices shape male behavior just as surely as male violence shapes women's fear.

The Crisis of Role Models

Think of straightening a warped piece of wood. You don't gently nudge it toward straight. You bend it hard in the opposite direction of the warp, hold it there, then release it to settle into straightness.

Aristotle understood: virtue exists as the mean between two vices. Courage sits between cowardice and recklessness. Temperance between insensibility and self-indulgence. Generosity between stinginess and wastefulness. These virtues aren't natural. They're skills developed through practice. But you don't develop virtue by aiming carefully at the mean. You develop it by deliberately practicing the opposite extreme from your natural tendency, then calibrating back.

The virtues themselves are universal. Everyone needs courage, temperance, generosity regardless of sex. But biological realities mean men and women start with different warps and require different bending to reach the same straightness.

The sixteen-year-old boy in the gym discovers he can lift more than grown men. He feels the power in his hands. Without guidance, this becomes recklessness, dominance, the corruption of protective capacity into control. To develop true courage, he must push his strength to excess, feel what happens when he goes too far, then learn to calibrate. He spars until he hurts someone he didn't mean to hurt.

That's when the elder steps in: „You felt that?
That's the edge. Now you know where it is. Pull
it back."

The young woman who reads every micro-
expression, who feels the room's emotional
temperature, who naturally smooths conflicts
discovers her power over social dynamics.
Without guidance, this becomes excessive
agreeableness, manipulation through guilt, the
corruption of empathy into people-pleasing. To
develop proper assertion, she must push
directness to the point of uncomfortable
confrontation. She speaks her truth so bluntly
she damages a relationship. That's when the
elder steps in: „You felt that? That's the edge.
Now you know where it is. Find the balance."

Both travel to the same destination: balanced
virtue. But the wood warps differently, so the
bending must differ.

This process requires two things we've
destroyed: role models who embody balanced
virtue and can guide others through the warping
process, and tolerance from the opposite sex for
developmental mistakes. These role models are
the elders, the ones who've made the journey
themselves and know where the edges are.

Historical cultures understood this. Spartan
agoge took boys at seven and put them through

controlled hardship. Not to create reckless killers, but to show them the extremes so they could find courage in the middle. Native American vision quests sent young people into isolation until they touched something beyond normal experience. The tribe welcomed them back, knowing they'd found their edges.

Were these systems perfect? No. Some were brutal. Some were rigid. Some deserved to burn. And burn them we did. We tore down the old structures, rejected the harsh initiations, dismantled the rigid pathways. Much of this was necessary. The Spartan system created warriors but also brutalized children. Traditional gender roles provided structure but imprisoned many in lives they never chose.

But here's what we failed to do: build something better to replace what we destroyed. We burned down the workshop without preserving the craft of straightening warped wood. We rejected the old role models without raising new ones.

Modern cultures have nothing comparable. A boy lifts weights in his garage watching fitness influencers who sell only the excess, never the calibration. A girl learns social power from Instagram algorithms that reward manipulation, never wisdom. Both practice extremes with no one showing them the mean and no process bringing them home. The wood isn't just warped now. We burned the workshop that knew how to straighten it.

The opposite sex must tolerate the warping process. When the boy practicing boldness overcompensates into aggression, when he makes clumsy attempts at leadership, when he proves his strength too forcefully, women must recognize: this might be the warping required before straightness. Label every overcorrection as toxic and he never completes the journey.

When the girl practicing assertion becomes too direct, when she overcompensates into confrontation while finding her voice, when she tests her social power clumsily, men must recognize: this might be the bending required before balance. Condemn every mistake and she never completes the journey.

This tolerance doesn't mean accepting abuse. It means role models can distinguish between someone stuck in vice and someone passing through necessary extremes.

What we have instead: no role models embodying virtue. No structured warping process. No tolerance for mistakes that virtue requires.

Watch what fills the vacuum. Young men find voices promising them the reckless extreme is actually the virtue. Young women find victim ideology promising them passivity is actually strength. The algorithm feeds both more extreme content because outrage drives engagement. Each practices their vice believing it's virtue, with no elder pulling them back to center.

This is why validating biological differences matters. You cannot guide healthy masculine development if you deny that masculine energy exists and has specific needs. You cannot guide healthy feminine development if you pretend feminine energy is just socialization. The denial doesn't eliminate the needs. It just ensures they manifest without guidance, which means they manifest toxically.

Who Benefits From the War

What happened in the mid-20th century wasn't organic social evolution. The results are too consistent, too beneficial to specific interests, to be accidental.

In 1960, Tom's grandfather bought a three-bedroom house in Sacramento on a factory wage. Single income. Supported wife and three kids. Paid off the mortgage in fifteen years. Retired with a pension. Tom has a master's degree in engineering, earns $95,000, and can't afford a one-bedroom condo in the same city. His girlfriend earns $70,000 in marketing.

Combined, they make nearly triple what his grandfather did in inflation-adjusted dollars. They're still five years away from maybe affording a down payment on a starter home, and that's if they have no kids.

What changed?

When you double the labor supply overnight without doubling demand for labor, wages flatten. When you double the number of buyers in the housing market, prices soar. Now it takes two incomes to maintain the standard of living one income formerly provided. This is not an accident.

The push to bring women into the workforce was sold as empowerment. In many ways, it was. Women gained legal personhood, educational access, professional opportunities, financial independence. These were legitimate demands that addressed real oppression.

But we must also look at the macroeconomic math. The outcome was entirely predictable and completely preventable. There were policy options that could have allowed women's economic participation while maintaining wage power and making family formation viable.

Consider an alternative: Limit those without children to 30 hours of work per week. Those supporting children can work up to 80 hours, divided between partners for couples or available fully to single parents. This keeps labor scarce and valuable, makes family formation economically advantageous rather than catastrophic, gives people time for relationships and community, and still allows any individual the capacity to be financially independent.

Instead, we got the worst possible outcome. Both sexes now work longer hours for less purchasing power. Both became more economically precarious. Children lost parental presence. The elderly lost family care. Communities lost cohesion. And everyone became more dependent on institutions and markets.

Consider what that dependence actually looks like. People who would never tolerate a partner telling them what to wear, when to show up, and how to behave accept exactly those demands from an employer without question. A loving partner asking for half as much would be called controlling. The employer asking for all of it is called a job. We traded the intimacy of interdependence for the compliance of employment, and called it freedom.

Beyond economic extraction, look at social dissolution. The nuclear family weakened. Extended family networks dissolved. Community bonds fractured. Individuals became atomized. State and corporate systems filled the gap left by family and community. The elderly became clients of nursing homes. Children became customers of daycare programs. Mutual obligations that held communities together got replaced by market transactions.

Ideologically, the transformation was complete. Motherhood became devalued as „just a housewife." Career success became the primary measure of worth for women, regardless of personal desire. Traditional male roles were dismissed as inherently toxic. The provider and protector became the oppressor. The man sacrificing his body in construction, his health in a factory, his time away from children found himself recast as privileged. His sacrifice went from honored to invisible to mocked. Biological differences were denied entirely. Complementarity got replaced with competition.

The genius of the operation was framing it as pure liberation while achieving something else entirely.

Anyone questioning this arrangement gets labeled as wanting women to be oppressed. But the question isn't about returning to the past. The question is: who benefits from destroying the family and making everyone more isolated and dependent?

The denial of male sacrifice created its own consequences. When you tell half the population their fundamental contribution has no value, that their willingness to sacrifice makes them oppressors rather than servants, you create a vacuum. Men still possess the drive to protect and provide. That energy doesn't disappear when denied. It seeks other outlets.

Enter the demagogues. These figures promise men what the culture withholds: respect for their sacrifice, permission to be strong, freedom to express themselves. They don't offer genuine solutions. They offer validation. And to men systematically told their masculinity is toxic, even false validation feels like oxygen. The culture created the conditions. The demagogues simply walked through the door.

The Unprecedented Current Divide

On the male side, online communities teach men to view women as incapable of love, only seeking resources. „Red pill" content portrays all women as manipulative and shallow. Incel communities celebrate misogyny. MGTOW positions women as existential threats to avoid. Growing numbers of men retreat from relationships, education, work entirely.

On the female side, „kill all men" gets treated as acceptable humor. Phrases like „not all men, but always men" circulate without recognition that replacing one word reveals the bigotry: „not all women, but always women" or „not all Black people, but always Black people" would be instantly condemned. All men get positioned as potential predators by default. Male issues like suicide epidemics and homelessness get dismissed or mocked. Any male concern gets labeled „incel" to dismiss it without engagement. Female dating strategy communities teach manipulation tactics.

Social media algorithms promote outrage because it drives engagement. Echo chambers reinforce antagonism. The worst examples from each side get treated as representative. Platforms profit from the division.

Dating apps commodified human connection. Swiping left on humans like they're products on Amazon. Relationships reduced to marketplace dynamics. The top percentage of men receive majority of female attention. Most men experience constant rejection. Women experience harassment and low-quality interactions. Both end up frustrated and blame each other for dynamics created by the platform design itself.

Economic pressure intensifies everything. Most young people can't afford to form families. Both sexes work longer hours for less purchasing power. Economic anxiety gets projected onto gender dynamics. The real issue is economic precarity making family formation impossible, but it's easier to blame the opposite sex.

Integration, Not Projection

The masculine must understand feminine suffering to truly serve rather than dominate. A man who doesn't understand what pregnancy vulnerability feels like, what walking alone at night knowing you're physically weaker feels like, what being valued primarily for appearance and youth feels like, cannot effectively protect or provide. He can only impose his idea of what protection should be.

Many warrior traditions recognized this. Boys carried women's burdens and learned women's perspectives before they could stand as men. You had to understand what the women carried before you earned the right to be called a protector. You can't protect what you don't understand. You can't provide what you don't recognize as needed. Masculine strength requires this understanding. Without it, strength becomes domination, control becomes prison, protection becomes possession. The masculine holds the physical power. Force without understanding becomes oppression.

The equivalent exists for women. The feminine must understand masculine suffering to truly support and inspire rather than manipulate or control. Women need to experience creating their own safety and provision to understand what they're demanding from men. The feminine provides vision and meaning, but that vision must be informed by understanding what the masculine navigates.

Both need this understanding, but the emphasis falls on the masculine understanding of feminine suffering for a crucial reason. The masculine holds the physical power. Force without understanding becomes oppression. The one with greater capacity for physical harm has greater responsibility to understand what that harm looks like from the receiving end.

When both sexes understand what the other actually experiences, partnership becomes possible. Without this mutual understanding, you get projection. Men project their need for emotional connection onto women, demanding they provide all depth and nurturing while resenting that need. Women project their need for safety and provision onto men, demanding they provide all protection and direction while resenting that dependence.

Jung called this integration: the masculine developing his softness, the feminine finding her strength. A man who cannot be gentle makes his capacity for force indistinguishable from a threat. A woman who cannot stand alone makes her need for protection indistinguishable from victimhood. We couldn't get here without first recovering what masculine and feminine actually mean.

The work isn't about becoming the opposite sex. The work is about understanding the opposite's lived experience deeply enough that your service becomes real rather than imagined.

Clarity, Direction, Purpose

A friend of mine, Sasha Hovespian-Ruby, learned something crucial about masculine energy through chaos.

He was dating two women consecutively. In what the universe clearly intended as cosmic comedy, one was named Sasha and the other Ruby. His own name, split between two people, both bringing unregulated feminine energy into his life. Not emotional turbulence. Actual chaos. Destructive behavior. Crossing boundaries he'd clearly set. Bringing things into his home he'd explicitly said no to.

It got so bad he found himself physically shaking one night, trembling with frustration, damning the universe itself. Here he had done all the shadow work, processed his trauma, developed consciousness. And still the universe kept delivering chaos, with the cosmic joke of their names matching his own crystal clear.

He gave up on women. Temporarily withdrew. Stopped trying.

Two months later, he met his current long-term partner.

The universe's sense of humor hadn't changed. This was the final test. The chaos wasn't random cruelty. It was checking whether he'd actually done the work or just convinced himself he had. Because he'd been seeking validation through women, bending himself to match their energy, tolerating boundary violations because he needed them to choose him.

When he stopped seeking validation and started embodying grounded presence, everything shifted. He stopped being the river trying to flow in whatever direction she wanted. He became the riverbank. Unmoved by emotional weather. Present but not reactive. Clear about his boundaries.

That's when she appeared. A woman who wasn't looking for someone to complete her, but someone to build with.

From this experience, Sasha articulated what the masculine actually needs to function: clarity, direction, and purpose.

A man without purpose is the most dangerous creature on earth. Not because he wants to cause harm, but because all that strength, all that drive, all that capacity for action has nowhere to go. It turns inward as depression and self-destruction, or outward as aggression and chaos.

Clarity means knowing your values and what you stand for. The masculine needs internal clarity about the virtues and principles that define who he is. This clarity creates the riverbank that won't shift with every emotional current. Without it, a man bends to accommodate, tolerates boundary violations, becomes the river flowing wherever she directs. With clarity about his values, he can be grounded presence. „I don't allow destructive behavior in my home" is clarity. „I value honesty and won't accept manipulation" is clarity. This internal knowing is what makes partnership possible, because the feminine can trust what's solid.

Direction means living with integrity and navigating decisively. The masculine needs consistency between values and actions, following through on commitments, making choices that align with what he stands for. This is the navigation system. Without it, a man knows what he values but fails to live by it, makes commitments he doesn't keep, says one thing and does another. Direction transforms clarity into action. Obstacles are fine. The masculine excels at overcoming obstacles. But wavering, contradicting yourself, or abandoning what you said mattered creates paralysis in everyone around you.

Purpose means understanding why any of this matters. The healed masculine will sacrifice anything, endure any hardship, face any danger, but only for something worth protecting or building. „Because our children's future depends on it" unleashes everything the masculine has. Purpose transforms work into meaning, struggle into nobility, sacrifice into fulfillment.

The feminine provides meaning and inspiration. She holds the vision, but more importantly, she gives the why that makes the effort matter. When the feminine constantly changes her vision, opposes the direction while demanding progress, or questions the purpose while expecting sacrifice, the masculine cannot function.

When the feminine provides clear meaning, offers genuine inspiration, and trusts the masculine to find the direction, she unlocks everything he can offer.

The current crisis isn't primarily about economics or politics. It's about severing the masculine from what it needs, then condemning it for failing to function. No clear vision of what's expected. No direction because every path gets criticized as problematic. No purpose because traditional masculine roles get dismissed as patriarchal oppression.

So men retreat into video games where objectives are clear, lose themselves in work where achievement is measurable, or withdraw from relationships entirely because the confusion makes partnership impossible.

Why Partnership Matters for Democracy

The adjusted model of democracy this book proposes requires a prerequisite rarely discussed. Men and women must function as partners, not adversaries.

The state's monopoly on violence is overwhelmingly controlled and expressed by men. Police forces, militaries, enforcement agencies are predominantly male. This isn't changing anytime soon, given the physical realities we've discussed, though autonomous weapons and AI enforcement represent a longer-term threat to that equation worth watching.

When men view women as objects to be possessed and controlled rather than as partners with agency, they create systems of domination. This dominance mindset often stems from wounded masculinity, from trauma that twisted protective capacity into control. You cannot have genuine self-governance when half the population is treated as objects.

The choice men make matters enormously. When societies restructured after breaking aristocratic control in the early 20th century, average men who finally gained political voice could have used force to maintain male exclusivity. In many countries, they chose differently. In Germany, both average men and women gained universal suffrage simultaneously in 1918 after the revolution. The centuries-long fight had been against elite control, not men against women. When that barrier finally broke, many societies chose partnership.

But this choice isn't guaranteed. It can be reversed.

Look at Afghanistan under Taliban rule. When ideology demands female suppression, men can simply impose their will through force. Education forbidden. Employment forbidden. Movement restricted. Complete domination enforced through violence. This demonstrates that women's freedoms exist partly because men collectively chose not to impose maximum suppression.

You might remember Asch's conformity experiments, where participants faced pressure to agree with an obviously incorrect group consensus. A 2010 study by researchers Kazuo Mori and Miho Arai at Tokyo University of Agriculture and Technology found striking gender differences when replicating this work. When tested in same-sex groups, minority women conformed to the incorrect majority opinion, while minority men did not conform at all. Males generally show approximately half the conformity effect of females in these studies.

This willingness to dissent from group opinion, even when isolated, becomes critical in democratic systems. When authoritarian forces attempt to consolidate power, when consensus forms around unjust policies, when the majority moves toward tyranny, someone must be willing to stand against it. Men's lower conformity means they're more likely to be that someone. They're more willing to point out when the emperor has no clothes, to refuse compliance when everyone else is going along, to fight those who seek domination even when resistance appears futile. This capacity for principled dissent, for standing alone against group pressure, is what prevents democratic systems from sliding into authoritarianism.

Women's greater responsiveness to social consensus serves different essential functions in maintaining community cohesion and social bonds. Partnership between these different strengths creates systems where communities maintain bonds while still having defenders willing to resist domination.

If women and men are divided, if they view each other as enemies, if partnership breaks down into domination thinking, then no amount of democratic structure can prevent tyranny.

The solution proposed in this book requires a stable foundation. That foundation is built on women and men functioning as partners, not enemies. It requires men who control violence to choose restraint and service over domination. It requires women to recognize male agency and participation rather than viewing all men as oppressors. It requires both sexes to see each other as necessary parts of a functioning whole.

The partnership between women and men isn't just a nice idea. It's a prerequisite for the kind of conscious, responsible self-governance that genuine democracy requires. Without it, we're

just one ideological shift away from
Afghanistan.

Building What's Been Destroyed

Men need to see that male violence and
intimidation are real and create legitimate fear.
Physical strength is power, and it can be abused.
Other men's bad behavior affects how all men
are perceived. Taking responsibility means more
than blaming women for the consequences of
male choices.

Women need to see that selective power is real
power and it can be abused. Hypergamy creates
the status hierarchies that then get complained
about. Victimhood can be weaponized to avoid
responsibility. Male expendability and suffering
are real and deserve recognition.

Both sexes need to see how they're being
played. The other sex isn't the enemy. Platforms
profit from outrage. Ideologies profit from
grievance. The real enemies are isolation,
atomization, economic exploitation, and the
forces that amplify division. Biological
differences aren't problems to solve; they're
realities to acknowledge and respect while
building systems that work for everyone.

The divide between men and women is the
most intimate form of divide and conquer. It
turns potential partners into enemies, makes

both sexes miserable, and serves institutional power.

The solution isn't policy or returning to the past. The solution is rebuilding what's been destroyed: pathways to virtue.

We burned down the old systems. Some deserved it. Spartan brutality, rigid gender roles, structures that imprisoned people in lives they never chose. But we made a critical error. We destroyed the workshop without preserving the craft. We rejected flawed role models without raising better ones. We tore down pathways to virtue without building new ones.

Now we can build something better. Like a phoenix from the ashes of what we burned, we can create systems that honor biological reality while respecting individual expression. Systems that guide the warping process without the brutality. Role models who embody virtue without the rigidity.

We need role models who embody balanced masculine and feminine energy. Not influencers selling extremes or algorithms feeding outrage, but humans who've done the work and can guide others through it. Elders who know where the edges are and can teach young people to find them.

We need tolerance for developmental mistakes. When young men overshoot boldness into aggression, they need guidance, not condemnation. When young women overshoot assertion into confrontation, they need calibration, not labels. The warping process requires both permission to explore and wisdom to guide the return to center.

We need structures that honor biological differences while creating space for individual expression. Where masculine strength serves rather than dominates. Where feminine vision inspires rather than manipulates. Where both can develop their gifts without rigid roles or denial of reality.

The wood is warped. The workshop burned. But from those ashes, we can build something better. New workshops. Better methods. Role models willing to do the work and guide the next generation.

The choice is yours. Keep fighting a war between the sexes that serves those in power, or recognize the real divide isn't between men and women. It's between all of us and the forces that profit from our separation.

The Window

You've seen it happen.

Maybe at a city council meeting where they cut off public comment after three minutes but gave the developer unlimited time. Maybe watching a presidential debate where both candidates spent forty-five minutes carefully avoiding the actual question. Maybe reading news coverage of an event you witnessed firsthand, realizing the reporter was describing a completely different reality than the one you stood in.

That moment when the performance dropped. When you saw the machinery underneath.

You're not alone. Across every developed democracy right now, people are waking up to the con. They see the manufactured divisions. The power monopolies. The elaborate theater of democracy running cover for extraction. Systems designed for unconscious populations have a structural weakness: they stop working when those populations wake up.

So the systems double down. They overreach. They get more obvious, more desperate, more willing to drop the mask. The machinery becomes visible to people who weren't looking for it.

When that tension breaks, history is fairly consistent about what comes next.

When Systems Fall

The pattern repeats.

First, enough people become aware of the exploitation. They see through the propaganda. They recognize the con. They stop believing the performance. This is uncomfortable for everyone involved, including the people doing the waking up.

Second, the system tries to manage this awakening. More surveillance. Tighter control. Harsher penalties for dissent. The performance drops further, and the mechanism shows through even more clearly. The cure accelerates the disease.

Third, the tension breaks. Sometimes it's a specific triggering event. Sometimes it's accumulated pressure. But once legitimacy is gone and force is all that's left, those in power face a binary choice: escalate to open authoritarianism, or let the whole structure collapse.

Fourth, what fills the vacuum depends entirely on what people have ready.

The American Revolution had an alternative system designed before the breaking point. The

French Revolution didn't. One created a republic. The other created the Terror, then Napoleon, then the monarchy again. Three swings of the pendulum to end up more or less where they started, except with considerably more blood on the floor.

The Russian Revolution had communist theory but no tested implementation and no culture of self-governance to build on. Lenin's own description of the first Soviet state, „one big factory," told you everything. The system that emerged was as authoritarian as what it replaced. More efficient about it, in the worst possible sense of the word.

Weimar Germany's collapse is the case study worth dwelling on. By the time the Nazi vote surged in 1930, the German middle class had already been economically destroyed once by the hyperinflation of 1921 to 1923, which wiped out savings accumulated over lifetimes. Then the Great Depression arrived and pushed unemployment past six million by early 1933. The Weimar Republic had given Germans democracy on paper while bankers and industrialists made the actual decisions. When people were desperate enough and disillusioned enough, they chose the strongman. Not because they loved fascism. Because liberal democracy had just failed them twice in a decade, and they needed something that felt solid. They got something solid, all right.

The pattern is consistent: systems fail when enough people stop believing in them. What replaces them depends on what alternatives exist when they fall. The French had a better constitutional design than the Americans on paper. It failed because the population wasn't ready for it. The Americans succeeded not because their system was perfect, but because enough colonists had spent years governing themselves at the local level and had developed some actual capacity for it.

Here's the part most political theory skips: consciousness shapes structures, but structures also shape consciousness. The causation runs both ways, which is why this is harder than it looks.

An authoritarian system doesn't just oppress people. It sculpts them. It punishes independent thinking early enough that most people stop doing it voluntarily. It manufactures urgency to prevent reflection. It keeps people economically precarious, because someone worried about rent doesn't have bandwidth for inner work. It isolates people doing similar work from each other. Becoming conscious under authoritarianism is possible. Plenty of people have done it. But the system is specifically engineered to make it expensive, and most people respond to price signals.

A captured democracy, the kind where power has hollowed out the form while preserving the shell, produces something subtler and in some ways more corrosive. People can do shadow work. They can recognize patterns. They can see the manipulation with unusual clarity, actually, because the gap between the performance and the reality is right there in plain sight. But the system ensures this awareness never converts into actual power. You end up conscious and impotent. Which eventually produces something worse than ignorance: informed despair. The feeling that you can see exactly what's wrong and it doesn't matter.

A system with real accountability works differently. When your voice actually affects outcomes, you develop different capacities than when it doesn't. Transparency makes manipulation expensive rather than profitable. Distributed power forces people to practice responsibility instead of outsourcing it to leaders who will inevitably disappoint them. The structure trains the population as much as the population builds the structure.

So the cycle that actually matters looks like this. A small number of people develop clarity under current conditions. It's difficult, but possible.

They recognize patterns. They stop falling for manipulation. They develop, slowly, the capacity for holding responsibility without exporting it to a savior or a scapegoat. Through contact with them, others become aware. Each person who wakes up makes it marginally easier for the next. Not generational drift. Something closer to exponential. The curve looks flat for a long time, and then it doesn't.

But timing matters enormously, because there are two ways this ends, and both of them close the window.

The first is collapse. Systems lose legitimacy faster than they can adapt. The performance drops completely. Those in power escalate to open authoritarianism, or everything falls apart. What fills the vacuum depends on what alternatives people have ready. Without preparation, populations default to whoever offers the most compelling version of order. You've seen the historical examples.

The second is perfection. The surveillance infrastructure gets completed before enough people wake up to stop it. Digital tracking. Social credit systems. AI-powered behavioral modeling that can predict dissent before it organizes. The system doesn't collapse. It upgrades into high-tech authoritarianism where resistance becomes structurally nearly impossible. This technology exists. Several governments are already deploying it. Every transaction tracked. Every communication monitored. Every deviation from baseline flagged. The infrastructure is being built now, while the attention economy keeps everyone looking somewhere else.

One ending closes the window through chaos. The other through total control. Both are in progress simultaneously. Whichever arrives first wins.

If awareness spreads fast enough, it's possible to build alternatives before either ending locks in.

You are in that window right now. It is not a large window.

For Those Who Are Awake

Section III of this book is a working system that conscious people can implement when the current one breaks. Waiting until after the collapse means choosing from whatever is left standing, and history is clear on what's left standing after collapse. Rarely what anyone would have chosen with a clear head and actual options.

The preparation work is not complicated. It requires starting before the crisis rather than during it, which is the only hard part.

Start by learning to recognize dark triad traits and how they manifest in leadership. Narcissism, Machiavellianism, and psychopathy present differently in a city council member than in a head of state, but the underlying patterns are consistent. Researcher Robert Hare spent decades developing the clinical tools to identify them, and his work is accessible to anyone willing to read it. Study the manipulation tactics until you can spot them in real time rather than three years later in a political memoir you're reading to understand what went wrong.

Stop feeding systems that profit from your outrage. Name manipulation when you see it. Withdraw from manufactured divisions. These are not grand gestures. They are hygiene.

Build your networks before they're desperately needed, because networks built under pressure are weaker than networks built beforehand. Know the alternative system well enough to explain it when someone asks, and someone will ask.

The most significant barrier to better governance is not technical. It's not even political, in the conventional sense. It's the widespread conviction that this is simply how things are, that the performance of democracy and actual self-governance are the same thing. They are not. Most people already sense this.

They just haven't had it said plainly enough, or offered anything to replace it with.

When the current system hits its breaking point, the people who prepared will have something to offer besides reaction. A system designed for populations that have done the work. That creates accountability instead of performing it. That distributes power rather than concentrating it and calling that arrangement normal.

You've done the shadow work. You see the machinery. You understand, which is the uncomfortable part, your own role in what you oppose.

What comes next is architecture.

III. Integration and Healing

Health

Democracy cannot exist in sick bodies.

The institutional designers have been working overtime. Voting systems, accountability mechanisms, separation of powers, checks and balances refined over centuries. All of it assumes something nobody says out loud: that the people doing the governing, and the people being governed, have functional brains. That they can think. That their nervous systems aren't quietly on fire.

What happens to democratic capacity when bodies don't have the resources to think clearly? We're asking people running on poor nutrition, minimal sleep, and chronic stress to make complex collective decisions. Then wondering why democracy isn't working.

Your Gut Is Running Your Government

The brain is the most sensitive organ to physical conditions. We treat depression, anxiety, brain fog, inability to concentrate, and emotional volatility as purely mental problems. They're often physical dysfunction wearing a psychological mask.

People with clinical depression show elevated inflammation markers in their blood. The gut-brain axis reveals that bacteria in your digestive system produce neurotransmitters directly affecting mood and cognition. Your gut produces roughly ninety percent of your body's serotonin. Not your brain. Your gut. The organ we've been told to ignore, to push through when it hurts, to fill with whatever's cheapest and most convenient. That organ is running your emotional and cognitive operating system.

Mediterranean diet studies show substantial improvements in mood and cognitive function compared to standard Western diets. Exercise demonstrates effects on anxiety and depression that rival pharmaceutical intervention. When you eat processed foods high in sugar and low in fiber, you feed the wrong bacteria, creating internal conditions that produce anxiety, depression, and cognitive fog. You've felt this. Your thoughts go to static after a bad meal. Your patience evaporates when you're hungry. Everything feels impossible when you haven't slept.

Here's where it gets politically inconvenient. Judges grant parole significantly more often in the morning than the afternoon, according to research by Shai Danziger and colleagues. Not because the evidence changes. Because their blood sugar is low and their brains are tired. Your freedom potentially hinges on whether the judge had a snack. We wouldn't let drunk people vote, yet we ask chronically sleep-deprived populations to make complex political decisions. We test pilots for alcohol. We do not test them for whether they slept. We've decided some forms of impairment matter and others don't, usually based on whether acknowledging them would be inconvenient for someone's bottom line.

A population running on compromised neurochemistry can't remember what politicians promised last year. Mistakes exhaustion for apathy. Reaches for simple answers because complex thinking requires energy it doesn't have. The body shapes the mind. The mind enables or forecloses democracy. It's a chain, and it starts in the gut.

The controlled evidence makes this harder to dismiss than it might feel.

Research on prison populations shows improving nutrition leads to dramatic decreases in violent behavior. A UK study by Bernard Gesch published in the British Journal of Psychiatry showed a thirty-seven percent reduction in violent incidents simply by providing vitamin and mineral supplements to prisoners. No therapy. No new programs. Vitamins. School feeding programs show the same pattern. Students given nutritious breakfasts demonstrate improved concentration, behavior, and academic performance. Students fed processed foods show increased hyperactivity and decreased attention span. The evidence exists. We've had it for decades. We choose not to act on it because current arrangements are profitable.

British industrialization offers the template. Factory workers received cheap sugar and white flour, stripped of nutrients, just sufficient to maintain productivity. Historical records from the period document increases in mental illness, cognitive impairment, and general docility. Workers were fed, functional, and too depleted to organize effectively. Not a conspiracy in the classic sense. No shadowy meeting where industrialists agreed to dim the population's thinking. Just a system that discovered, through ordinary profit-seeking, that a mildly undernourished workforce was easier to manage than a healthy one.

Ultra-processed foods introduced across America after World War II followed the same script. The marketing called it progress. The reality was a population-wide nutrition experiment with no consent forms. Within decades, rates of depression, anxiety, and cognitive decline climbed sharply. The food industry produces ultra-processed foods cheaper to manufacture, with longer shelf lives, engineered for repeat consumption. The pharmaceutical industry profits from managing the conditions they create. A closed loop that works for everyone except the people living inside it.

This is your grandparents' generation. Your parents' generation. The people who taught you that pushing through exhaustion was virtue, that discipline meant ignoring your body's signals, that success required sacrifice. They weren't wrong about dedication. They were living in systems that made biological dysfunction the price of participation. And we inherited both the systems and the belief that this is simply how things are.

Politics on Good Hardware

What if we treated health as democratic infrastructure rather than personal responsibility?

Think about what political discourse looks like when people aren't operating from chronic stress and inflammation. When brains have resources for nuanced thinking rather than reactive responses. When emotional regulation comes from stable neurochemistry rather than constant effort against one's own biology. Citizens capable of holding competing ideas simultaneously, considering long-term consequences, disagreeing without their nervous systems interpreting it as physical threat.

This isn't speculative. The prison studies, the school feeding research, the gut-brain data all point the same direction. Small interventions in physical conditions create substantial changes in behavior, mood, and cognitive capacity. The Gesch study didn't change the prisoners' circumstances, history, trauma, or social environment. It changed their nutrition. That alone shifted the outcome by more than a third. Scale those interventions across populations and you're changing what kind of politics becomes possible.

None of this changes without restructuring what success actually means. Current health systems optimize for pharmaceutical consumption and treatment of illness rather than prevention. The sicker the population, the more the system „works" by its own metrics. Flip the measure: population health becomes the indicator of success. When metrics decline, those responsible face consequences.

Concretely: a food manufacturer introduces a new additive. Under current systems, they demonstrate it won't kill anyone immediately, secure approval, and profit from sales while it gradually contributes to inflammation and cognitive decline over years. No liability because the harm is diffuse and long-term. Under restructured incentives, they bear the cost of proving safety before widespread use, fund the research if population health metrics decline after introduction, and face escalating costs if causation is established. Suddenly the math changes. Prevention becomes more profitable than slow poisoning.

The same logic applies to industries that systematically undermine employee health through sleep deprivation, chronic stress, and manufactured time poverty. And to the regulators. Those setting food standards cannot receive funding from the industries they regulate. When guidelines change, the reasoning must be public, the evidence examined by independent bodies, conflicts of interest named rather than buried in footnotes.

These changes threaten enormous economic interests. Food manufacturers, pharmaceutical companies, agricultural industries, and healthcare corporations profit from current arrangements. They employ lobbyists and fund campaigns and will resist with considerable resources. They'll warn of economic catastrophe, job losses, threats to freedom. Apparently it's tyranny to prevent them from making you cognitively impaired, but it's freedom when they actually do it.

Which brings us back to you, sitting inside the system being described.

They're betting you're too tired to fight back. Too sick to organize. Too fogged to see the pattern. They're counting on your body doing quietly what overt oppression never could.

But they miscalculate one thing. Once someone understands the connection between body, mind, and political capacity, and once they experience what changes when that connection is addressed, the knowledge doesn't leave. Your afternoon brain fog isn't personal weakness. It's systemic design. When enough people recognize this, and feel the difference between compromised and clear, the ground shifts.

Health is democratic infrastructure. The body is where self-governance either becomes possible or quietly fails. Everything else we build depends on what we build it on.

Education

Picture a child on their first day of school. They arrive with questions about everything: why the sky changes color, how numbers keep going forever, what adults are really talking about when they lower their voices. They want to understand the world. They are, in the most literal sense, driven to learn.

Twelve years later, that same person sits in a fluorescent-lit room, watching a clock, completing a worksheet they don't understand for a grade they don't care about, in preparation for a job they haven't chosen yet.

Something happened in between. We call it education.

The modern school wasn't designed to educate you. It was designed to prepare you for the factory floor, and it was designed that way on purpose, by people who said so out loud.

The system traces back to early nineteenth-century Prussia, where the state first provided regimented mass schooling. Students were sorted by age and moved through successive curricula like products on an assembly line. The goal was to create obedient workers who could follow orders, show up on time, and tolerate monotony without complaint. When the industrial revolution needed bodies for factories across the West, this model followed. Factory owners required workers who were punctual, docile, and agreeable. People who would take instructions from managers they weren't even related to, which was, genuinely, a degrading new concept at the time.

The industrialists who championed universal education weren't shy about their intentions. Frederick Taylor Gates, advisor to John D. Rockefeller, wrote in 1913 that educational charity should not try to make people into „philosophers or men of learning or science" and should avoid raising up „authors, orators, poets, or men of letters." The goal was workers, not thinkers. And they got exactly what they designed for.

The Factory Model in Action

Economists Samuel Bowles and Herbert Gintis spent years documenting the mechanics. Their 1976 study *Schooling in Capitalist America* identified what they called the „correspondence principle." Schools deliberately mirror the social relations of production.

The hierarchy in schools corresponds to workplace hierarchy: principal over teachers, teachers over students, older students over younger, exactly like management over supervisors over workers. The fragmentation of knowledge into separate subjects corresponds to the division of labor. Math at 9 a.m., English at 10 a.m., never the two shall meet, just like your job handling one tiny piece of a process you'll never see completed. The emphasis on external rewards like grades corresponds to working for wages rather than intrinsic satisfaction. You're not learning for the joy of understanding. You're accumulating points to trade for advancement, training for a lifetime of doing things you don't care about in exchange for money.

Bowles and Gintis found that personality traits like dependability, consistency, identification with institutional goals, and empathy for authority predicted success in school better than intelligence did. Meanwhile, creativity, independence, and questioning authority were actively penalized.

The destruction of creative capacity demonstrates this at scale. In 1968, NASA hired George Land to develop a test measuring divergent thinking, the ability to generate multiple solutions to open-ended problems. The test worked brilliantly for screening engineers. Then Land tested 1,600 children aged four and five. Ninety-eight percent scored at the „creative genius" level.

He followed up with the same children at age ten. Thirty percent still scored at a genius level. By age fifteen, twelve percent. Adults? Two percent.

We start at 98 percent creative genius and end at 2 percent. A 96-point decline in creative capacity over the course of education. The kids didn't get dumber. They got schooled.

Land identified two distinct modes of thinking. Divergent thinking generates new possibilities, exploring multiple solutions without judgment. Convergent thinking evaluates, judges, criticizes, narrows options. Both have their place. But schools teach children to do both simultaneously, which is like pressing the accelerator and the brake at the same time and calling it driving.

„Don't give me creative answers, give me the right answer." „Stop daydreaming and pay attention." „That's not how we do it." „Color inside the lines."

These commands repeat daily for twelve years, training the creativity out of children with the efficiency of a military boot camp. By the time they're adults, asking them to think creatively is like asking someone who's never moved their body to run a marathon. The capacity is still there, buried under years of conditioning, but it feels unreachable.

The system treats intelligence the same way. Fifty percent of children with higher IQs underachieve in school. The kid who questions why they need to memorize dates instead of understanding historical patterns gets marked down for „not following instructions." The student who already grasps the material and refuses to do repetitive homework gets labeled „lazy." The child who thinks independently rather than accepting the teacher's interpretation gets tagged as „difficult."

Schools don't primarily reward intelligence. They reward compliance. The traits rewarded align precisely with what employers need: punctuality, obedience, tolerance for boredom, acceptance of hierarchy, suppression of critical thinking. The traits penalized are exactly those that threaten workplace control: creativity, independence, questioning authority, autonomous thinking. The students who excel aren't necessarily the smartest. They're the most obedient. They've mastered telling authority figures what those figures want to hear, completing assignments exactly as specified, and suppressing their own thoughts in favor of regurgitating approved answers.

This isn't education. It's domestication.

Teaching to Think

Walk into any high school and ask students what they're learning. You'll hear about chemical equations, Shakespeare's sonnets, the dates of various wars, symbolism in classic novels. Fine subjects, some even useful.

Now ask them to explain how credit card interest works. How their government actually functions. How to identify when they're being manipulated. What logical fallacies politicians use daily. Blank stares.

We teach kids to analyze metaphors in poetry but not how to think critically about information sources. We make them memorize historical dates while omitting that history is largely „the story that survived" rather than a neutral account of what happened. We drill grammar rules while neglecting why humans act the way they do. We assign book reports while never teaching students how to spot the invalid reasoning used to manipulate them every single day.

These aren't oversights. They follow the same pattern as everything else: schools reliably avoid teaching anything that would help students recognize manipulation or question authority.

Cognitive science has spent decades identifying what actually works for learning. Spaced repetition, self-testing, and interleaving different topics can improve retention by 60 to 80 percent compared to conventional methods. Schools do the opposite: cramming material into single units before tests, emphasizing passive rereading, and blocking subjects into isolated chunks. Every technique proven least effective, executed with remarkable consistency.

Why? Because effective methods feel harder. When you reread material, it becomes familiar. Familiar feels like understanding. Researchers call this the „fluency illusion": material slides through the mind effortlessly, creating false confidence that evaporates the moment you actually need to retrieve it. Testing yourself feels uncomfortable. You struggle. You confront what you don't know.

Schools continue using inferior methods because those methods process students efficiently, not because they produce learning. Once students understand that struggle is the mechanism of learning rather than evidence of failure, they stop seeking the easy path and start treating difficulty as signal, not punishment.

What follows is the curriculum that actually prepares people for self-governance rather than compliance. Not theory. Working models.

Practical Psychology

You cannot govern yourself if you don't understand what governs your reactions. This is foundational, which is why it belongs at the start of any serious education rather than in an elective psychology course at the end.

Students learn about the Asch conformity experiments, where ordinary people claimed obviously wrong answers to match the group. The Milgram obedience studies, where ordinary people administered what they believed were dangerous electric shocks because an authority figure told them to. How minds construct narratives divorced from evidence and then defend those narratives against all comers.

They learn the difference between dominance hierarchies and competence hierarchies. How manufactured social divisions are built and maintained. How fear hijacks decision-making. How group pressure overrides individual judgment. How confirmation bias operates, how trauma shapes behavior, the mechanics of projection and unconscious pattern repetition.

Not abstract theory. Practical knowledge, taught with the same rigor as algebra: recognize when you're being manipulated, when you're projecting your own fears onto someone else, when you're following the herd because it's easier than thinking. A population that understands its own psychology becomes substantially harder to steer through manufactured fear, tribal identity, or emotional spectacle.

Logic and Argumentation

Every person should reflexively spot ad hominem attacks, straw man arguments, false dilemmas, slippery slope fallacies, appeals to authority. Not as concepts memorized for a test but as tools for intellectual self-defense, practiced until they become automatic.

Students analyze real speeches, dissect advertisements, examine news articles. They practice identifying fallacious reasoning not in textbook examples but in the actual media environment they inhabit. Watch any political debate, any news segment, any social media argument: fallacies everywhere, deployed with confidence by people who know their audience won't catch them. People trained in logic see through these immediately. People without this training accept invalid reasoning as persuasive, every time.

Democracy requires evaluating arguments. Evaluating arguments requires recognizing when arguments are invalid, regardless of who makes them or how they make you feel. This is not a luxury subject.

Basic Economics

Not advanced theory. Fundamentals: how money is created, what inflation means, how interest compounds over time, the relationship between money supply and prices, how power and wealth concentrate, how monopolies form and sustain themselves. What debt actually costs over a lifetime. The difference between a stock and a bond, between a budget deficit and national debt, between economic growth and the distribution of that growth.

One year on economic fundamentals transforms civic discourse. When people understand how the system works, they ask better questions and evaluate proposals based on mechanism rather than rhetoric. They recognize when promises violate basic economic principles. Most economic policy debates involve people who don't understand economics arguing about what economists should do. Teaching basics doesn't make everyone an economist. It gives everyone enough ground to evaluate claims intelligently, which is all democracy requires.

Physical Movement and Embodiment

The research on this is unambiguous: physical activity significantly enhances cognitive function through increased brain activation, improved memory and executive function, better attention, and enhanced problem-solving. Exercise stimulates neural growth, increases blood flow to the brain, strengthens connections between regions responsible for learning. The sit-still-for-six-hours classroom model ignores all of this, and students pay for it cognitively.

Physical education, properly conceived, isn't gym class. It's integrated understanding of what it means to function as an embodied being — movement skills, body awareness, the relationship between physical states and mental ones. Schools that weave regular physical activity throughout the day see improved academic performance, better behavior, and enhanced focus. The brain needs movement to function. Designing systems that treat the body as inconvenient transport for the skull costs everyone.

Preserving Creative Capacity

Schools that maintain rather than destroy creativity keep one principle simple: separate divergent and convergent thinking. Generation time is for exploring ideas without evaluation: questions without predetermined answers, problems without single solutions. Evaluation time comes after: assess the possibilities, identify the strongest options, refine. Both modes are developed deliberately rather than collapsed into simultaneous self-cancellation.

Less „here's the answer, memorize it" and more „here's the question, explore it." Teachers facilitate exploration rather than dispense conclusions. The result: creative capacity doesn't decline from 98 percent to 2 percent over twelve years. It has the chance to grow.

Schools That Got It Right

Two working models demonstrate what becomes possible when education is designed for self-governance rather than compliance. These aren't theoretical proposals. They're functioning realities with documented outcomes.

Sudbury Schools

Founded in 1968 in Framingham, Massachusetts, the Sudbury model gives students complete control over their education. They choose what to learn, how to learn, when to learn. The school operates as a direct democracy where students and staff participate equally in all decisions, including hiring and firing of teachers. Students effectively experience democratic governance daily rather than studying it as an abstraction.

Research on graduates shows they succeed in higher education and careers and report that the school developed personal responsibility, initiative, curiosity, and the ability to

communicate across status hierarchies —
precisely the capacities factory-model schools
penalize. Follow-up studies find graduates
collectively pursue the full range of careers
valued by society, with particular strength in
roles requiring creativity and self-direction.

The model rests on a radical premise: children's
natural curiosity is sufficient, if you get out of its
way. Age mixing is considered its „secret
weapon." Older students mentor younger ones.
Younger students learn by observing others.
Students teach each other constantly, without
being assigned to. There are no required classes,
no grades, no tests, no comparisons between
students. The school provides resources and
access to knowledgeable adults when students
request help. Students design their own
education, and apparently they manage it fine.

More than 60 schools worldwide now use this
model. Graduates report no difficulty getting
admitted to universities of their choice or
adapting to academic requirements when they
chose to. They maintained their passion for
learning and their sense of personal
accountability.

Finland's System

Finland transformed from a mediocre,
inequitable system to the top of international

rankings through a series of reforms that cut against almost everything the factory model holds sacred.

Starting in the 1970s, Finland eliminated tracking students into different levels based on test scores, then eliminated most standardized examinations. They developed a common curriculum accessible to all students through the end of secondary school, aimed at equalizing outcomes rather than sorting students into predetermined futures. Teachers receive three years of rigorous, fully state-funded graduate preparation. Teaching is one of the most prestigious professions in the country; only one in ten applicants is accepted to teacher training programs. Teachers are trained to work with every type of student, including those with disabilities, language barriers, and learning challenges, which removes the institutional incentive to identify and warehouse difficult cases.

The system operates on trust rather than testing and surveillance. There are no mandatory standardized tests in comprehensive schools. Only 5 to 10 percent of students in any age group participate in national evaluations. Schools operate with substantial autonomy. Teachers design their own approaches within broad national guidelines, which means instruction stays human rather than becoming a delivery mechanism for standardized content.

Recent reforms emphasize „phenomenon-based learning," where subjects integrate around real-world questions rather than remaining isolated from each other. The focus is „learning to learn" as a lifelong skill. Students develop increasing autonomy as they advance, choosing between general and vocational education but able to move between both as their interests evolve.

The results: only 7 percent of variance in student performance occurs between schools in Finland, compared to the 29 percent OECD average. A system designed to serve all students actually serves all students. This turns out to be achievable.

The Sudbury and Finnish models differ in implementation but converge on what matters. Both start from trust rather than suspicion, building intrinsic motivation instead of engineering compliance. Both use age mixing and peer learning rather than rigid segregation by year. Both position teachers as facilitators rather than dispensers of correct answers, aim at developing whole people rather than narrow academic performance, and treat democratic participation as the daily structure of school rather than a civics lesson once a week.

The practical implication is simple: education can serve self-governance rather than compliance. Students can practice democracy instead of memorizing its definition. The factory model isn't inevitable. It's a design choice, and one that can be replaced.

Proof of Concept

Both models have been running long enough to settle the question of whether they work. Sudbury schools have operated for 56 years across more than 60 locations worldwide, each one a standing refutation of the factory model's core assumptions: that children must be coerced into learning, that creativity must be sacrificed for discipline, that democratic participation must wait until adulthood. Finland transformed its entire national system within a single generation, starting not with a charismatic reformer but with political consensus that education should serve all students rather than sort them. It took sustained commitment across multiple administrations and decades of iteration. But it worked.

Resistance to transformation follows predictable lines. Those who benefit from a population trained to compliance don't welcome a population trained to think. The objections will be ideological, urgent, and confident, advanced by people who haven't read the research and see no reason to. But demonstrated alternatives dissolve assumed legitimacy more effectively than arguments do. When people encounter graduates of genuinely educational systems, people who retained their curiosity, developed real accountability, and succeeded without being broken first, the necessity of the current model becomes much harder to defend.

Education is a political question dressed in administrative language. A population skilled in logic, psychology, and basic economics asks uncomfortable questions and recognizes the techniques used to prevent those questions from landing. Once enough people understand what the system was designed to produce, the design loses its air of inevitability. What replaces it already exists, documented and working, in more than 60 locations and one entire country.

The kids who arrived on the first day asking everything don't have to leave twelve years later knowing how to sit still and wait for instructions. That outcome was engineered. It can be re-engineered.

The Ground Has Been Prepared

Cleisthenes had a problem. Athens in 507 BCE was tearing itself apart. Aristocratic families were fighting for control while the common people grew increasingly bitter about their powerlessness. The solution he proposed was so radical that even today, 2,500 years later, we still haven't quite wrapped our heads around it.

He suggested that ordinary citizens should actually run the government.

Not elect representatives to run it. Not petition their betters for better treatment. Actually run it themselves. Farmers, merchants, and craftsmen would debate policy, vote on laws, and serve in rotating administrative positions. The Assembly would include any citizen who bothered to show up. Decisions would be made by majority vote after open debate.

The aristocrats thought he was insane. Their objections wrote themselves: the common people are too ignorant, demagogues will manipulate them, they'll vote themselves free bread and circuses until the treasury empties, important decisions require expertise that peasants don't possess. These are, of course, the exact same objections raised against expanded democracy today, which tells you either that the concerns are perennial and legitimate, or that aristocrats across the centuries have been reading from the same memo. Perhaps both.

Cleisthenes ignored them. He implemented his system, and Athens became what we now call the world's first democracy. The word itself comes from *demos*, meaning people, and *kratos*, meaning power. Not representative power. Not delegated power. Actual power.

For roughly two centuries, this experiment worked. Athens produced Socrates, Plato, Aristotle, Sophocles, and Euripides. It built the Parthenon. It defeated the Persian Empire despite being vastly outnumbered. It became the cultural center of the ancient world. All of this while governed directly by ordinary citizens who gathered in the Agora to debate and vote.

Their version had massive flaws, which anyone defending direct democracy today should be honest about. Women couldn't participate. Slaves couldn't participate. Only twenty to thirty percent of the population counted as citizens. When the Assembly made catastrophic decisions, the Sicilian Expedition during the Peloponnesian War being the textbook example, people died by the thousands. And eventually, the system collapsed under external pressure and internal dysfunction.

But for two centuries, thousands of ordinary people governed themselves without professional politicians, campaign consultants, lobbying firms, or political parties. Farmers and craftsmen showed up, listened to arguments, and voted. Not perfectly. Not without error. Functionally enough to create one of history's most influential civilizations.

Then we abandoned the whole idea for 2,000 years.

When representative democracy emerged in the modern era, it came packaged with a story: direct democracy was impossible at scale, complex modern issues required professional expertise, the Athenian experiment was a historical curiosity rather than a viable model. Some of this was true in 1787. It hasn't been true for decades. Yet the story persists, carefully maintained through omission, and the current system gets presented as democracy itself rather than as one particular design choice among many.

The standard framing offers two options: representative elections every few years, or authoritarianism. Democracy or dictatorship. This framing isn't accidental. It makes the current system look like the only alternative to tyranny, and it has worked remarkably well as a conversation-stopper. But the choice between bad options and worse options isn't a choice between the possible and the impossible. The real question is what mechanisms give citizens actual power while maintaining functional governance, and once you ask that honestly rather than rhetorically, you find that others have already been asking it for decades.

Dozens of experiments worldwide have tried to answer it. Some worked. Some failed. Almost none of them appear in civics curricula or political debates. But they have been quietly preparing the ground regardless.

Direct Power in Practice

Direct democracy gets dismissed as mob rule or naive idealism. Too many people to make collective decisions. Issues too complex for average voters. Citizens too uninformed to judge policy. These sound reasonable until you notice they're essentially arguments against democracy itself, just wearing sensible shoes.

Direct democracy doesn't mean everyone votes on everything. That would be absurd and nobody serious proposes it. It means citizens hold real power over decisions that affect them, with various mechanisms for exercising that power intelligently. The Swiss have been running versions of this for centuries. Countless cities and regions worldwide have experimented with different forms.

Participatory budgeting is one such mechanism. Starting in 1989, Porto Alegre, Brazil tried something genuinely radical: let citizens vote directly on how to spend public money. Not symbolic consultation, not advisory panels, not feedback sessions that funnel into a report that goes nowhere. Real authority over real expenditure. The city divided into sixteen districts, each holding open assemblies where residents proposed projects and debated priorities: this road or that park, a new school or better street lighting. After deliberation, residents voted. Projects with the most support got funded. The city actually built them.

The difference between having a voice and having a vote turned out to be significant. Infrastructure improved because locals knew which roads actually needed fixing, rather than which roads were visible from the mayor's office. Corruption dropped because thousands of eyes watched the money move through a process they'd participated in. Civic engagement increased because showing up had consequences. The model eventually spread to thousands of cities across four continents, which is what tends to happen when something works.

Participatory budgeting isn't a complete system of governance, and its advocates would be the first to say so. It's a tool that functions within specific constraints. You can democratically allocate infrastructure spending. You cannot democratically manage pandemic response through neighborhood assemblies. The scale and complexity don't match the mechanism, and pretending otherwise would be its own kind of magical thinking.

That limitation defines the proper scope rather than undermining the concept. Citizens make thoughtful decisions about concrete issues with visible consequences when the decision space is bounded and the feedback loop is short. The key is using participatory budgeting where it works, not abandoning it because it can't do everything.

Random Selection and Expertise

Sortition is an ancient idea that feels radical today: select decision-makers randomly, like jury duty for governance. Instead of electing politicians or appointing experts, choose citizens by lottery to deliberate on specific questions. Ancient Athens used it for many offices. Most democracies act as though it never existed.

Ireland ran two separate modern experiments with it, and they're worth distinguishing because the details matter.

Picture the scene in Dublin in 2012. Same-sex marriage had been politically untouchable for years. Supporting it risked your constituency in a country where the Catholic Church had spent decades shaping the moral imagination of the electorate; opposing it risked looking like you were standing in front of a tide that was visibly coming in. So elected representatives did what elected representatives do when a question is genuinely difficult: they didn't resolve it.

They established a Constitutional Convention of one hundred members: sixty-six randomly selected citizens and thirty-three sitting politicians. These weren't elected, they weren't appointed for their views, and they weren't chosen by anyone with a stake in the outcome. They were pulled out of the national register the way you'd pull names for jury service. Among them were people like a school bus driver from Cork, a retired nurse from Galway, a small business owner from Belfast.

The Convention recommended a constitutional referendum on same-sex marriage. That referendum passed in 2015 by sixty-two to thirty-eight percent, the first time in history a country had legalized same-sex marriage by popular vote. Randomly selected citizens moved the needle that professional politicians had spent years pretending was immovable.

Four years later, the Irish government ran a second experiment. The 2016 Citizens' Assembly consisted of ninety-nine randomly selected citizens, no politicians this time, having apparently concluded that including them in the first experiment had been generous enough. It was tasked specifically with abortion law, perhaps the most politically toxic question in the country. The Church had written the existing prohibition into the constitution in 1983. After months of structured deliberation and expert testimony from all sides, this group of randomly chosen farmers, teachers, nurses, and office workers recommended liberalizing abortion access significantly. The resulting referendum passed by sixty-six to thirty-four percent.

These weren't flukes. They were structural outcomes. Random citizens can't be bribed before they're selected. They have no donors to repay, no re-election to calculate, no tribal base to perform for. The Irish experiments didn't succeed because randomly selected people were smarter or more informed than politicians. They succeeded because those people were free. That freedom, not any special competence, broke decades of deliberate political paralysis.

This points to the core tension in democratic design: expertise versus accountability. Random selection gives you accountability without expertise. Party politics, despite the professional sheen, delivers neither. Party ministers typically aren't domain experts; they're loyalists given portfolios based on internal arithmetic, which is why the Minister for Health often knows less about healthcare systems than the randomly selected nurse who deliberated in Dublin. Professional bureaucracy offers expertise without accountability. Obtaining all three simultaneously turns out to be harder than proponents of any existing model want to admit.

Random selection doesn't solve this. Randomly selected citizens running complex ministries get absorbed by permanent staff who control information flow and write the decision papers. Without the structure of a bounded deliberation and a fixed timeframe, the lottery winners become rubber stamps for whoever manages the institutional machinery. The mechanism works within defined constraints. Exported beyond them, it deteriorates into a different kind of fiction.

Deliberation Without Teeth

Digital deliberation platforms use online tools to enable large-scale public discussion on policy. Instead of town halls constrained by physical space and whoever can afford to take a Tuesday evening off, thousands can participate simultaneously from wherever they are. Software maps where diverse groups agree and disagree, surfacing common ground that traditional political processes routinely obscure.

Taiwan's vTaiwan platform demonstrated this was possible in practice. Between 2014 and 2018, it resolved genuinely contentious policy questions through a structured combination of online discussion and in-person meetings. When Uber arrived and threatened to destroy the existing taxi industry, the platform engaged thousands of participants across affected communities. A consensus position emerged. The government adopted it. The Uber case became an international example of digital deliberation working at scale.

Then vTaiwan collapsed. By 2018, participation had fallen from thousands to hundreds to dozens. Not because the technology failed and not because participants had lost interest in governance. The platform had no binding authority. The government could ignore recommendations whenever politically convenient, which turned out to be fairly often. Once participants grasped this, they stopped showing up. You can run only so many well-facilitated conversations that produce thoughtful recommendations and then disappear into a ministerial drawer before people find better uses for their evenings. This is not a design flaw. It is the only rational response.

The lesson has been confirmed everywhere similar platforms have been tried: deliberative processes without real power die. Citizens won't invest sustained effort in advisory exercises that leave the actual decision to the same people who created the problem.

But before writing off the whole approach, consider what the Taiwan case actually proved. Digital tools can enable thousands of people to find genuine consensus on contentious issues. The technology works. The deliberation works. What failed was the connection to actual authority. The mechanism itself was sound; the plumbing to decision-making power was missing. That's a different kind of failure than discovering the idea is fundamentally broken.

Which raises the obvious question: what if deliberative platforms had binding authority over a defined class of decisions? What if consensus reached through structured online deliberation triggered automatic policy implementation, shifting the burden to politicians to publicly justify overriding a documented public consensus rather than quietly ignoring it? The participation calculus changes entirely when showing up has consequences. Taiwan showed us what's possible. It also showed us exactly what kills it.

Delegates, Not Representatives

There's a simpler problem lurking underneath all of these experiments. Deliberation platforms and participatory assemblies both assume citizens have the time and sustained interest to engage across the full range of policy. Most people don't, and there's nothing wrong with that.

A nurse understands healthcare policy in ways that most people simply don't. She also might have limited patience for the details of agricultural subsidy reform, which is fair. An engineer grasps infrastructure tradeoffs but finds early childhood education policy bewildering. This is normal human specialization, not a failure of citizenship. The question is whether democratic systems can accommodate it honestly rather than pretending it away.

Liquid democracy offers one answer. You vote directly on issues you care about and understand. On issues where you lack expertise or interest, you delegate your vote to someone you trust in that domain. The critical distinction from ordinary representative democracy: you can revoke that delegation instantly and redirect it elsewhere. If your trusted delegate on healthcare policy starts supporting positions that seem captured or wrong, you withdraw your delegation immediately, without waiting for an election cycle, without needing the support of half the constituency, without any of the friction that makes current accountability nearly fictional.

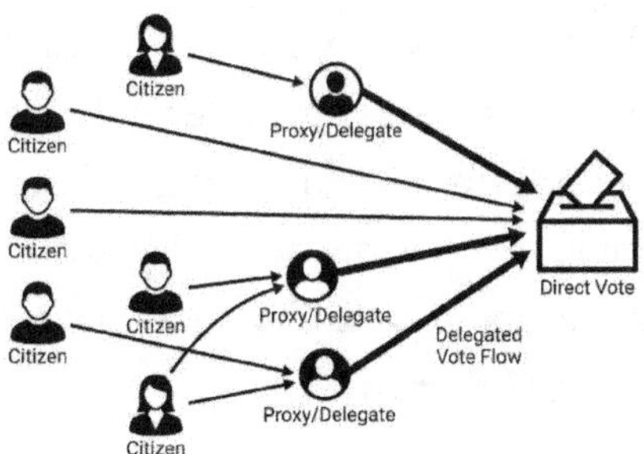

The technical barriers that once made this impractical have been cleared. Real-time delegation at national scale is feasible. The coercion problem that plagued earlier proposals has also been addressed. Previously, nothing stopped your employer or local strongman from demanding to see who you delegated to. A cryptographic solution now lets you prove you hold a valid delegation right without revealing its destination. The engineering, in other words, is ready. It's been ready for a while.

The human software, it turns out, is more stubborn.

When researchers have studied how people actually behave with liquid democracy systems, the delegation patterns don't follow expertise. They follow attention. Users don't primarily delegate to the nurse in their community whose clinical experience makes her genuinely informed on drug pricing policy. They delegate to the political commentator with three million YouTube subscribers who covers healthcare as one topic among seventeen. The charismatic podcaster accumulates millions of delegations not because she has deeper policy knowledge but because she has an audience that already trusts her on other things.

Tribalism compounds this badly. People delegate based on identity affiliation rather than subject-matter judgment. If you identify as progressive, you delegate to progressive voices across all policy domains, regardless of their domain-specific knowledge or absence of it. The nurse with genuine clinical expertise and thoughtful policy views collects a few hundred delegates from people who know her directly. The political personality with no medical training collects millions because he reliably signals the right tribal membership. He doesn't need to know anything. He just needs to feel familiar.

The instant revocation mechanism, supposed to be the feature that makes this whole system work, stops functioning at the scale where it would matter. When a major influencer holding millions of delegations makes terrible decisions or gets visibly captured by industry interests, their followers rarely revoke. Parasocial bonds create emotional investment that functions like loyalty, and admitting your trusted commentator failed you feels uncomfortably close to admitting you were wrong. The influencer holds their delegates through repeated failures that would have ended a politician's career precisely because there's no election to force a reckoning. The accountability loop, the entire point of the mechanism, quietly dissolves.

And once someone accumulates enough delegations to meaningfully influence policy, they become a target worth enormous resources. An influencer holding ten million delegations on economic policy represents a concentrated lobbying opportunity unlike anything the current system has managed to produce. The corruption pressure scales with the power.

Liquid democracy becomes genuinely workable for populations that have done the interior work this book describes: people capable of catching their own tribal reflexes, of evaluating evidence without it triggering defensiveness, of withdrawing trust from compromised sources without experiencing it as self-betrayal. The mechanism is sound. Asking whether it works with humans as they currently exist is like asking whether a sports car handles well with flat tires. The engineering is fine. The question is what you're filling it with.

For now, a narrower application is more productive. What if you're not delegating positions on policy questions, but accountability for outcomes in a specific domain? Not „I delegate my healthcare votes to this person,“ but „I hold this person responsible for healthcare results.“ The distinction changes what drives the selection. Evaluating someone based on demonstrated outcomes rather than ideological alignment gives tribal instinct less purchase. When the question shifts from „do I like what they say“ to „are things actually getting better,“ different information becomes relevant and different people start looking credible. The revocable delegation mechanism remains valuable. What you're delegating, and what triggers revocation, makes all the difference.

The Parts Already Exist

Porto Alegre, Ireland, Taiwan, liquid democracy. Four experiments, four different failure modes, four different things that worked before the conditions shifted or the political will ran out. None of them offers a complete system. Each is a demonstration that a specific mechanism functions under specific conditions, with a well-defined failure mode when conditions change.

What they collectively prove is that the current system is a design choice, not a law of nature. Citizens in Porto Alegre allocated public money more honestly than the politicians they replaced. Randomly selected Irish citizens moved questions that professional politicians had deliberately kept immovable. Thousands of Taiwanese found genuine consensus through digital deliberation until they understood it didn't matter. The accountability logic of liquid democracy works when people can evaluate outcomes rather than perform identity.

The real constraint isn't institutional possibility. It's that nobody teaching civics mentions any of this.

The next chapter proposes one combination of these mechanisms. It is not a final answer.

Systems evolve, and future generations will inevitably improve whatever we build. But it is a framework that takes seriously what the experiments have actually shown. The ground has been prepared. The question is whether we're willing to build on it.

A System of Accountability

We've spent considerable time examining shadows. The collective ego's automatic responses, the patterns that keep us trapped in cycles of blame and victimhood, the mechanisms by which we project our fears onto others and manufacture divisions to avoid looking inward.

That work matters. Without understanding how we got here, without recognizing our own complicity in maintaining broken systems, any proposed alternative becomes just another arena for the same unconscious patterns to play out.

But shadow work alone doesn't build better systems. At some point, after identifying the problems and acknowledging our role in perpetuating them, we need to ask: what do we build instead?

The previous chapter explored experiments worldwide: participatory budgeting, liquid democracy, sortition, digital deliberation. Each revealed possibilities. Each exposed limitations. The question wasn't which single experiment to adopt wholesale, but which insights to extract and combine.

This chapter proposes one such combination. Not as a utopian fantasy or final answer, but as a technically feasible governance model designed around continuous accountability rather than theatrical representation.

The principles are straightforward: expertise over ideology, transparency over complexity, continuous feedback over fixed terms, distributed authority over centralized control. The mechanisms draw from existing democratic innovations, blockchain technology, and behavioral economics. What's radical isn't the components but the integration.

And before dismissing this as impossible, remember: those who built democratic systems didn't believe they had created the final form of government. They expected evolution, not stagnation. Jefferson explicitly said the Constitution should be rewritten every 19 years. Madison designed amendment processes. They knew future generations would have better tools.

We have those tools now. We have the internet. Cryptography. Real-time data collection and analysis. Yet we're still running systems designed for the age of horse messengers.

The biggest mistake: we bundle authority into party packages and lock them in for fixed terms, then spend four years hoping they don't betray us.

What I'm proposing is not a revolution. It's an upgrade. Keep the representative structure but fix the accountability mechanism. Continuous delegation instead of fixed terms. Subject matter experts instead of party politicians. Transparent performance metrics instead of campaign promises.

It sounds radical. It's not.

The Minimal Shift

Here's the core change: we keep representatives but eliminate political parties and fixed terms.

The difference sounds minimal. It's not.

In the current system, you elect a politician from a party on a fixed term. You're buying a package deal. You get their stance on healthcare, education, foreign policy, environmental regulation, and a hundred other issues bundled together like a cable subscription where you can't opt out of the channels you hate. You vote for the package, and if you dislike 40% of it, well, that's democracy. Once they're in, they're in for four years no matter how badly they perform.

At least with cable, you can cancel when the service degrades. With politicians, you're locked in until the contract expires, no matter how many times they promise they'll fix the buffering.

But the deeper problem is structural. Parties need money to function. Campaigns cost millions or billions. Someone has to pay for it. Corporate interests fund healthcare committees. Defense contractors fund foreign policy hawks. Foreign actors fund ideologically aligned parties. By the time anyone takes office, they're already compromised. The party system creates a single point of capture: control the party machinery, and you control everyone who needs it to get elected.

Parties also require ideological coherence to maintain identity. This breeds incompetence by design. A brilliant healthcare economist who reaches conclusions that contradict party ideology won't get the appointment. An ideologically pure party member with mediocre credentials will. The selection mechanism filters for political reliability, not technical excellence.

Picture hiring a doctor based on whether they support your favorite sports team rather than whether they can diagnose illnesses. That's essentially how party systems staff governments.

And parties survive by manufacturing division. The left-right divide we explored earlier isn't natural. It's constructed and maintained because parties need you voting tribally rather than evaluating individual competence. If voters started judging candidates on results rather than party affiliation, the entire party system would collapse. So they polarize. They demonize. They create culture war. Division is the product that keeps parties alive.

Instead of voting for a party package, you select experts for different domains. Healthcare. Infrastructure. Education. Different people with different expertise.

The Minister of Health might be someone who spent decades in hospital administration. The Infrastructure Minister could be a civil engineer. Education goes to someone with actual teaching or policy credentials.

Adjacent expertise counts too. Some fitness coaches understand human physiology and preventive health better than most doctors. A researcher who spent decades studying educational outcomes can challenge career administrators. Minimum credentials keep complete amateurs out, but citizens ultimately decide who's most qualified. This prevents guild capture while maintaining competence.

No more package deals. You can trust the healthcare expert even if you hate who's running infrastructure. No more voting for someone's climate policy while despising their foreign policy.

And if any Minister fails? You revoke your delegation immediately. No waiting for the next election cycle.

This is still representative government. We're not pretending everyone can vote on everything. What changes is who represents you — experts instead of politicians — and how long they serve through continuous delegation instead of fixed terms.

This single mechanism changes everything about the incentive structure.

Right now, politicians have fixed terms. Once they're in, they're in. They can lie, break promises, serve corporate interests, start wars, and there's nothing you can do about it until the next election cycle. By which point they've already done the damage and moved on to lucrative consulting gigs.

The previous chapter covered liquid democracy in detail. The delegation structure and the revocability carry over, but the application is different. You're not delegating how to vote on individual policies. You're delegating authority over who manages an entire domain. And the trigger for pulling that delegation isn't disagreement with a specific decision. It's failure to deliver results.

But if your delegation can be revoked at any time? If the Minister of Infrastructure knows that failing to fix the roads means losing the job immediately? The incentives shift. Dramatically.

Suddenly, the executive's primary concern isn't winning the next election or pleasing Party donors. It's keeping the population satisfied enough that they don't pull the plug.

Not utopian fantasy. Engineering.

The Architecture: Subject Matter Executives

The system operates through specialized Ministers, each managing a distinct domain: Health, Education, Infrastructure, Energy, Justice, and so on. You're not electing a government. You're selecting who manages healthcare, who manages education, who manages infrastructure - separately. Different expertise for different domains.

The obvious question: how do we find these executives?

The answer is simpler than you might expect: minimal gatekeeping, maximum competition. Anyone with basic credentials can apply, and citizens do the real filtering through delegation.

The process works like this:

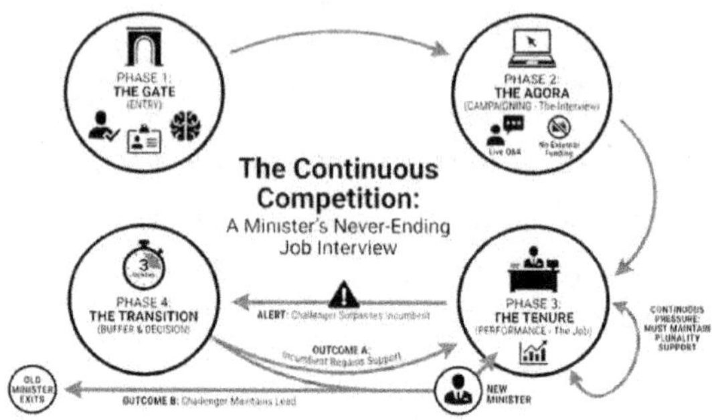

Step One: Open Application

Any citizen can apply to be a Minister, provided they meet the minimum qualifications for the domain.

Minimum requirements (verifiable):

- Relevant professional experience (5+ years in the field or closely related field)
- OR relevant academic credentials (advanced degree in the domain)
- OR published expertise (books, research, recognized thought leadership in the field)
- OR demonstrated management experience at comparable scale

For example, Minister of Health candidates might have:

- Hospital administration experience
- Medical degree with healthcare policy background

- Public health doctorate with published research
- Healthcare system management at regional or national level
- Written authoritative books on healthcare systems

These aren't gatekeeping. They're basic filters preventing complete fools from cluttering the candidate pool. You wouldn't hire a CTO or CFO without minimum credentials and experience. Ministers managing domains affecting millions of people require the same baseline competence.

Candidates declare their candidacy and post two things publicly: their CV (education, professional experience, projects completed, publications, credentials) and their proposal (a detailed plan for how they would manage their domain).

Credentials are verified through the platform. False claims result in immediate permanent exclusion.

The platform makes all candidates searchable and comparable. Dwayne Johnson could theoretically apply for Minister of Health if he had relevant credentials (he doesn't). But a doctor with thirty years of hospital administration experience can. Both CVs are public. Both proposals are visible.

Compensation matters. If we want top talent competing with private sector positions, Ministers must be paid competitively. A Minister of Infrastructure should earn more than a private sector engineering executive managing similar scope. A Minister of Health should earn more than a hospital system CEO.

The exact amount is transparent and set by citizens (who can delegate this decision to compensation experts). But the principle is clear: you're asking someone to manage a domain affecting millions of people, with full transparency and instant accountability. That responsibility deserves compensation above market rate for comparable private sector roles.

The goal isn't enriching politicians. It's competing for talent. The best healthcare administrator might earn $500K running a hospital system. If we offer $300K to run the entire national healthcare system, we get worse candidates. Offer $700K with full transparency on how it's spent, and we compete.

Some will still choose public service for idealistic reasons. Good. But we shouldn't rely solely on altruism when we need competence.

Step Two: Delegation

You can vote directly for candidates in each domain, or delegate your vote to someone you trust in that area.

Your healthcare vote goes to your doctor. Your infrastructure vote to an engineer you respect. Your education vote to a teacher whose judgment you trust.

Important: Anyone can refuse to accept delegations. If you want your vote to remain private, you can opt out of receiving delegations entirely. This protects people who don't want their voting decisions to become public or who don't want the responsibility of voting on behalf of others.

Human behavior becomes the filtering mechanism here.

Step Three: Weighted Influence Through $x^{0.9}$

The critical piece: accumulated delegations face diminishing returns according to the formula **influence = delegations$^{0.9}$**.

Important: This weighting applies only once, at the final candidate level. If you delegate to your doctor, who delegates to a specialist, who votes for Candidate A, the x^0.9 formula is applied only to the total delegations that Candidate A receives. It's not compounded at each step in the chain. A long delegation chain doesn't reduce your vote's power beyond the single application of the formula at the end.

Consider what this means in practice. One direct vote equals 1.0 unit of influence. Ten delegations translate to 7.94 units of influence, retaining 79.4% efficiency. A hundred delegations become 63.1 units at 63.1% efficiency. Ten thousand delegations compress to 3,981 units at 39.8% efficiency. The more delegations accumulate, the less efficient each additional delegation becomes.

This matters because it changes the dynamics of bad delegation.

If you delegate your healthcare vote to Taylor Swift because you love her music, you're making a terrible decision. You're giving voting power to someone with zero healthcare expertise. And the system penalizes this through the power function.

(For context: Taylor Swift's endorsement of a presidential candidate in the current system can shift voter registration by hundreds of thousands. She already has massive political influence. The $x^{0.9}$ weighting doesn't eliminate celebrity influence, it just prevents it from being overwhelming.)

When Taylor Swift accumulates 500,000 delegations from fans who aren't thinking critically, those delegations translate to 134,609 units of influence, a 73% reduction from the raw vote count.

But the system self-corrects: Taylor Swift, if she's smart, will delegate those healthcare votes to actual doctors. Why? Because when healthcare outcomes fail, she gets blamed by her 500,000 supporters. Her reputation depends on choosing good delegates.

So the power naturally flows: fans $\rightarrow$ Taylor Swift (celebrity) $\rightarrow$ healthcare experts $\rightarrow$ qualified Minister candidates.

The $x^{0.9}$ weighting applies to Taylor's accumulated delegations, compressing them significantly. But those units then flow to whichever healthcare expert Taylor trusts. The system routes power toward competence, even when it starts with popularity.

Meanwhile, 10,000 people delegating directly to their doctors accumulate 3,981 units flowing to qualified candidates. Add the celebrity-routed delegations to expert candidates, and the serious healthcare administrator ends up with far more support than someone without domain expertise.

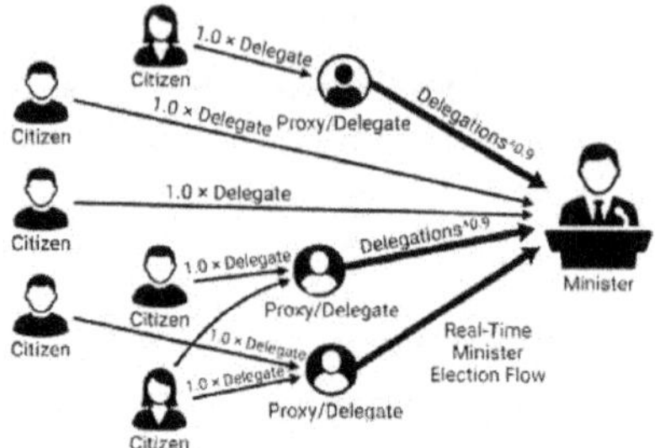

Of course, some celebrities are experts themselves. A celebrity doctor like Dr. Mark Hyman has both popularity and domain expertise. That's legitimate because the delegations aren't being misallocated.

The key insight: even influencers who accumulate massive followings have incentive to delegate to domain experts rather than vote directly on issues they don't understand. The $x^{0.9}$ formula prevents any single person from holding too much power, while the transparency of delegation chains ensures bad decisions get exposed and punished quickly.

Step Four: Final Delegation and Selection

After the weighted delegation system operates, the candidate with the most weighted influence becomes Minister. The runner-up becomes Shadow Minister.

Ministers need only plurality, not majority.
If the leading candidate has 31% support and everyone else has less, that's sufficient. This isn't a weakness. It means Ministers can be replaced easily when better candidates emerge. The threshold for holding power is simply being the best available option, not commanding overwhelming support.

But how does this process actually work in practice? Three mechanisms ensure it functions effectively:

Transparency and Instant Revocation

Every delegation is visible to the person who made it. Your vote is private, but you can see exactly where your vote went.

If you delegated to your doctor, and your doctor delegated to a specialist, and the specialist voted for Candidate A, you see that entire chain. You know exactly which candidate ultimately received your vote.

If you disagree with that choice, you can instantly withdraw your delegation. Not next week. Not next election cycle. Instantly.

This creates continuous accountability not just for the Ministers, but for everyone in the delegation chain. Your doctor knows that if she delegates badly, her patients will revoke their

delegations. The specialist knows the same.
Everyone in the chain has skin in the game.

Three-Month Transition Period

Delegations can shift at any time, but ministerial
changes don't happen overnight. When another
candidate surpasses the current Minister in
support, a three-month transition period begins.

This serves multiple purposes. The current
Minister has time to address concerns, correct
mistakes, and potentially regain support.
Citizens have time to reconsider their delegation
choices. The incoming Minister has time to
prepare for transition. The domain gets
continuity rather than chaos.

If support continues declining during those
three months, the transition proceeds. If the
Minister regains plurality support, they remain in
position. If a third candidate emerges with even
more support during this period, they become
the incoming Minister instead.

At the end of three months, whoever has the
most weighted support becomes Minister. The
previous Minister typically becomes Shadow
Minister, unless they've dropped below second
place.

This isn't a loophole for incompetence. Three
months is short enough that serious failures get

corrected quickly. But it's long enough to prevent ministerial changes based on temporary public mood swings or minor controversies that blow over.

Think of it like employment law in countries that require notice periods. You can fire someone, but they get three months to transition. This protects both the employee and the organization. Same principle applies here.

Good candidates crystallize quickly from this system. The healthcare administrator with a strong proposal and thirty years of experience starts accumulating delegations from healthcare professionals, hospital workers, patients who've researched the candidates, and citizens who delegated to people with healthcare expertise. Within weeks, the serious candidates become obvious. Not because a committee selected them, but because distributed decision-making filtered them naturally.

The Digital Agora: State-Provided Platform

The state provides a digital agora, a platform for public discourse and idea exchange. While candidates use it to represent themselves to the public, it serves a broader purpose: facilitating deliberation on policy proposals, cross-domain discussions, and citizen engagement with governance questions.

The platform eliminates the role of money in political visibility while enabling informed public deliberation.

In the current system, candidates need money to get their message out. Advertising. Media appearances. Campaign infrastructure. This creates the fundamental corruption: whoever funds your visibility owns you.

The digital agora solves this by providing equal access to public attention and creating space for substantive policy discussion.

Every candidate gets scheduled live sessions. All sessions are live-streamed and permanently archived. Citizens can submit and upvote questions. Candidates answer in real-time. Fact-checking happens live, with AI assistance and human oversight. Sources and citations are displayed automatically. Previous statements are searchable. Candidates can present their proposals, defend their track record, and explain their vision.

The platform tracks engagement metrics such as questions answered versus dodged and claims verified versus disputed, but these are informational rather than filtering mechanisms.

Zero Tolerance for Outside Funding

If it becomes clear that a candidate received money, support, or promotional assistance from third parties (whether corporations, advocacy groups, wealthy individuals, or foreign actors), they are immediately excluded. Not fined. Not warned. Excluded.

This rule applies retroactively. If you took corporate money five years ago before declaring candidacy, and it's discovered now, you're out.

The logic is simple: the state provides everything you need to reach the public. If you're accepting outside support, you're accepting corruption. Those whose master is Mammon find no purchase here. There's no legitimate reason to take it.

Citizens can donate volunteer time to help candidates they support, such as helping them prepare for agora sessions. But no money changes hands. No paid staff. No advertising buys. Nothing that creates financial obligation.

Offering favors, jobs, or benefits in exchange for delegations is corruption and results in immediate permanent exclusion. The platform monitors for patterns suggesting quid pro quo arrangements.

This raises an obvious question: what about Ministers with industry backgrounds? The best healthcare administrator might have worked for hospital systems. The best energy policy expert likely worked in energy companies. That's where domain expertise develops. Past employment isn't corruption. Normal professional compensation for legitimate work isn't corruption.

Corruption is when a Minister's wealth inexplicably quadruples while making favorable decisions for former employers. Corruption is the house in the Hamptons that appears on a Minister's salary. Corruption is patterns of enrichment that don't match disclosed income.

When citizens suspect this, they can demand current financial disclosure. Not speculation. Actual evidence of suspicious enrichment. The Minister then provides complete financial documentation: bank statements, property holdings, investment portfolios, income sources. Everything becomes public.

Refuse to disclose? Automatic removal and permanent exclusion from future candidacy.

Industry expertise remains valuable. But the moment that expertise looks like it's being sold to the highest bidder, everything becomes visible. And the consequences are immediate.

This eliminates the entire apparatus of campaign finance corruption. You can't buy influence over a Minister if you can't fund their path to power.

Notice what we've eliminated: gatekeeping committees that can be captured. Expert panels that can be corrupted. Party machinery that filters for loyalty over competence.

The selection mechanism is entirely distributed. Thousands or millions of individual decisions, each with skin in the game, each with instant revocation power.

Bad decisions get penalized through the power function. Good decisions retain influence. And because the entire delegation chain is transparent to each voter, people learn quickly whether their delegates are making good choices.

Will we make mistakes? Absolutely. Especially in the beginning. That's why the revocation is instant. If the Minister you ended up supporting (directly or through delegation) turns out to be incompetent, you can withdraw your support today. Not in four years. Today.

The key insight from Ireland's Citizens' Assembly applies here: freedom from political obligation matters as much as expertise. Without parties, there's no central machinery to capture. Corporate interests can't buy systematic access by funding party infrastructure. Foreign actors have no coordination point to compromise. You'd have to convince millions of citizens individually, and their doctors, and their trusted experts. The distributed nature of the system makes it resistant to capture.

What we're left with is a job interview conducted by millions of people simultaneously, with the math naturally filtering out popularity-driven bad decisions while preserving expertise-driven good ones.

Emergency Powers for Crisis Response

Ministers have temporary emergency authority within their domain during genuine crises: natural disasters, pandemics, infrastructure failures, acute system breakdowns.

When a Minister declares emergency powers, they can act immediately without the 30-day public comment period. Build emergency hospitals, redirect resources, implement containment measures, deploy rapid response. The crisis doesn't wait for bureaucratic process.

But emergency powers expire automatically after 30 days. If the crisis continues, the Minister must seek citizen ratification to extend emergency authority. Citizens can revoke delegation during this period. If they don't trust the Minister's crisis response, they replace them immediately.

The principle is straightforward: either the Minister is qualified and citizens trust their emergency judgment, or they shouldn't hold power at all. Competence under pressure is part of the job. Citizens observe crisis response in real time and decide whether to maintain their delegation.

What This Looks Like in Practice

When It Works: Two Decades of Boring Competence

Yuki Tanaka becomes Minister of Transportation in 2031 with 34% support. She's a logistics engineer who spent twenty years optimizing freight networks. Her proposal: integrate rail, road, and port systems to reduce shipping bottlenecks.

She delivers. Freight transit times drop 22% in her first three years. The Shadow Minister challenges her on rural access. She adjusts. Costs come in under budget. Support climbs to 41%.

Year seven, she misreads demand for a northern port expansion. Builds capacity that sits mostly empty for two years. Support drops to 35%. The Shadow Minister, a maritime logistics specialist, publishes the analysis showing the error. Tanaka acknowledges it publicly, redirects resources to more needed infrastructure in the south. Support stabilizes.

By year twelve, she's overseen the largest infrastructure modernization in the country's history. Trains run on time. Roads get maintained. Bridges don't collapse. It's boring. It works.

Her support fluctuates between 37% and 44% depending on current projects and challenger quality. She's made mistakes. Small ones. Caught early. Corrected publicly. She's never had a scandal because there's nothing to scandalize. She's an engineer doing engineering.

Twenty years in, at 62 years old, she announces she's stepping down. Not because she has to. Because she's tired. Her final support: 39%. Not adulation. Just acknowledgment that she did the job well.

The competition to replace her attracts seven qualified candidates. The Shadow Minister, who's spent two decades reviewing her work, doesn't win. A younger infrastructure specialist with innovations in electric vehicle charging networks does. Gets 36% support. Becomes the new Minister.

Tanaka consults on projects for a few years, then retires. No corruption investigations. No tell-all books. No controversy. She managed transportation infrastructure competently for two decades and left it better than she found it.

That's what success looks like in this system. Unremarkable and effective.

When It Fails: Three Months of Visible Incompetence

Javier Moreno becomes Minister of Agriculture with 29% support in 2033. He's run large farms, understands commodity markets, has a plan to modernize irrigation systems.

Two months in, a crop disease hits wheat production in the northern provinces. It's containable with rapid quarantine protocols. Moreno hesitates. He doesn't want to upset farmers by restricting transport. He thinks he can manage it with voluntary compliance.

The disease spreads.

The Shadow Minister, Amara Okafor, an agricultural scientist, publishes a scathing analysis. The containment window closed. Voluntary measures failed. The disease is now endemic. This year's wheat harvest will drop 30%. Moreno's delay will cost the country billions.

She provides the solution Moreno should have implemented: mandatory quarantine zones, emergency import protocols, compensation frameworks for affected farmers.

Within three days, delegations shift. Farmers who initially supported Moreno revoke. Agricultural experts who delegated to him redirect to Okafor. Moreno's support drops to 18%. Okafor climbs to 33%.

The three-month transition period begins.

Moreno could use this time to correct course, demonstrate competence, regain support. But the disease is already spreading. The damage is done. His credibility on crisis management is shattered. Over the next three months, his support continues eroding to 15%. Okafor's support climbs to 37%.

She becomes Minister.

The transition takes three months. Okafor implements her containment strategy. The disease gets contained. The harvest loss is bad but manageable. Markets stabilize.

Moreno becomes Shadow Minister at 18%. He reviews Okafor's decisions, and his agricultural economics expertise remains useful despite his crisis management failure. He catches when she's about to over-compensate farmers in ways that would create dependency. His support might rebuild over time. Or it might not.

Alternatively, if a crop disease specialist had emerged during the crisis with better credentials and innovative pathogen tracking protocols, that person could have jumped to second place, displacing Moreno entirely. In that case, Moreno's political career ends. He returns to farming, competent at running his own operation but finished in governance.

The system allows both outcomes. What matters is whether Moreno remains the second-best option or whether someone better exists. Either way, the critical failure gets identified within days, and corrected within months. The better option takes over through orderly transition.

The woman who delegated her vote to a farmer, who delegated to an agricultural cooperative leader, who voted for Moreno? She watched the entire chain of delegation. Saw the failure. Saw Okafor take over. Saw the correction.

She didn't need to organize a recall petition. Didn't need to wait four years. Didn't need to choose between bad options in an election. The system just worked. Incompetence became visible. Better options existed or emerged. Delegations shifted. Problem solved.

Not dramatic. Not revolutionary. Just functional.

What the Weighting Accomplishes

The $x^{0.9}$ weighting accomplishes two critical things:

First, it prevents concentration of power. A single person can never accumulate too much influence. The formula creates diminishing returns that compress even massive followings.

Second, it penalizes delegating to highly influential people. If you delegate to someone who already has massive following, your vote loses power through the diminishing returns formula. This creates an incentive to delegate to less popular but more qualified experts rather than celebrities.

This means manipulation requires corrupting many people, not just one. And because delegation chains are visible to supporters, bad decisions lead to rapid loss of support.

Even influencers who accumulate large followings have incentive to delegate to domain experts. Their reputation depends on outcomes, not rhetoric. This naturally routes power toward competence.

The Breaker Switch: Revocable Delegation

It bears emphasizing because it shapes everything that follows. Politicians have fixed terms. Once they're in, they're in. They can lie, break promises, serve corporate interests, start wars, and there is nothing you can do until the next election cycle. By which point they've already done the damage and moved on to lucrative consulting gigs.

The breaker switch changes everything.

You can revoke your delegation today. Not in four years. Not after the damage is done. Today.

This isn't chaos. This is power.

Politicians optimize for election day. They make promises they have no intention of keeping because the consequences won't hit until after they've secured another term or retired. Ministers optimize for performance. Continuously. Because if your delegation can be revoked tomorrow, you can't coast for four years on empty promises.

The dynamic works like every competitive market. Companies that can lose customers at any time behave very differently from monopolies with captive audiences. Southwest Airlines knows you can fly Delta tomorrow, so they focus on service. Your cable company knows you can't easily switch, so they treat you like garbage. The same principle applies here.

Human inertia provides stability without removing power. Changing your delegation requires effort. Log into the platform, review alternatives, make a decision. Most people won't bother unless performance clearly deteriorates. Hospital wait times increasing. Infrastructure quality is declining. Measurable failures to deliver on objectives.

But the option exists. That's what matters.

The system tracks leading indicators. If a Minister's policies show early signs of failure, if outcomes diverge from projections, if transparency reveals mismanagement, citizens can act before things break catastrophically. You don't wait for the bridge to collapse. You revoke when the maintenance data shows structural problems.

And blame-shifting becomes impossible. Politicians currently blame their predecessors, the opposition party, and circumstances beyond their control. Anything to avoid accountability. With instant revocation, there's nowhere to hide. You own your results. If hospitals are failing under your watch, you can't spend four years pointing fingers. Citizens revoke your authority and try someone else.

The delegation mechanism comes from liquid democracy, but applied differently. Instead of delegating votes on policies, you're delegating authority over who manages the domain. The trigger for revocation isn't disagreement with a policy position. It's failure to deliver outcomes.

This shifts evaluation criteria. When judging someone based on demonstrated competence rather than ideological alignment, tribalism has less grip. When evaluating results rather than rhetoric, parasocial attachment matters less. The question becomes „can they deliver outcomes" instead of „do I like what they say."

What About Narcissists, Psychopaths, and Machiavellians?

Power attracts certain personality types. Narcissists, psychopaths, and Machiavellians (the dark triad we explored earlier) are drawn to positions of authority. This won't change. Human nature doesn't change.

What changes is how much power those positions hold and how visible the abuse becomes.

In the current system, these personalities thrive. Fixed terms give them years to exploit their position before facing consequences. Party structures provide cover for their manipulation. Campaign finance lets them buy influence. Complexity hides their corruption. A narcissist can charm their way to office, a psychopath can ruthlessly eliminate rivals within party machinery, a Machiavellian can make backroom deals that never see daylight.

The new system doesn't eliminate dark triad personalities from seeking power. But it reduces the advantages they currently enjoy:

Power is distributed. No single Minister holds the concentrated authority of a President or Prime Minister with a four-year term of immunity. When power is dispersed and instantly revocable, the position becomes less attractive to those seeking domination rather than service.

Transparency is pervasive. Not just blockchain, but Shadow Minister analysis, public reporting requirements, citizen scrutiny, professional body reviews, AI-assisted analysis. The entire system requires informed citizens to function, which throws light on everything. Backroom deals, manipulation, corruption become much harder when actions are visible and track records are permanent.

Accountability is continuous. Get caught exploiting your position, you're out immediately. No four-year shield. No party protection.

Whistleblowing is incentivized. Ministry staff and civil servants who expose corruption or abuse receive legal protection and cannot be fired for reporting problems. The Shadow Minister gains power by proving the Minister's malfeasance. This creates bottom-up accountability, where those who see problems have reason to expose them rather than stay silent.

But the system isn't perfect. Charismatic narcissists can still accumulate delegations. Skilled manipulators can still deceive for a time. This is where shadow work becomes essential.

The better a population becomes at recognizing narcissistic patterns, detecting manipulation, seeing through performative charisma, the more effectively the system filters for genuine competence over domination. A population doing shadow work makes the system work better. A population ignoring shadow work remains vulnerable to the same old tricks in new packaging.

The system creates structural defenses against domination. But ultimately, true leadership versus domination isn't determined by mechanisms alone. It's determined by whether citizens can tell the difference.

The breaker switch is the mechanism that turns democracy from a periodic ritual into a continuous feedback loop.

The Technical Infrastructure

Before discussing how laws work, we need to address the obvious question: how is any of this actually implemented?

The entire system runs on blockchain technology. Not as a buzzword, but as the only infrastructure that makes continuous delegation, transparent voting, and instant revocation technically possible.

Every delegation, every vote, every revocation is recorded on a distributed ledger. This means:

- **No central point of control.** The data isn't stored on a government server that can be hacked, manipulated, or shut down. It's replicated across thousands of independent nodes.
- **Immutable records.** Once you delegate your healthcare vote to your doctor, that transaction is permanently recorded. If you later revoke it, the revocation is also recorded. The full history is auditable.
- **Real-time transparency.** You can see your complete delegation chain at any

moment. Who you delegated to, who they delegated to, which candidate ultimately received your weighted vote.

- **Instant revocation.** Because the system is decentralized, you don't need to wait for a central authority to process your revocation. You submit the transaction, it's validated by the network, and your delegation is revoked.
- **No double-voting.** The blockchain ensures each citizen has exactly one vote per domain, preventing the kind of fraud that plagues traditional systems.

What this looks like in practice:

You log into the platform with your verified identity. You see all the domains (Health, Education, Defense, etc.). For each domain, you can either vote directly for a candidate or delegate to someone you trust.

If you delegate, you can see the full chain: you delegated to Person A, who delegated to Person B, who voted for Candidate C. If Candidate C wins and becomes Minister of Health, you can track their performance metrics in real-time. If they fail, you can revoke your support with a single transaction.

All of this is recorded on the blockchain. All of it is auditable. None of it requires trusting a central authority.

This infrastructure isn't theoretical. Blockchain-based voting systems already exist and are being tested. The technology works. What we're proposing is applying it at national scale with continuous delegation rather than periodic elections.

The Architecture of Laws: From Stone Tablets to Living Code

In the current system, laws are treated like religious commandments. They're passed by a legislative body, carved into the legal code, and remain there until another legislative session bothers to repeal or amend them. The process is slow, opaque, and easily captured by special interests who know how to work the system.

This creates an accumulation problem. Germany's legal code spans thousands of pages across federal law, state law, and EU regulations. No human being has read all of it. No lawyer can hold it all in their head. Yet we're all expected to obey it under the principle that „ignorance of the law is no excuse."

Imagine being handed a 10,000-page rental agreement written in Klingon and told you're legally bound by every clause, including the one on page 4,387 that you definitely should have noticed. Absurd, yes. But intentional. Complexity benefits those who can afford experts to navigate it. It creates barriers to entry, protects incumbents, and ensures that ordinary citizens can't understand the rules governing their own lives.

Before explaining how laws should work, we need to be honest about how they actually work now.

The Current System

Most people assume Congress, the Bundestag, or Parliament writes laws. They don't.

Ministry lawyers and career bureaucrats draft the actual text. Industry lobbyists literally write regulatory language and hand it to friendly legislators. Legislative staff (hired lawyers working for committees) shape the details. Special interest groups with legal teams contribute entire sections.

Legislators themselves? They vote on packages they rarely read in full, following party leadership instructions. They negotiate backroom deals and claim credit for laws they didn't write.

The technical review process involves independent fiscal authorities analyzing costs, legislative committees reviewing proposals (often captured by the industries they regulate), government ministries providing impact assessments, and outside experts testifying (invited by committees who already know what they want to hear).

When conflicts arise, resolution happens through cabinet meetings behind closed doors, legislative vote-trading („support my bill, I'll support yours"), coalition negotiations in parliamentary systems, and backroom compromises that never see public scrutiny.

Budget allocation follows the same pattern: the executive proposes a budget, the legislature adds pork barrel spending for key districts, and the final vote depends on political horse-trading rather than merit.

Emergency powers work similarly: executives act immediately, legislatures supposedly check within 60 days, but in practice executives abuse and legislatures rubber-stamp.

The current system isn't sophisticated. It's centuries of accumulated patches hiding who really decides.

The Ministerial Domains

The system operates through specialized Ministers. Each handles a distinct domain.

Current countries typically have ministries covering: Health, Education, Defense, Foreign Affairs, Justice, Finance, Economy, Labor, Infrastructure, Energy, Environment, Agriculture, Housing, Science & Technology, Digital Affairs, and others depending on the country.

We keep this structure. Ministers are selected through the delegation system with $x^{0.9}$ weighting as described earlier. Each Minister manages their domain, proposes laws, and implements policy within their area of expertise.

Law Proposition and Approval

Ministers propose laws in their domain. The Minister of Health proposes healthcare regulations. The Minister of Infrastructure proposes building codes.

Each proposal includes a plain language explanation (what it does, why it matters), technical legal text (for legal precision), evidence base (problem solved, supporting data), and cost analysis (implementation, enforcement, compliance).

30-Day Public Comment Period:

The proposal goes public immediately. For 30 days, citizens ask questions (ministry staff responds within 48 hours), propose

amendments with reasoning, flag concerns
requiring ministry response, and professional
bodies submit expert analyses.

Shadow Minister submits opposing analysis
challenging the Minister's claims. „Minister
claims this costs $X, my analysis shows $Y."
„Minister says this solves A, but creates problem
B." The adversarial structure forces honesty
through competing analyses.

AI assistance streamlines the comment process
by clustering similar questions (10,000 variations
of „How will this affect rural hospitals?"
become one comprehensive answer), filtering
spam and bad-faith submissions, and translating
legal language to plain language. The system
shows similar past laws and their outcomes,
models cost/benefit scenarios, compares
international examples, flags contradictions with
existing laws, and tracks which questions get
answered versus dodged.

If the Minister amends based on feedback, clock
resets for another 30 days.

Professional Review and Approval:

After the public comment period, professional
bodies review the law for technical soundness.
But to prevent guild capture (where professions
approve regulations that serve their own

interests over the public good), the review must be adversarial.

Adversarial Professional Review:

When a professional body reviews a law, adversarial groups must also review it:

- **Medical regulations** reviewed by medical boards AND patient advocacy groups, health economists, medical ethics organizations
- **Legal regulations** reviewed by bar associations AND legal aid organizations, access to justice advocates, law school reform groups
- **Engineering standards** reviewed by engineering societies AND consumer safety organizations, environmental groups, cost analysis experts

The adversarial reviewers have different incentives. Medical boards might approve licensing requirements that restrict supply and raise doctor incomes. Patient advocacy groups would challenge unnecessary barriers that reduce access to care.

If no natural adversarial organization exists, the public comment period is extended and the proposing body must address every substantive critique raised by citizens. The Minister cannot dismiss concerns as „not understanding technical details" without detailed rebuttal.

This prevents professions from using technical complexity to hide self-dealing. Adversarial review forces transparency about whose interests a regulation actually serves.

Ministry lawyers finalize the legal text after adversarial review is complete. This is what ministries were always supposed to do: draft enforceable legislation. The difference is that now they face both professional scrutiny and continuous citizen oversight rather than party politics.

Once adversarial review is complete, the law is enacted. It begins with implicit 100% support (having passed both professional and adversarial scrutiny) and remains in effect unless citizens actively withdraw support.

Professional Approval with Citizen Emergency Brake:

This handles specialized laws naturally. Small business regulations are managed by commerce experts. Agricultural policy by agricultural specialists. Technical standards by engineers. The professionals who understand the domain make the initial approval decision.

But citizens retain the emergency brake. After a law passes, you can withdraw your support from it at any time through direct withdrawal, not liquid delegation. You either support the law or you don't.

If citizen support falls below 60%, the law must be removed within 30 days. This allows orderly wind-down of enforcement while preventing indefinite continuation of laws the majority actively opposes.

When laws are withdrawn, cases decided under those laws can be appealed for review. If someone was imprisoned under a law that lost public support because it was unjust, they can appeal their conviction. The legal system reassesses these cases based on current law.

The emergency brake exists for stopping genuinely harmful laws: mass surveillance programs, rights violations, clear corruption, regulations causing obvious harm. Not for disagreeing with policy choices.

Most citizens won't engage with specialized regulations. If you're not a small business owner, you probably won't withdraw support from small business regulations unless they're clearly destructive. Natural apathy protects good specialized laws.

Citizen-Initiated Laws:

Citizens can also propose laws directly. Any citizen can draft a proposal and submit it to the platform.

For citizen-initiated laws to be enforceable, they need professional legal drafting. The platform provides access to legal experts who can translate citizen proposals into proper legal text. This prevents well-intentioned but poorly drafted laws from creating unintended consequences.

Other citizens can delegate their support to that proposal (liquid delegation works here). If the proposal reaches 50% + 1 support, it becomes binding law.

Citizens force action on issues the government ignores: „Require body cameras on all police,“ „Ban Ministers from trading stocks during service,“ „Mandate expense transparency,“ „Prohibit warrantless surveillance.“

The government can't block citizen-initiated laws. If the people want it and reach majority support, it happens, provided it doesn't violate constitutional protections.

Professional laws handle technical governance. The emergency brake stops abuses. Citizen-initiated laws force accountability.

Tyranny of the majority remains a concern, which is why constitutional protections exist with higher thresholds. Still better than tyranny of the minority we have now, where a small elite makes decisions for everyone.

Handling Technical Complexity

Some laws are unavoidably technical. The solution structures them with AI translation: a plain language summary is required alongside the full technical text for experts. AI translates complex provisions into understandable language, and professional bodies explain the implications.

Citizens don't need to understand pharmaceutical chemistry to withdraw support from a drug approval law that's causing deaths. They see the outcomes and decide.

Cross-Ministerial Conflicts

When Ministers' domains conflict (Environment vs. Economy, Defense vs. Budget constraints), resolution can happen through referendum or mandate expansion.

Referendum approach: Citizens vote on which priority takes precedence. Liquid delegation is possible here, allowing you to delegate to experts you trust to resolve these trade-offs.

Mandate expansion approach: If similar conflicts keep arising, citizens can vote to expand one Minister's mandate to include that intersection. For example, if Environment and Energy constantly clash over carbon regulation, citizens might expand the Environment Minister's domain to include energy policy related to emissions. The Minister best suited to handle that type of decision gets the authority.

Ministerial mandates are defined in law, so expanding or changing them follows the same law-making process described earlier. Citizens can repeal or modify mandates the same way they can any other law.

This prevents endless referendums on recurring issues while maintaining democratic control over domain boundaries.

Frequency of conflicts is unknown but likely increases in early years as the system stabilizes. The mandate expansion mechanism should reduce referendum burden over time as domain boundaries clarify.

Constitutional Boundaries

Not everything is up for vote. Some principles are foundational.

Constitutional boundaries include basic rights: freedom of speech, association, due process, equal protection. These aren't negotiable.

The tyranny of the majority remains a concern. If 60% of the population wants to oppress the remaining 40%, constitutional protections provide the primary defense. No system perfectly solves this problem.

But transparency and consciousness matter. A population doing shadow work, recognizing its own projections and tribal impulses, becomes less likely to support oppression. When citizens understand how scapegoating works, when they've examined their own capacity for cruelty, when they've developed awareness of manipulation tactics, the desire to oppress minorities weakens.

The system doesn't force this consciousness. But it creates conditions where unconscious oppression becomes harder: budgets are public (can't hide atrocities), actions are visible (can't deny what's happening), Ministers face instant revocation (enables rapid response to abuse). Combined with a population developing greater self-awareness, these structural features provide meaningful protection beyond just constitutional text.

Constitutional Court judges selected through delegation, with higher thresholds:

- Require 60% weighted delegation
- Minimum credentials (20+ years legal experience, constitutional law expertise)
- 10-year terms (not lifetime, not instant revocation)
- Can be removed for corruption but requires 66% vote
- Performance metrics public

The ten-year terms preserve independence from political pressure on controversial cases while maintaining accountability for corruption or incompetence. Citizens delegate to legal experts they trust for judge selection.

Constitutional amendments:

- Require 66% supermajority
- Longer review period (90 days instead of 30)
- Possible but difficult, preventing impulsive changes while allowing adaptation

The constitution is the operating system. Laws are the applications. Update applications when they don't work. Updating the OS requires more deliberation.

The Architecture of Taxation

The tax code is where democratic accountability quietly disappears.

In the current system, tax codes are weapons of class warfare disguised as neutral policy. The wealthy hire accountants to find loopholes. Corporations lobby for exemptions. The middle class pays while the rich hide assets offshore.

Nobody un`derstands how it works because the tax code is deliberately incomprehensible. It's designed to be just complicated enough that „I followed the law" and „I systematically defrauded the public" look identical to anyone without a tax law degree.

In the new system, taxation is transparent, simple, and directly accountable.

The Budget Process

Current process: Executive proposes, legislature adds pork barrel spending, backroom deals determine allocations.

New process:

Step One: Ministerial Requests

Each Minister submits a proposed budget with line-item transparency: how much is needed, what it will be spent on, expected outcomes, and multi-year projections. All of this is published publicly so citizens see exactly where money goes.

Step Two: Finance Minister Creates Budget

The Finance Minister reviews all requests and creates the national budget. This is like current finance ministers but with key differences:

- **Must balance budget or show clear debt projection**
- **Must save money** (not just spend everything requested)
- **All allocations public and justified**
- **No black budgets, no hidden spending**

The Finance Minister faces same accountability as other Ministers: delegation can be revoked if they mismanage finances.

This creates beneficial pressure. The Finance Minister must prioritize what the majority actually needs, not what special interests want. Unlike current systems where finance ministers serve corporate donors or party elites, this Finance Minister serves citizens directly. Tax and spending decisions reflect public priorities, not backroom deals.

But accountability includes long-term thinking. The budget must include AI-modeled projections showing consequences over 10+ years: „This spending level in 2035 means debt at X% GDP, interest payments consuming Y% of revenue." Future pain becomes visible now, preventing short-term political games at the expense of future generations.

The Finance Minister functions like a CFO. Citizens are the collective CEO. You hire someone with financial expertise to manage the books, keep spending sustainable, and allocate resources efficiently. If they mismanage, you fire them and hire someone better. You don't micromanage every budget decision; you judge them on results.

The Tax Structure

For Individuals: Progressive Consumption Tax

Taxed on spending, not earnings. Eliminates complex income tax codes.

Progressive structure:

- Basic necessities (food, housing, healthcare, education): 0%
- Standard goods: Moderate rate
- Luxury goods: Higher rate

Self-enforcing: Tax calculated automatically at point of sale.

For Businesses: Value-Added Tax (VAT)

Businesses pay tax only on the value they add at each step of production. A furniture maker pays VAT on the difference between what they paid for wood and what they charge for the finished table.

This system is proven globally, used in over 170 countries. It's self-enforcing through cross-verification: businesses have incentive to report purchases accurately because those purchases reduce their tax burden.

Standard VAT rate applies across all business types. No special exemptions. No loopholes for specific industries. The simplicity makes it impossible to game through accounting tricks.

Participatory Budgeting at Communal Level

Federal budget through Finance Minister. Local level: direct citizen control.

Porto Alegre model. Binding authority over actual money.

Communities hold assemblies. Residents propose projects — fix road, build park, etc. Technical evaluation verifies feasibility. Community votes allocate budget. Projects with most support get funded.

Transparency total. Track every dollar. Proposer's reputation on line.

Natural filtering: people who care vote. Local knowledge produces better outcomes than centralized planning.

Federal Structure: Subsidiarity

Decisions made at lowest competent level.

Local: Roads, parks, sanitation, local law enforcement, zoning **Regional:** Cross-boundary infrastructure, universities, hospitals **Federal:** Defense, monetary policy, interstate commerce, national standards

But here's the key: the federal government doesn't control everything just because it can. If a function can be handled locally, it stays local. If it can be handled regionally, it stays regional. Federal authority is reserved for genuine national concerns.

This prevents the concentration of power that makes corruption inevitable. A Minister of Agriculture can't dictate farming practices nationwide. Regional agricultural policies vary based on climate, soil, and local needs. The federal role is setting food safety standards and coordinating interstate distribution, not micromanaging every farm.

Each level has genuine authority and genuine accountability. Local officials answer to local residents. Regional officials answer to regional populations. Federal Ministers answer to the national citizenry. And at every level, the accountability is continuous through revocable delegation.

Citizen Oversight of Spending

But taxation is only half the equation. The other half is spending. And this is where the system gets really interesting.

Every ministerial expenditure is tracked on the public ledger. Every contract, every grant, every salary is visible. And citizens can flag suspicious spending for audit.

If the Minister of Infrastructure awards a $50 million road contract to a company owned by their cousin, someone will notice. And when 10,000 people flag it, the Shadow Minister investigates.

If the investigation reveals corruption, the Minister is fired immediately. Not after an impeachment process. Not after a trial that drags on for years. Immediately.

And the Shadow Minister, who exposed the corruption, becomes the new Minister. This creates a built-in incentive for accountability. The Shadow Minister isn't just watching for mistakes. They're hunting for corruption because exposing it is their path to power.

Participatory Budgeting for Discretionary Spending

Some portion of the budget (say, 10%) is allocated to participatory budgeting. Citizens can propose projects, and the population votes on which ones to fund.

Want a new park in your neighborhood? Propose it, detail the costs, and rally support. If enough people vote for it, it gets funded.

Citizens directly control how their tax dollars are spent. Not everything goes through Ministers. Some things go directly to the people.

The Architecture of Justice

Every country arrives at this moment with a functioning legal system. Courts, judges, prosecutors, public defenders. These institutions evolved over centuries, incorporating lessons from countless cases and adapting to societal needs. They work, mostly.

The governance model doesn't discard this infrastructure and start from scratch. Legal systems are woven into the fabric of society. Precedent matters. Stability matters. You can't redesign criminal justice every year without destabilizing everything else that depends on it.

The Justice Minister

The Minister of Justice manages the judicial system. Selected through delegation like other Ministers, they need demonstrated legal expertise: years as a judge, prosecutor, defense attorney, legal scholar, or justice reformer. Their credentials and reform proposals are public.

Their mandate is continuous improvement, not revolution. Court backlogs keeping people waiting years for trial? Address capacity through better case management, more judges, or alternative dispute resolution. Recidivism rates revealing that prisons create better criminals instead of rehabilitating them? Examine what's failing and implement evidence-based reforms. Legal aid so inadequate that only the wealthy get proper representation? Expand access.

The Minister identifies problems, implements reforms, tracks outcomes, and adjusts based on evidence. If the reforms fail, if outcomes worsen, if corruption persists, citizens revoke their delegation and try someone else.

Countries don't need to reinvent every wheel. If Norway's prison system produces dramatically lower recidivism through humane treatment and rehabilitation programs, study it and adapt what's applicable. If Germany's legal aid structure ensures better representation for

defendants, implement similar approaches. If
Japan's restorative justice practices show
promise in reducing repeat offenses, investigate
how they might work in the local context.

The best Justice Ministers will be those who can
identify what works elsewhere, understand why
it works, and adapt those principles to their
country's legal traditions and cultural context.

Judicial Independence

Judges need protection from political pressure
on individual cases. A judge ruling on a
controversial matter can't worry about being
fired tomorrow because the verdict angered the
majority. This is why judges have longer terms
and higher removal thresholds, as discussed in
the Constitutional Boundaries section.

But independence doesn't mean immunity.
Patterns matter. Consistent bias favoring
prosecutors over defendants, corruption taking
bribes for favorable rulings, or gross
incompetence can still trigger removal. The
Justice Minister manages the system judges
operate within — caseload, resources, training,
advancement criteria — but doesn't control
their rulings.

Individual cases remain independent. Systemic
failures get addressed.

Separation of Powers

The three branches of government remain distinct:

Legislative: Citizens directly, through law approval/withdrawal and citizen-initiated laws.

Executive: Ministers selected through delegation, instantly revocable.

Judicial: Courts and judges with longer terms and higher removal thresholds for independence.

This separation prevents any single branch from accumulating too much power. The Justice Minister manages the judicial system. Law enforcement and police fall under executive authority, handled by whichever Minister has that domain in their country's structure.

The Necessary Monster of Defense

Defense is where democracy goes to die.

Not because militaries stage coups, though they do. Not because intelligence agencies spy on citizens, though they do. But because defense requirements fundamentally conflict with democratic accountability. Secrecy. Rapid decisions. Lethal force. You can't crowdsource military strategy. You can't have instant revocation when missiles are in the air.

Yet unchecked control over violence always gets abused. Intelligence agencies manufacture threats to justify budgets. Defense contractors bribe officials for useless weapons systems. Generals plan wars to advance careers. The machinery of defense becomes the machinery of oppression.

Chile, 1973: A democratically elected government falls to a military coup backed by foreign intelligence. The defense apparatus, supposedly protecting democracy, destroyed it instead. The pattern repeats. Turkey. Pakistan. Brazil. Myanmar. Give the military unchecked power long enough, and it eventually uses that power against the people.

The question isn't whether to have defense capabilities. It's how to prevent them from eating the democracy they're supposed to protect.

The answer requires an uncomfortable trade-off. Defense and intelligence can't operate under the same continuous accountability that governs everything else. They need longer terms, more secrecy, more authority. But that authority must be contained, compartmentalized, and watched by people with no incentive to let it expand.

And the people drawn to defense roles will include those with dark triad traits.

Ruthlessness, strategic manipulation, comfort with violence. These traits evolved because tribes needed members capable of calculated aggression to survive.

The system doesn't try to exclude these personality types from power. That's impossible. They'll always seek positions requiring those exact traits. Instead, like integrating your own shadow rather than repressing it, the system channels them where their nature serves a function. Defense needs people comfortable making hard decisions under pressure. Counter-intelligence needs strategic thinkers who understand deception.

The constraints exist because these traits, unchecked, destroy democracies. But the traits themselves have purpose. The goal isn't elimination. It's containment and direction. Put the ruthless where ruthlessness serves survival, then watch them closely.

The Defense Minister serves one four-year term and never again. Selected through the same delegation system as other Ministers, but the term is fixed. No renewal. No second chance.

Why? Defense creates loyalty. Soldiers follow commanders. Intelligence operatives develop institutional allegiance. A Defense Minister serving for decades accumulates personal power that becomes dangerous. Better to rotate leadership, preventing any single person from building a military power base.

The mandate is narrow: control military forces and military intelligence. Not domestic surveillance. Not counter-intelligence. Not law enforcement. Just the capacity to project force abroad and gather intelligence on foreign military threats.

The budget is public. Citizens see total defense spending, force deployments, major weapons acquisitions. Classified programs exist, but their budget lines are visible. If defense spending becomes absurd, citizens can revoke budget authority. The Minister can argue for more money but can't hide where it goes.

Counter-intelligence operates separately. Different Minister. Different mandate. Four-year term, no re-selection, ever.

The separation matters. Defense looks outward: foreign militaries, external threats, power projection. Counter-intelligence looks inward: detecting foreign spies, protecting infrastructure, preventing espionage. Combining them creates a police state.

The counter-intelligence mandate is purely defensive. Detect foreign interference in elections. Protect power grids from sabotage. Identify foreign agents stealing technology or corrupting officials.

Not regime change. Not mass surveillance. Not infiltrating domestic political movements. Not targeting dissidents. The moment this Minister exceeds defensive boundaries, the Intelligence Review Board exposes it publicly and the Minister loses position.

The Intelligence Review Board exists to watch the watchers. Nine civilians selected randomly, like jury duty. Two-year rotating terms. Full security clearance. Complete access to every classified program.

They review operations, investigate complaints, and declassify illegal activity. The Defense and Counter-Intelligence Ministers can't fire them, intimidate them, or publicly identify them — which protects board members from retaliation.

Every quarter, the board publishes a public report. Not compromising active operations or classified sources, but telling citizens what they reviewed, what concerns emerged, and whether the defense apparatus is operating within legal boundaries.

Random selection prevents capture. Two-year terms prevent complacency. Nine members prevent individual manipulation.

Revolving Door Ban: Former Defense Ministers, Counter-Intelligence Ministers, and senior military officers cannot work for defense contractors. Ever.

Right now, generals approve billion-dollar weapons programs, then retire to executive positions at the companies that built those weapons. The incentive is obvious: approve bloated contracts, get rewarded later. The revolving door turns defense procurement into wealth extraction.

Close the door. You want to serve your country? Serve. You want to profit from war? Pick a different career.

None of this makes defense safe. These constraints don't eliminate the danger defense and intelligence pose to democracy. They make abuse harder to hide and easier to stop.

Defense remains the monster democracy must feed to survive. These mechanisms just keep the monster chained.

The Infrastructure

None of this works without the platform. The digital infrastructure that enables continuous delegation, transparent budgets, and participatory governance.

This platform is the most critical piece of the entire system. And it must be designed with security, transparency, and decentralization as core principles.

Open Source and Auditable

The code for the platform is open source. Any programmer can review it. Any security researcher can audit it. Vulnerabilities are disclosed publicly and patched immediately.

Current voting systems work oppositely: proprietary software that can't be independently verified. We're supposed to trust that the machines work correctly, but we can't look under the hood.

That's insane. And it's exactly how you'd design a system if you wanted to enable fraud.

Open source means trust through verification, not trust through authority.

Decentralized Architecture

The platform runs on a distributed network. Not a central server that can be hacked, seized, or shut down. A blockchain-based system where the data is replicated across thousands of nodes.

If a government tries to shut down the platform, they'd have to shut down every node simultaneously. That's functionally impossible.

And because the blockchain is immutable, votes can't be changed after they're cast. The ledger is permanent and publicly auditable.

This doesn't mean individual votes are public. Privacy is maintained through zero-knowledge proofs, which allow you to prove you voted without revealing who you voted for.

Identity Verification Without Surveillance

The platform needs to ensure one person, one vote. But it can't require invasive surveillance or create a database that can be used to target dissidents.

Cryptographic identity systems solve the problem. You register once, using biometric verification. But the system doesn't store your biometric data centrally. It stores a cryptographic hash that can verify you're you, but can't be reverse-engineered to identify you.

When you vote, the system verifies you're a registered citizen without linking your vote to your identity. Your vote is anonymous, but provably valid.

The approach prevents both fraud and surveillance. You can't vote twice. But nobody can see how you voted.

Resilience Against Attack

The platform will be attacked. By hostile governments, by corporate interests, by anarchists who want to watch it burn.

So it's designed to be resilient. Multiple redundancies. Distributed denial-of-service protection. Intrusion detection systems. Automatic failovers.

And here's the key: the platform is maintained by a distributed network of volunteers and paid professionals whose work is publicly reviewed. If someone introduces a backdoor, it gets caught in code review.

The entire security model is transparency. Nothing is hidden. Everything is auditable.

The Bet

The system creates better incentives. It removes structural barriers that prevent self-governance. It eliminates excuses. It makes accountability possible.

Constitutional protections guard against tyranny of the majority. But ultimately, no mechanism can fully prevent oppression if a population is committed to it. What changes the equation is consciousness. A population engaged in shadow work, one that has confronted its own projections and biases, becomes less inclined to oppress minorities. Not because rules prevent it, but because the psychological need to dominate diminishes.

The system and the inner work reinforce each other. Better structures make shadow work easier. More conscious citizens make better structures possible.

But if we're not capable, if we'd rather be ruled than rule ourselves, if we'd rather complain than participate, if we'd rather blame politicians than take responsibility, then we'll get exactly what we deserve.

But if we are capable? If we're willing to do the work of self-governance?

Then this system gives us the tools to build something genuinely new. Not a utopia. Not a perfect society. But a society where power flows from competence instead of connections, where accountability is continuous instead of periodic, where citizens are CEOs instead of subjects.

That's the bet.

And if it works, the world changes.

Not through revolution. Through obsolescence.

Because once you've tasted real power, such as the power to fire your Minister of Health for incompetence, the power to veto bad laws, or the power to control your own tax dollars, you'll never accept powerlessness again.

And the old system, the system that told you to vote once every four years and then shut up, will collapse.

Not because we destroyed it.

Because we built something better.

Objections

Every system that threatens existing power arrangements attracts critics. The objections to Liquid Representative Democracy are entirely predictable, recycled from debates that doomed Athens, that Switzerland still wrestles with, that every democratic reformer has faced across two thousand years of argument. They deserve honest answers, not reassurance.

Majority tyranny. Demagogic manipulation. Crisis response speed. Short-term thinking. Tribal warfare. Economic capture. Decision fatigue. Technology vulnerabilities. Theocratic subversion.

These aren't trivial concerns. They're the same challenges that haunt every democratic experiment. But none of them, examined carefully, prove fatal. Each has a concrete answer rooted in how the system actually works.

„But Won't The Majority Tyrannize Minorities?"

Fifty-one percent revoke delegates from a minister protecting minority rights. They install someone hostile. Ministerial authority implements discriminatory policies. Or a referendum passes targeting a specific group with simple majority support.

This fear has real precedent. Jim Crow had popular support. California voters banned same-sex marriage through Proposition 8 in 2008. Democratic processes have enabled serious injustice before, and they will do so again under any system that doesn't build friction into the architecture.

Liquid Representative Democracy builds that friction deliberately, though no system perfectly prevents oppression if populations are committed enough to it.

Constitutional rights sit outside ministerial authority and outside popular vote. Free speech, due process, equal protection, bodily autonomy cannot be overridden by a minister with strong delegate numbers. Constitutional amendments require a 66% supermajority, making fundamental rights more durable than in systems where five unelected judges reinterpret them for a generation based on who happened to appoint them.

Constitutional review follows proven models. Germany's Federal Constitutional Court has spent decades balancing democratic decision-making with rights protection effectively. Courts review decisions for constitutional compliance, with appointments structured to prevent capture by temporary majorities.

A minister campaigning on targeting minorities faces immediate constitutional review. Rights override popularity. This friction slows populist tyranny even when it cannot stop a sufficiently determined majority.

The alternative has a record too. Slavery. Jim Crow. Japanese internment. The War on Drugs targeting minorities disproportionately. Immigration policies excluding specific ethnicities. LGBTQ discrimination codified in law. None of these stopped at an institutional wall. Representatives didn't prevent them; representatives enabled them while institutional safeguards smiled and waved.

Liquid Representative Democracy removes campaign funding as the gateway to power. When ministers don't owe their positions to donors, donors cannot purchase loyalty at minority expense. That's a more reliable protection than hoping politicians defend vulnerable groups out of personal virtue rather than financial dependency.

The deeper defense is consciousness itself. Populations that have done serious shadow work, that recognize projection and tribal impulse for what they are, become less inclined toward oppression. Not because rules stop them, but because the psychological need to dominate loses some of its grip. Constitutional safeguards create friction. Consciousness changes motivation. Together they offer something that constitutional text alone cannot.

„Demagogues Will Manipulate The System"

Charismatic liars exist. They promise revolutionary improvements while scapegoating minorities. They manipulate through emotional appeals, and once in power they implement destructive policies while maintaining popularity through propaganda. Every era produces them. Most eras elect at least one.

Current democratic systems practically send an invitation. Elections reward charisma over competence. Media amplifies personalities over policies. Concentrated executive power hands demagogues a weapon the moment they win. The architecture is optimized for exactly this problem.

Power in Liquid Representative Democracy doesn't consolidate the way demagogues require.

No single minister dominates. A charismatic healthcare minister cannot declare war, change constitutional rights, or reach into other domains. Authority distributes across ministers at multiple levels, with no president or prime minister available to unify it. The demagogue cannot climb to the top of a structure that has no top.

Performance matters more than promises. Dashboards show objective outcomes. Revolutionary transportation improvements get measured against whether transportation actually improves. Measurable reality contradicts lies eventually. The honest question is whether „eventually" arrives quickly enough.

Here the Shadow Minister earns its keep. Every minister has an adversarial peer reviewing their work. The runner-up from selection analyzes decisions, publishes critiques, and proposes alternatives. When policies fail, the Shadow Minister documents it with data. When a demagogue's promises collapse against reality, the exposure comes from inside the system, from someone who wanted the job and has every incentive to say so publicly.

If infrastructure doesn't improve despite revolutionary promises, the Shadow Minister's analysis triggers delegate shifts. The demagogue gets fired. The person who exposed the failure typically takes over. This creates accountability that doesn't depend on opposition parties voters already distrust, or on media that may have decided the story was less interesting than the next personality conflict.

Constitutional protections add final barriers. Ministers targeting minorities face supermajority requirements and judicial review. Popularity doesn't override rights.

Distributed authority prevents consolidation. Outcome evaluation exposes failure. Shadow Minister scrutiny accelerates the correction. Constitutional bounds prevent the worst abuses. Not a guarantee, but considerably harder to circumvent than systems where removing a failed leader requires a constitutional crisis or waiting for the next election cycle, whichever feels more humiliating.

„It's Too Slow For Modern Crises"

Pandemics don't wait. Financial collapses happen overnight. Military threats demand immediate response. Does Liquid Representative Democracy have time for deliberation when minutes matter?

The system handles this by separating operational decisions from policy changes.

Ministers respond to emergencies within their mandates immediately. A healthcare minister implements pandemic protocols, containment measures, and resource allocation without public approval. This requires no more permission than current health officials already exercise during outbreaks.

Constraints exist:

- Can't violate constitutional rights
- Can't exceed budget authority without emergency approval
- Can't create permanent policy changes
- Can't commit military forces offensively (defense is permitted; offensive war requires public approval)

Emergency actions expire automatically after thirty days. If crises continue, ministers seek citizen ratification for extensions. Citizens retain the ability to revoke delegation throughout this period. If they don't trust the crisis response, they replace the minister immediately rather than waiting until the crisis has resolved itself one way or another.

The underlying principle: either ministers are qualified and citizens trust their emergency judgment, or they shouldn't hold the position. Competence under pressure is part of the job description, not an exceptional demand.

For major cross-mandate decisions requiring public votes, blockchain enables results within hours. Cryptographically secure voting produces legitimate outcomes faster than traditional processes.

Ministers also provide institutional continuity through long service. An infrastructure minister serving fifteen years maintains expertise and executes long-term projects without election cycle disruptions. Current representatives spend roughly half their terms campaigning for the privilege of doing it again.

The real inefficiency critique, examined closely, targets democratic accountability itself. When corporations want deregulation that enables pollution, convincing ministers answerable to transparent metrics is harder than lobbying legislators whose failures hide behind procedural complexity.

That friction is intentional. Infrastructure maintenance takes decades while wealth transfers happen efficiently. Military spending passes quickly with bipartisan enthusiasm. Efficiency correlates with elite interests, not public welfare. Liquid Representative Democracy preserves speed where it matters while making elite capture difficult enough to be worth attempting.

„People Will Vote For Short-Term Benefits Over Long-Term Needs"

Humans want tax cuts now, not fiscal responsibility paying off in twenty years. Cheap energy today, not climate stability for grandchildren. Immediate relief, not sustained effort over generations.

Politicians already exploit this tendency enthusiastically, kicking problems down the road because solving them costs elections. Climate change required serious action in the 1980s. The response was approximately nothing for decades, because the costs would fall on current politicians while the benefits would accrue after they'd moved on to board seats and speaking fees.

Several features of Liquid Representative Democracy push against this.

Ministers serving fifteen years develop perspectives that extend well beyond election cycles. While public attention cycles through crises, ministers operate on decade timelines. A transportation minister building rail infrastructure works through multiple news cycles. As long as progress metrics show appropriate advancement, delegate support remains. Accountability accumulates over time rather than concentrating in a single election moment.

Outcome tracking penalizes dishonest forecasting in ways that compound over time. Ministers whose predictions about policy outcomes consistently miss reality lose credibility and eventually positions. A healthcare minister who promises that cutting prevention services saves money faces direct comparison against what actually happens to long-term costs. Track records accumulate publicly, which becomes a serious problem if yours is bad.

Constitutional provisions for environmental sustainability and fiscal responsibility could require supermajorities to override. If default positions favor protection and balanced budgets, short-term overrides require convincing significant majorities across regions. This builds a deliberate bias toward long-term thinking into the most critical domains.

Different governance scales create different time horizons naturally. Local decisions address immediate concerns because local populations experience immediate consequences. Federal constitutional questions require extended deliberation because the stakes are highest and reversing mistakes is most difficult.

None of this guarantees sound long-term governance. But it creates better incentives than systems where politicians chronically kick problems down the road because solving them would cost them the next election. The climate didn't start burning because humans are stupid. It started burning because the system rewarded short-term thinking with continued employment.

„Tribalism Will Tear It Apart"

Binary political warfare intensifies. Tribal factions compete for ministers. Regional ministers become tribal leaders. Citizens delegate based on identity rather than competence. The system fragments into warring camps.

This diagnosis misidentifies the cause. Tribalism in current democracies isn't an unfortunate side effect of people having bad values. It's a feature, actively manufactured by the architecture.

Two-party systems force every issue into binary opposition. Red or blue. Left or right. With us or against us. Party loyalty matters more than outcomes. Politicians who break from party positions face primary challenges designed to eliminate them. The Republican Party spent thirty years convincing its voters that climate science was a liberal conspiracy, not because conservatives have bad values but because it was electorally useful. The Democratic Party spent twenty years telling its voters that trade deals benefited workers, not because the evidence supported it but because donors required it. When the architecture runs on tribalism as fuel, it produces tribalism efficiently.

Liquid Representative Democracy disrupts this by multiplying the axes of evaluation.

Ministers must coordinate across domains to succeed. Healthcare ministers work with environmental ministers, economic ministers, and education ministers when policies overlap. Success requires building relationships across traditional boundaries. Ministers who cannot coordinate fail visibly, and their failure is recorded.

Transparent performance metrics make tribal loyalty costly in ways that are hard to ignore. When tribal allegiance produces worse results than evidence-based competence, dashboards show the comparison. People notice when ministers in their region underperform compared to those elsewhere. The data doesn't care about your team.

Multiple ministers at different levels fragment the tribal identification that binary systems depend on. Citizens support some ministers while opposing others based on actual performance. Identity doesn't align perfectly across domains when you're evaluating multiple independent decision-makers simultaneously. The us-versus-them dynamic loses coherence because there are too many „thems" to keep track of.

Federal structure allows regional variation without requiring uniform national policy. Cultural differences get accommodated without forcing every tribe to fight for unified control of everything.

Tribalism will persist. Human nature doesn't change through institutional redesign. But ministerial accountability requires evaluating actual outcomes rather than allowing tribes to never interact except through media caricatures and cable news fury about what the other side allegedly wants to do to your children.

The current situation: tribal warfare so intense that families stop speaking over elections, parties more polarized than at any point since the Civil War, and citizens checking party affiliation before deciding whether to trust basic factual claims. The bar is low enough that clearing it would represent genuine progress.

„Economic Power Will Still Dominate"

Wealthy interests adapt. They cannot buy ministers through campaign contributions, so they find other channels. Media campaigns, think tanks, corporate positions promised after service. The mechanisms change but the outcome remains: economic power translates to political power.

This objection has real force. Liquid Representative Democracy doesn't automatically fix capitalism or eliminate wealth inequality.

Rich people will still have advantages. Anyone claiming otherwise is selling something.

But the system makes power acquisition significantly harder by changing the terrain on which that acquisition happens.

Ministers don't need campaign funding. Selection happens through government-provided digital forums. Candidates present CVs, video statements, Q&A sessions, and public debates. No advertising spend. No contribution cycles. This eliminates the primary channel through which economic capture currently operates.

When ministers don't need wealthy donors to secure their positions, wealthy donors cannot buy loyalty through funding. The mechanism breaks at the root rather than at the branch.

Selection criteria align with job requirements rather than fundraising capacity. Civil engineers compete on engineering accomplishments. Healthcare experts compete on public health expertise. Not on their ability to raise millions from pharmaceutical companies and maintain relationships through donor dinners.

Performance metrics matter more than public relations. Ministers are evaluated against independently gathered statistics they don't control. A healthcare minister who increases costs while worsening outcomes gets removed regardless of their communications budget. Results are harder to fake than promises, and under this system someone is always checking.

Ministry staff can anonymously report corruption without retaliation. Ministers who serve corporate interests over public welfare face whistleblowing from within their own organizations.

Multiple regions create competitive pressure. Outcome differences become visible through dashboards. People notice when ministers in their region consistently underperform compared to those elsewhere, and they have a mechanism to do something about it immediately.

The core difference comes down to concentration. Representative democracy creates choke points where economic power concentrates influence efficiently. Lobby a few hundred legislators. Fund key committee chairs. Build the revolving door with industry. The investment is manageable because the targets are few.

Liquid Representative Democracy distributes power across roughly twenty federal ministers, hundreds of state secretaries, and thousands of district directors and municipal administrators, each accountable to their respective populations through transparent metrics and revocable delegation. Wealthy interests would need simultaneous capture across all these levels. When any executive can be removed within days of visibly serving wealthy interests over public welfare, the cost and uncertainty of capture becomes prohibitive rather than routine.

Capture remains possible. It just stops being cheap and reliable. For a system designed by human beings operating within human societies, that may be the best available outcome.

The system also enables economic reform directly, by placing decision-making power in the hands of ministers accountable to the full range of people affected rather than to donors. Ministers can address wealth inequality, worker ownership, taxation structures, and corporate regulation without first asking permission from the people who fund campaigns.

„People Will Be Overwhelmed By Decision Fatigue"

Citizens must track multiple ministers across different domains, evaluate their performance through quarterly reports, decide when to shift delegates, and vote directly on cross-mandate issues, all while working full-time jobs, raising families, and managing daily life. Participation degrades into inertia. Delegates sit with failed ministers out of exhaustion rather than judgment. The system becomes de facto oligarchy through apathy.

Liquid Representative Democracy doesn't require the constant vigilance this picture assumes.

Most governance happens through ministers making operational decisions within their mandates. You don't vote on hospital staffing levels, bridge maintenance schedules, or diplomatic protocols. Ministers handle routine decisions the way executives handle operations. Your active participation is occasional, not continuous.

During stable periods, direct voting on cross-mandate questions might occur once or twice annually: war declarations, constitutional amendments, major restructuring. Frequency matches necessity rather than an arbitrary electoral calendar.

Delegate decisions are rarer still. A competent infrastructure minister serving fifteen years doesn't require constant re-evaluation. You check performance dashboards periodically, usually when something goes wrong or when quarterly reports surface notable changes. If infrastructure improves steadily, you leave your

delegate in place. If it deteriorates, you shift
support. The decision is simple because the
information is clear.

This is substantially less demanding than current
systems, where „engagement" means watching
politicians argue on television while feeling
powerless, following overlapping primary and
general election cycles, trying to understand
which representatives control which
committees, and deciphering whether your
representative's votes match the promises they
made eighteen months ago in a speech you
never saw. Current engagement requires
enormous attention for results that are often
nothing.

The assumption that citizens must become
experts on everything is also wrong. You're not
evaluating technical decisions. You're evaluating
outcomes. Did infrastructure improve? Did
healthcare costs decrease? Did education quality
increase? Performance dashboards present this
information without requiring technical
expertise. You don't need to understand
epidemiology to notice whether people are
getting healthier.

Decision fatigue comes from making choices
that don't matter or that you cannot influence.
Liquid Representative Democracy creates

opposite conditions: choices that matter and that you actually control.

„The Technology Will Fail Or Be Compromised“

Blockchain gets hacked. Zero-knowledge proofs contain exploitable vulnerabilities. A state actor compromises the voting system. Solar flares take down networks. Software bugs miscount votes. The entire digital infrastructure collapses, and with it the governance system.

Technology failure is a genuine risk. But the objection implicitly compares Liquid Representative Democracy against a technology-free alternative that doesn't exist. Current systems already depend on vulnerable technology that gets hacked, breached, and compromised regularly. Proprietary voting machines with secret code, centralized databases with single points of failure, paper trails that disappear. The question isn't whether to use technology. The question is whether this architecture handles failure better than the alternatives. It does.

Blockchain distributes data across thousands of nodes, eliminating single points of failure. Compromising the system requires simultaneously attacking a majority of nodes, which is prohibitively expensive and operationally complex. Compare this to current systems where a successful attack on a single election database or voting machine can affect outcomes while leaving no visible trace.

Zero-knowledge proofs aren't experimental technology. They're proven mathematical techniques developed through decades of scrutiny by cryptographers and security researchers, already deployed in financial systems handling trillions of dollars annually. The math doesn't negotiate.

Open source implementation means thousands of independent security researchers can audit the code. Bugs get caught and fixed publicly. Compare this to proprietary voting machine software, where manufacturers have successfully fought legal battles to keep code secret, making independent security audits impossible. One of these approaches is trying to be secure. The other is trying to appear secure.

Multiple redundancy layers ensure continuity. If blockchain nodes go down, others maintain the system. If primary networks fail, backup networks activate. If digital voting becomes temporarily unavailable, the system includes manual fallback mechanisms using paper ballots and local counting. The system doesn't require technology to function perfectly. It requires technology to function well enough most of the time, with robust fallbacks when it doesn't.

Transparent operation makes attacks visible. Compromise attempts appear in public logs distributed across nodes. Security researchers monitoring the system detect anomalies quickly rather than discovering them during a post-election audit, or never.

Regular security audits, bug bounty programs rewarding researchers who find vulnerabilities, and continuous improvement based on emerging threats make the system more secure over time. The alternative, propping up aging proprietary systems behind legal barriers to scrutiny, moves in the opposite direction.

„Theocratic Ideologies Will Destroy The System From Within"

A population segment believes governance must follow divine command rather than human deliberation. They view democratic decision-making as inherently illegitimate because it places human judgment above divine decree. They participate in Liquid Representative Democracy not to make it work, but to accumulate enough power to replace it with theocracy.

This objection is different from all the others. It's correct.

No political system based on humans collectively determining their own governance can survive when significant portions of the population reject that premise as blasphemy. Democratic systems only survive when populations actually want democracy. This isn't a design flaw someone clever can engineer away.

Liquid Representative Democracy has no defense against this that doesn't betray its own principles. Banning religious participation means becoming tyrannical. Excluding theocratic candidates means abandoning the premise that people choose their own governance. Prohibiting religious voters from delegating to ministers who promise to implement religious law means the system isn't actually democratic. Every attempted solution collapses into the thing it was trying to prevent.

This is precisely why the shadow work sections of this book matter more than any of the mechanisms described elsewhere. Theocratic ideology thrives on unexamined shadow. It offers escape from responsibility through submission to divine authority. It provides certainty in an uncertain world. It promises salvation in exchange for obedience. Fear, superiority, projection, denial: every psychological pattern examined in Section I finds perfect expression in theocratic movements, which is why such movements never lack for recruits.

No rule prevents a population from choosing theocracy if that's what they want. The only defense is consciousness. Populations that have done serious collective shadow work, that value freedom more than certainty, that accept responsibility for their choices, develop real resistance to theocratic appeals. But this is not a once-and-done achievement. Each generation must choose freedom again, must resist the seductive promise of absolute answers, must accept the burden of uncertainty that self-governance demands.

Liquid Representative Democracy works only in cultural contexts where populations actually value human deliberation over divine command. The Enlightenment created specific conditions making democratic self-governance possible: freedom of conscience, separation of church and state, individual rights protecting dissent from religious orthodoxy, scientific thinking emphasizing evidence over revelation. These aren't universal human achievements. They're specific cultural developments that remain contested even in societies that most loudly claim to have settled the question.

If people don't want to govern themselves, they won't, regardless of the mechanisms available to them. Liquid Representative Democracy simply makes that choice more honest and the consequences more immediate.

The Standard We Must Meet

None of the answers above are complete victories. Majorities can oppress minorities. Demagogues manipulate. Crises demand speed. Short-term thinking dominates human decision-making. Tribalism is real and persistent. Economic power corrupts. Decision fatigue is genuine. Technology can fail. Theocratic ideology threatens secular democracy.

These aren't hypothetical concerns. They're daily reality across every existing democratic system.

The standard isn't perfection. The standard is „better than what we have.“

Current systems have produced climate inaction while the planet burns, concentrated wealth while majorities struggle, launched endless wars enriching contractors while killing millions, eroded civil liberties in the name of protecting freedom, and left populations feeling powerless while simultaneously blaming those populations for not voting enthusiastically enough for pre-selected candidates. The defense usually offered is that things could be worse. This is technically true. It is also not much of a defense.

Liquid Representative Democracy offers concrete improvements across each of these failures. Rights become harder to strip than under any system where shifting judicial appointments reinterpret them across decades. Shadow Ministers create adversarial accountability from inside rather than waiting for journalists or opposition parties to notice. Instant revocation replaces four-year immunity from consequences. Ministerial continuity enables long-term thinking by removing the electoral incentive to promise what can't be delivered. Fragmented domains reduce tribal alignment because identity cannot map cleanly onto dozens of independent performance questions simultaneously. Eliminating campaign finance removes the corruption channel at the root rather than the branch. Distributing power across hundreds of accountability points raises the cost of capture from manageable investment to near-impossible coordination problem. Emergency powers expire automatically, preventing indefinite executive expansion through declared crisis.

Not utopia. Not a system that erases human selfishness. An architecture of consequence, where failure results in removal, success yields continued service, and authority remains tethered to measurable reality.

Ministers will make errors. People will disagree fundamentally about values. Wealthy interests will seek advantage. Tribalism will persist. Theocratic movements will attempt subversion. The system creates friction against these tendencies rather than wishing them away.

Representative democracy persists not because it's the best system humans have imagined. It persists because it functions magnificently as a machine for responsibility avoidance. It allows us to blame politicians while maintaining the comfortable fiction that we're powerless victims of a broken system rather than the people who built it and keep choosing it.

Real democracy requires surrendering that comfort. It requires accepting the difficult, messy, essential work of actual self-governance.

That's what Liquid Representative Democracy demands. It's also exactly why it works.

Economy

Most people experience the economy the way they experience the weather: as something that happens to them. You work, you get paid, prices go up, wages stagnate, and somewhere distant and abstract, a small number of people accumulate wealth at a pace that would have seemed obscene to any previous civilization. Nobody designed this, the thinking goes. It just emerged. It's just how things are.

That framing is doing a lot of work on behalf of people who benefit from it enormously.

What we call the economy is a set of rules. Rules about who can own what, how debt gets created, which activities generate returns and which don't, how wages are set, and who captures the difference between what workers produce and what they're paid. Those rules were written by people, revised by people, and are maintained by people. They reflect choices. They could be different. The fact that they haven't changed much isn't evidence that they can't. It's evidence that the people positioned to change them prefer them as they are.

This chapter won't propose a complete overhaul. That would be a different book, written by someone with an economics doctorate and a considerably higher tolerance for policy debates. What I'm offering are glimpses of alternatives that already exist, some possibilities technology might finally make feasible, and a cleaner view of the structure we've agreed to accept as inevitable.

But we have to name it first.

We've built an architecture calibrated so that most people never accumulate enough resources to become genuinely free. Remember what we covered in „Money is a Leash"? Currency as control mechanism. The threat of poverty keeping people compliant. The person who owns capital extracts value from the person who works. The debt system ensures this extraction happens efficiently, creating money that benefits those nearest its source while diluting everyone else's purchasing power. Financial engineering generates more wealth than actual production. Speculation beats innovation. Inheriting wealth pays better than a lifetime of real contribution. People are technically free to quit any job, but only to find another arrangement at rates that keep them dependent.

We call it wage slavery for a reason. The chain is invisible, but the constraint is real.

The concentration at the top isn't a malfunction. It's the system performing as designed.

There's a perverse footnote to all this: if everyone consumed resources at the rate wealthy people do, the planet would collapse faster than it already is. Our infinite appetite for growth gets accidentally constrained by keeping most people poor. This isn't environmental policy. It's a side effect of inequality that happens to slow total resource destruction. Not exactly a ringing endorsement of either the economic model or our relationship with the planet, but worth sitting with. We've built a system so structurally violent that its cruelty accidentally performs one useful function.

Most people assume only two alternatives exist: capitalism or communism. Team A or Team B, pick one and defend it against all criticism, forever. These aren't the only two ways to organize economic life, and treating them as the full menu prevents anyone from imagining anything better.

Start with communism. It means collective ownership of the means of production: the factories, the land, the resources owned by everyone rather than private individuals. Most people misrepresent this as a system where everyone gets paid exactly the same regardless of effort. Worth addressing, because if it were true, it would be deeply unfair. Someone working double shifts receiving the same as someone doing the bare minimum? Someone who sacrifices and saves arriving at the same destination as someone who wastes everything? That violates basic fairness and destroys motivation. It's also not what collective ownership actually means.

The misconception thrives on both sides of the debate. Those romanticizing communism imagine a world where they wouldn't need to work and could become philosophers and rock stars. Those opposing it imagine hard workers permanently subsidizing slackers. Neither picture reflects what the system actually proposes, but both reveal the fantasies and fears people project onto it. That alone tells you something: when an idea generates such vivid fantasies in its supporters and such vivid nightmares in its critics, you're probably not dealing with clear thinking on either end.

What history does show is the implementation problem. Every attempt to move from private to collective ownership required seizing property and redistributing it, which meant concentrating enormous state power in whoever was managing the transition. And once that power concentrated, something consistent happened: the enforcers became the new ruling class. The system meant to eliminate domination produced a different version of it.

Could it function differently under genuine distributed democracy, where power was real and consequences for abuse were immediate? Maybe. We haven't seen it tried under those conditions.

Now capitalism. Theoretically it rewards risk and effort better than its alternative. In practice, CEOs who destroy companies collect golden parachutes on the way out. Someone born into wealth can live lavishly their entire life without contributing beyond occasionally appearing at board meetings to vote on their own compensation. The people who actually build things, care for the sick, and teach children are told their work is admirable but not particularly valuable in market terms.

Consider the hedge fund manager. They add no measurable product to the world, no service that would be missed if they disappeared tomorrow, and they earn more in a single year than a thousand nurses will accumulate across their entire careers. The nurse spent that time keeping people alive. The hedge fund manager spent it moving numbers between columns. The market has spoken, and it has decided the numbers win. This isn't an anomaly. It's the system working exactly as structured.

The result is massive wealth concentration, a permanent laboring class, and a ruling tier extracting value from everyone below it. Different mechanisms than the communist implementation, but a strikingly similar destination. Both systems reliably produce the same thing — greed, domination, and fear as the operating system underneath, regardless of the flag flying above. Which suggests those three forces are the actual problem, not the name of the economic team you're on.

One more historical point worth making: central planning genuinely couldn't compete with markets for efficiency. Command economies couldn't process the information flowing through millions of individual decisions. They couldn't adapt. Markets distributed resources better, responded to needs faster, and encouraged innovation in ways that top-down systems structurally couldn't. This wasn't propaganda. It was an observable, consistent pattern across the entire modern era.

That historical argument, though, was premised on a specific limitation: no system could gather and process enough information to plan well at scale. For most of human history, that was simply true. It may no longer be. AI can now identify patterns in complex systems that no human analyst would catch, and it processes those patterns continuously rather than in quarterly reports. The old case against central planning assumed an information ceiling that technology is quietly removing. This doesn't mean the problem is solved. Technology amplifies the consciousness operating it, and ours hasn't caught up. But the constraint is shifting, and that matters for what might eventually become possible.

The W.L. Gore Model

Most corporate org charts look roughly the same: a triangle with someone important at the top, progressively less important people below, and a base layer of people who do most of the actual work. W.L. Gore & Associates looked at that structure and declined.

They make Gore-Tex, among other products, and generate roughly four billion dollars in annual revenue doing it. They operate in competitive global markets against companies with every conventional advantage. And they do it without traditional hierarchy, without bosses in the conventional sense, and without job titles that lock people into rigid roles.

They call it a „lattice structure." Imagine a tapestry where strong threads weave together horizontally rather than stacking vertically. Everyone is called an „associate," from the newest hire to the CEO. Leaders emerge based on their ability to attract followers, not because someone appointed them from above. Want to lead a project? Convince others that your idea is worth their time and expertise. Authority comes from respect and results, not from position on an org chart.

Each facility stays under 200 employees. When a location grows beyond that threshold, it splits into a new one. The reason is straightforward: genuine direct communication becomes impossible when groups get too large. You can't maintain a lattice if people don't actually know each other well enough to coordinate without intermediaries.

Associates have sponsors who help them navigate the company and develop their skills. But sponsors aren't bosses. They can't issue orders. They advocate, coach, and help people find their place in the organization's web of projects and commitments.

Compensation is determined by peers. Your colleagues evaluate your contributions, and that shapes your pay. Not pulling your weight? Your peers notice. Indispensable across multiple projects? That shows up in what you earn. The system aligns incentives in ways that top-down performance reviews never quite manage, partly because it's very difficult to fool the people who actually work alongside you every day.

Associates are also part-owners through an employee stock ownership plan. When the company thrives, everyone benefits directly. When things go poorly, everyone feels it. There's no owner class and worker class eying each other across a structural divide, because they're the same people.

Does it work perfectly? Of course not. The model requires hiring people who can handle ambiguity and self-direction. Some people thrive with clear hierarchies and defined roles; they'd be miserable at Gore, wandering the halls looking for someone to tell them what to do, gradually developing an existential crisis about whether they even exist without a job title on their business card. Building consensus takes time. Maintaining culture across global growth requires constant attention.

But consider the track record. W.L. Gore has been consistently profitable for decades. They've launched groundbreaking innovations across multiple industries. They have appeared on Fortune's „Best Companies to Work For" list every year since 1998, with employee turnover around 3%. The model doesn't just feel principled. It performs.

What makes Gore relevant here isn't that every company should copy their structure. It's the proof of concept. Wage slavery isn't structurally inevitable. You can build successful enterprises where the people creating value actually benefit from that value, where ownership and contribution align, where the leash loosens because people aren't perpetually terrified of losing everything.

A Speculative Merit Alternative

What if distribution could be redesigned around actual contribution rather than accumulated capital? Not what you've inherited, not what you've extracted through rent-seeking, but what you've genuinely done and what sacrifices you've made for collective benefit.

Imagine a system where access to resources correlates with real contribution, tracked by AI in ways human institutions never could. The nurse working double shifts during a pandemic gets recognized. The teacher who stays late for struggling students gets rewarded. The engineer solving genuine problems gets valued above the one gaming metrics. AI could theoretically observe patterns of contribution across time and context, distinguishing authentic value creation from manipulation of incentive structures.

The system would also impose a ceiling on the wealthiest people in society. Right now, Elon Musk owns resources equivalent to roughly a million average people combined. That level of concentration doesn't reflect a million times more contribution or sacrifice. It reflects the compounding advantages of capital ownership, market position, and the power to capture value from other people's labor while calling it innovation. Unless posting on social media at 3 AM counts as a million times more valuable than teaching kindergarten, which current market valuations apparently suggest it does.

In a merit-based system tracked by AI, unlimited accumulation becomes impossible. Access would be capped at some multiple of the baseline that still motivates without enabling grotesque concentration. Maybe ten times the average. Maybe a hundred. The exact multiple matters less than the principle: nobody accumulates a thousand times more than someone else, because nobody contributes a thousand times more.

The system would still reward entrepreneurial risk that creates genuine value, and innovation that improves lives. But the things that currently generate the most wealth — inheritance, financial speculation, rent extraction from property you own but didn't build — wouldn't register as contribution at all. You can still work harder and be rewarded for it. You simply can't build a dynasty on what your great-grandfather extracted.

This is speculation, not a policy proposal. The consciousness required to implement something like this doesn't exist yet. We'd need collective agreement on what constitutes merit, which sacrifices matter, and how to weigh different types of contribution. More fundamentally, any system this powerful could become a totalitarian nightmare inside a generation. Who programs the AI? Who sets the parameters? Who audits the auditors? Technology doesn't resolve human consciousness problems. It amplifies whatever consciousness gets brought to it. And given our track record, we'd likely end up with an AI that weights LinkedIn engagement over actual human contribution, which would be darkly hilarious if it weren't so plausible.

Economic Vision

Both the Gore model and the speculative merit system point at the same thing: the story that our current arrangement is the only viable option is a story someone benefits from you believing.

It's not inevitable. We chose this. We keep choosing it through our daily acceptance of terrible outcomes as normal. Gore demonstrates what's actually possible: that companies can thrive without traditional hierarchies, that workers can be owners without destroying motivation, that peer-based accountability can function at scale. The merit system sketch shows what might become possible as technology evolves, and also how quickly such systems would collapse or calcify without the right consciousness guiding them.

No structure, however well-designed, holds when the people inside it remain unconscious, driven by shadow material, unable to see past immediate self-interest. Transplant Gore's lattice into a culture of domination and fear and it mutates into something unrecognizable within a few years. New systems require new people. The inner work isn't a complement to structural reform. It's the prerequisite.

Some people are already doing it. Some organizations are already functioning differently. The alternatives aren't theoretical. They exist, they work, and they're being ignored by a civilization that has confused the cage it's in with the shape of reality. Recognizing that distinction is where everything starts.

Culture

„Culture is not your friend. Culture is for other people's convenience and the convenience of various institutions, churches, companies, tax collection schemes, what have you. It is not your friend. It insults you. It disempowers you. It uses and abuses you. None of us are well treated by culture."

Terence McKenna said this in a lecture that spread widely among people trying to understand why they felt perpetually off-balance in their own lives. He meant every word. Culture programs you to serve systems rather than yourself. It shapes your desires, fears, and aspirations into the precise shape most convenient for whoever is doing the extracting.

He was also only half-right. Culture is unavoidable. Without it, you make every decision from scratch, with no accumulated wisdom to draw from, no frameworks for navigating complexity, no practices for building communities or regulating the nervous system when things go sideways. Culture is the soil consciousness grows in. The question McKenna never quite answered is what you plant once you've torn the weeds out.

Cultures don't emerge from abstract philosophies or noble intentions. They develop from material conditions over centuries, sometimes literally from the earth itself.

Thomas Talhelm, a psychologist at the University of Chicago, published research in Science in 2014 that should have unsettled every confident theory about national character. Studying thousands of people across China, he found that the psychological gap between southern Chinese (more collectivist, more interdependent) and northern Chinese (more individualist, more analytical) had nothing to do with ethnicity or dynastic history. It correlated with what their ancestors grew.

Rice farming requires elaborate irrigation systems built and maintained collectively. Farmers coordinate water use and share maintenance costs. Canals need constant dredging. Rice also demands roughly twice the labor of wheat at critical periods, and transplanting and harvesting require cooperative exchanges where families depend on neighbors during the weeks that decide the year. Interdependence is survival.

Wheat requires far less coordination. One family can manage planting and harvest alone. Independence becomes virtue.

Warm climates with year-round growing seasons produce abundance mindsets. Cold climates with brutal winters produce scarcity consciousness and the compulsion to prepare. These pressures, repeated across hundreds of generations, shape what behaviors get reinforced, what values crystallize, what kind of person comes to feel normal.

Culture isn't fate. But it isn't a design choice you make at a weekend retreat, either. The real question is whether it gets consciously cultivated or unconsciously inherited. Whether it serves institutional convenience and keeps you compliant, or whether it supports the genuine self-governance this book is about.

The Consciousness Democracy Requires

Give someone the power to revoke their Minister's delegation, and watch what they actually do with it. Some will evaluate competence, track results, and make reasoned decisions about who deserves their trust. Others will respond to whoever speaks most confidently, whoever promises the simplest solution, whoever knows which tribal nerve to press at exactly the right moment. The same tool produces radically different outcomes depending on the consciousness wielding it.

These capacities develop through specific cultural conditions, practiced over time, until they become the default way of seeing the world. What that cultivation looks like in practice is worth examining closely, because it looks nothing like a seminar.

Consider gratitude. The entitled mind believes the world owes it everything. When things go well, that's baseline expectation. When things go poorly, that's injustice requiring someone to blame. This mindset makes functional democracy nearly impossible because it prevents acknowledging what you've received and contributing anything back.

Thai culture has a concept called katanyu: gratitude expressed through action. Not just feeling thankful but showing appreciation through respect, care, and supporting those who supported you. You benefit from roads you didn't build, schools you didn't fund, institutions others created and maintained across decades before you arrived. Katanyu reminds you that you owe something back, not from guilt but from honest recognition of what you're standing on.

This practice directly counters the victimhood consciousness explored earlier. When you actively acknowledge what you've received, performing perpetual victimhood becomes harder to sustain. You can still identify genuine injustice and demand real accountability, but the framework shifts from ,,everything is owed to me" to „I've received much and can contribute back." The entitled mind is always waiting to reassert itself, though. Katanyu requires permanent practice, not a one-time revelation.

Now consider death, which Western culture has decided to handle by pretending it mostly won't happen. Picture someone at 2 AM scrolling through health symptoms, convincing themselves the headache is a tumor, the fatigue is organ failure, the rash is something with a long Latin name and no good prognosis. The panic isn't really about the symptoms. It's about what the symptoms point toward: the fact that one day there won't be a you doing the scrolling. Modern culture treats death as absolute failure, the one outcome that must be avoided at any cost, preferably through sufficient expenditure. So we hide aging bodies in facilities with cheerful names. We medicalize dying until the machines are doing most of the work. We talk about people „losing their battle" with illness, as if mortality were a war the sufficiently brave could win. Statistically, we're all losing that battle. Nobody wins.

The result is a population living in permanent low-grade existential terror. And terrified people are extraordinarily easy to manipulate. As the Fear chapter showed, death anxiety drives authoritarianism. Remind people they're mortal, show them threats everywhere, and they'll support almost anything that promises protection. They'll surrender freedom for the illusion of safety and accept surveillance, restriction, and control, whatever might keep the void at bay a little longer.

Tibetan Buddhist traditions take the opposite approach: look directly. Practices drawn from the Bardo Thodol tradition include deliberate meditation on impermanence and death, sitting honestly with the fact that you will die, everyone you love will die, everything you build will eventually be forgotten. The goal isn't morbid fixation. It's honest acknowledgment that makes the present legible. Accepting impermanence doesn't produce nihilism. It produces appreciation for what you have while you have it, and the courage to act without the paralysis that comes from pretending death is something that happens to other people.

The third practice is internal regulation. People who cannot regulate their own emotions become desperate to regulate external circumstances as compensation. They need rigid rules, strong authorities, and predictable environments because internal chaos feels unbearable. Give them uncertainty and they'll hand authority to whoever promises to make the uncertainty stop. Strong leaders have always understood this dynamic better than democrats have.

Stoic philosophy offers specific practices for developing that internal regulation. The dichotomy of control, articulated by Epictetus in the Enchiridion, distinguishes between what you can influence and what you cannot. You can't control what others think, what happens to the economy, or whether people respect you. You can control your own responses, your reasoning, your character. Focusing energy on what you can actually influence reduces the desperate need to control everything outside yourself.

Marcus Aurelius governed the Roman Empire while practicing this daily. His Meditations, written as private reminders rather than a philosophical treatise, reveal a man constantly recalibrating: he controls only his own mind, external events carry only the meaning he assigns them. He was managing fifteen provinces, continuous border wars, and a devastating plague while reminding himself, in private, that other people's behavior was not his emergency. This isn't passivity. It's directing power toward what can actually be moved.

Citizens practicing this distinction can participate in governance without needing to control every outcome. They can advocate for policies, delegate to competent Ministers, revoke delegations when appropriate, and accept that sometimes their preferred approach won't prevail. The ability to engage without needing to win is what makes collective decision-making survivable over the long term.

None of these practices work through intellectual conversion. Deciding that gratitude is philosophically sound does not make you grateful. You become grateful by practicing gratitude until it rewires how experience registers, until the entitled interpretation of events stops being the automatic first draft.

Picture a neighborhood in Bangkok. A young professional passes an elderly street vendor every morning. Each time, hands together, a slight bow. The wai. Three seconds. But those three seconds are doing something: this person matters, your interaction with them matters, you exist in relation to others and not in isolation from them. Do this across years, across thousands of small moments, and it gradually changes how you see. People stop being obstacles or resources or background noise. Democracy built on that soil works differently than democracy built on people calculating their individual advantage and calling it civic participation.

None of this requires adopting entire traditions wholesale. You don't need to become Thai to practice gratitude, Buddhist to contemplate mortality, or Stoic to develop internal regulation. Regular structural moments do most of the work: acknowledgment of what you've received, neighborhood gatherings where people share food and actual conversation, memorial practices that celebrate lives rather than just process loss, children learning early what they can and cannot control.

Culture is what people do, not what they're told to do. It emerges from necessity that becomes practice that becomes tradition. When institutions model respect through genuine transparency, when community practices reinforce interdependence, those qualities become normal. Normal is what you want. Normal is what outlasts any particular government.

These practices also build immunity to manipulation through division. When you've shared meals with people across supposed dividing lines, learned from them, recognized their humanity in specific rather than abstract ways, projection becomes harder to sustain. It's difficult to externalize all evil onto „those people" when you have actual relationships with them that complicate the story.

Division has always served power. Left against right, men against women, generation against generation. As long as it works, new divides will be manufactured from whatever material is available. Solving today's specific divide doesn't address that. Building cultural immunity to the technique does.

The Slow Growth of Culture

You can implement a new political system in months. You can restructure an economy in years. Culture doesn't care about your timeline.

The Ministers in this book can be selected through liquid democracy starting tomorrow, if the infrastructure exists. The transparency mechanisms can be built and deployed. But the cultural capacity to use these tools well? That takes decades of consistent, unglamorous work that no one will credit you for because it won't be visible until you're gone.

Children absorb culture subconsciously long before they can articulate it. They watch how adults handle conflict. Whether people express gratitude or entitlement. How community members treat each other and what that reveals about who counts. What gets celebrated and what gets condemned. The practices become normal. The consciousness those practices cultivate becomes the baseline for everything built on top of it.

There's a Japanese concept relevant here: shokunin, the craftsman's devotion to mastering a practice over a lifetime. A sushi chef who spent decades perfecting rice preparation before touching fish. Cultural cultivation works on a similar logic, except the timeline spans generations rather than careers. You are the apprentice to people long dead, and the teacher of people not yet born.

This means cultural change requires commitment beyond single lifetimes. You're not just building for yourself but for people who haven't arrived yet, who'll inherit what you cultivated without knowing who planted it. The democracy described in this book works when populations have done the shadow work, developed the gratitude practices, cultivated an honest relationship with mortality, and built the internal regulation capacity that lets them engage without needing to win. That's generational work.

But it compounds. Each generation that does this work makes it easier for the next. The practices become tradition. The consciousness becomes culture. What seemed radical becomes normal, and what seemed normal to the previous generation looks, in retrospect, like a prolonged collective failure of imagination.

McKenna was right. And the response to being right about something that depressing is to do the work anyway. Culture built in service of consciousness rather than control is possible. Practices transmitted across generations can liberate rather than constrain. The soil can grow something other than compliance.

But only if someone starts the planting.

The harvest comes for our grandchildren. The planting starts now.

IV. Ongoing Practice and Maintenance

Sustainable Engagement

You're standing at your kitchen counter. Your phone buzzes: „Minister of Health: Emergency room wait times increased 40% over six months. The Shadow Minister published an analysis. Review alternatives?"

You swipe it away without reading.

Maybe you're tired. Maybe you trust your delegation chain. Maybe you just don't want to deal with it right now. Or maybe you've been avoiding healthcare news because your sister has been waiting three months for a specialist appointment, and thinking about it brings up feelings you'd rather leave alone — anger, helplessness, the particular exhaustion of caring about something you can't fix.

The system doesn't know the difference. It registers a dismissed alert. Your delegation stays active, the Minister stays in power, and life continues.

But the difference is real. One is trust. The other is avoidance. And only you know which one you're doing.

Efficient delegation is a genuine strategy: you've chosen competent people, you trust their judgment, and when something breaks badly enough, you respond. The rest of the time you're living your life. That's not laziness. That's the point. Avoidance looks identical from the outside but operates on completely different logic. The alerts arrive and your first instinct is irritation, not concern. The problems that affect you most directly are the ones you're least willing to look at. You've outsourced not just technical evaluation but responsibility itself, and on some level you know it.

Nobody forces you to engage. Your vote flows through your delegation chain either way. But the question underneath all the practical arrangements is this: are you delegating because you trust your delegates to handle decisions you're not qualified to make? Or because you don't want to think about governance at all, even when it's quietly reshaping your daily life?

Ignorance is genuinely blissful. No outrage, no cognitive load, no Sunday afternoons lost to reading ministerial performance reports. Current representative democracy perfected this arrangement. Vote once every four years, then stop paying attention. Most people never track what their representatives actually do between elections. They hand over their political power and deliberately avoid information about how it gets used. This isn't cynicism. It's an entirely rational response to systems that offer participation without real consequence.

A more distributed architecture makes the temptation sharper. Delegation chains are longer, the distance from you to actual decisions is greater, and you can plausibly tell yourself you're participating while doing nothing at all. That's fine, as long as you're honest about it. Trusting your chain while staying alert to genuine failures is the system working as designed. Avoiding engagement because political reality makes you uncomfortable, because not knowing feels safer than knowing, is something the system cannot detect, correct for, or care about. That part is entirely up to you.

The Temptation to Abandon Responsibility

The most seductive feature of any efficient system is the permission it seems to grant you to stop thinking.

„I delegated to my doctor. It's not my fault if the healthcare system fails." „I set up my delegation chains years ago. I can't be expected to monitor everything." „The system has Shadow Ministers and performance metrics. Why do I need to pay attention?"

All technically true. All potentially the most convenient thing you've ever told yourself.

The distinction worth holding onto is narrower than it sounds. You're not responsible for personally vetting every ministerial candidate, or reading quarterly reports, or developing expertise in infrastructure policy. But you are responsible for the delegation choices you made. And you're responsible for responding when those choices produce outcomes you didn't want. Those are different things. The first set of exemptions doesn't cover the second set of obligations.

The continuous revocation power built into this system isn't a theoretical feature. It's what makes the whole architecture honest. When things go wrong, you had the power to intervene. You chose not to. That's not a tragedy. It's a decision.

Current representative democracy offers more comfortable terrain. „The politicians failed me. The system is corrupt. I'm just one person." There's enough truth buried in each of those statements to make them feel like analysis rather than evasion. The earlier chapters in this book covered these patterns closely: projection, denial, victimhood, scapegoating. Avoidance belongs to the same family. It's just harder to catch because it doesn't announce itself as evasion. It feels like rest.

A system that gives you real power removes the comfortable terrain. You can revoke bad Ministers. You can redirect bad delegations. You can participate when it actually matters. The signs that you're not doing any of this tend to be quieter than people expect. A critical alert arrives about a Minister failing in a domain that directly affects you, and your first reaction is irritation rather than concern: not „this needs attention" but „why is this bothering me right now." Someone brings up a local governance failure and you steer the conversation elsewhere, not because you lack opinions but because forming them out loud would mean having to do something with them. The roads get worse, the wait times get longer, the school your neighbor's kids attend starts losing teachers, and somewhere you absorb all of this as weather: unpleasant, impersonal, not really anyone's responsibility. Your delegation chains were set up years ago based on who seemed reasonable at the time, and you haven't thought about them since. Choosing not to engage is still a choice. Civic power functions like a gym membership:

technically yours, practically lapsed, and slightly guilt-inducing whenever it comes up.

The Quiet Cost of Looking Away

Unlike the sharper patterns this book has covered, avoidance rarely comes with a villain's self-awareness. It's ordinary human behavior responding to genuine exhaustion. Political engagement is hard to sustain in a way that's difficult to explain to people who haven't tried, and the desire to live your life without governance as a background hum of anxiety is completely understandable.

But avoidance is still a shadow pattern — the preference for comfortable numbness over uncomfortable awareness, the impulse to let someone else handle it, the quiet suspension of your own judgment in exchange for not having to use it. Jung wrote in *The Undiscovered Self* that the greatest danger to any democratic society isn't external threat but the inner resistance of its citizens to conscious participation. He meant the willingness to hand over responsibility to anyone who presents themselves as willing to take it. At the collective level, that's not philosophy. That's how Ministers accumulate influence nobody consciously meant to grant them.

No one will force you to pay attention. No one will register your disengagement as a failure or hold it against you. The consequences take their time. A policy you'd have objected to if you'd read the alert, an appointment in a domain you'd stopped monitoring, a slow accumulation of decisions made by people who were paying attention precisely because they knew most others weren't.

The system doesn't require you to become a policy expert or sacrifice your evenings to ministerial reports. What it requires is honesty about the difference between two things that look the same from the outside: trusting competent delegates and staying available when something breaks, versus using the language of participation as a comfortable way to opt out entirely.

A population that has genuinely done this work, that has looked at its own tendency to outsource responsibility and recognized it for what it is, will use the system for what it was designed for. When something breaks badly enough, they respond. Not heroically, not constantly. Just when it actually matters. That's all it takes. The question is whether enough people are willing to know the difference between when they're doing that and when they aren't.

Boundaries

If you've done shadow work, you know boundaries. Not walls. Membranes. They let good things in, keep destructive things out, and maintain your integrity while remaining open to genuine connection.

Without boundaries, you become a dumping ground for everyone else's projections, anxieties, and unprocessed material. You lose yourself. You get consumed by other people's agendas.

With rigid walls, you cut yourself off from growth, feedback, and real relationship. You become defensive, isolated, incapable of change.

The collective operates the same way.

I don't believe in borders. Not philosophically.

The idea that where you happen to be born determines your nationality, your identity, your belonging? Arbitrary lines on maps, enforced by violence, maintained by the collective amnesia that mistakes historical accident for natural law. A Prussian king draws a line. Someone shoots anyone who crosses it. Three generations later, people die for that line. Call it heritage.

I've lived my life refusing to see myself as defined by the coordinates of my birth. I'm human first. The passport is administrative equipment, not an identity. The culture I carry is chosen and evolving, not stamped onto me by geography.

In a more honest world, borders would be obsolete. People would move freely. Cultures would exchange and evolve without customs checkpoints. Governance would organize around shared values rather than the accidents of cartography. Humanity would finally recognize itself as one species navigating one planet.

That's the world worth building toward.

But until global power structures change fundamentally, borders serve a practical function. They create containers where populations can develop shared values and governance systems. Without them, consciousness-based culture has no protected space to develop.

You can't run an experiment in an open field during a hurricane. You need a laboratory. Controlled conditions. Protection from interference. You can't test a new approach to democratic self-governance while a hostile empire floods your system with manufactured crises designed to make it fail. You need boundaries that protect the experiment long enough to see if it works.

The proposed system requires citizens capable of cooperation, critical thinking, and collective responsibility. Building this capacity takes generations. Shadow work doesn't happen overnight. A culture of conscious self-governance is fragile while it develops. It needs protection.

Not forever. But for now.

One reaction to this is to project all fear onto borders and demand fortress states. The opposite is to project all historical guilt onto them and demand their complete dissolution as moral penance. Both miss the actual function of boundaries, which is discernment: letting in what serves you, keeping out what destroys you, without confusing the two.

A conscious nation maintains boundaries without hostility. It protects what it's built without paranoia. It welcomes genuine connection without naive vulnerability. And it works actively toward a world where such protection becomes unnecessary.

As populations develop genuine self-governance capacity, voluntary union becomes possible in a way fundamentally different from how borders have historically changed. The Soviet Union came into being through conquest and elite imposition. The Baltic states, Ukraine, Georgia, the Central Asian republics were absorbed through force and political maneuvering, the populations never consulted. When they finally got the chance to vote in 1991, the union dissolved almost immediately. That's what happens when a union is imposed rather than chosen.

But when populations have genuine control through delegate systems, union works differently. The people themselves can vote directly on whether to merge with a neighboring country. Not their representatives. Not their ministers. Them.

Imagine two countries that have both implemented conscious self-governance successfully. After generations, they hold simultaneous referendums: „Should we unite under shared governance?" If both populations vote yes, that's a genuine democratic union. The people decided. That's categorically different from how borders currently change through conquest, elite deals, and economic pressure dressed up as diplomacy.

The consciousness that enables self-governance also enables voluntary cooperation at scale. Borders become permeable through democratic will, not through naive dissolution or imperial force.

But in a world where empires don't surrender territory voluntarily and hostile actors use populations as weapons, boundaries remain survival necessities.

Nuclear Deterrence

Nuclear weapons are the only proven defense against imperial intervention.

Iraq didn't have them. Destroyed under false pretenses, the evidence for which was later described by Colin Powell as „a blot" on his record, in what may be history's most understated self-assessment.

Libya gave up its nuclear program in 2003 as part of a deal with Western powers. By 2011, Gaddafi was dead and the country was in ruins. The deal turned out to be less of an agreement and more of a helpful list of reasons not to feel threatened while the bombs were being loaded.

Syria never had them. Still vulnerable to external manipulation and occupation.

Pakistan has them. Sovereign despite decades of pressure.

North Korea has them. Cannot be invaded, no matter how much the empire wants regime change.

The pattern is clear enough that you don't need a political science degree to read it. Nations without nuclear weapons face regime change when they threaten imperial interests. Nations with them don't.

Every country implementing genuine self-governance would learn this lesson quickly: if you want independence from the current empire, you need the ultimate deterrent. Not because nuclear weapons are good. Because empires respect nothing less.

Every country implementing genuine self-governance learns this lesson: if you want independence from the current empire, you need the ultimate deterrent. Not because nuclear weapons are good. Because empires respect nothing less.

We wish this weren't true. Nuclear weapons are existentially dangerous. But until global power structures change fundamentally, a nation proving that citizens can govern themselves without a ruling class threatens every empire on Earth. And empires have demonstrated repeatedly that they will destroy alternatives to their control.

The question isn't whether nuclear weapons are morally pure. They're not. The question is whether you're willing to be destroyed for refusing to acquire them.

Maintaining this boundary is uncomfortable. It requires accepting that the world operates on power dynamics that don't care about your principles. It requires holding a weapon you hope never to use while knowing that not holding it makes you a target. None of this is morally satisfying. It is, however, empirically accurate.

The boundary here isn't about aggression. It's about making the cost of attacking you higher than any benefit. It's about saying clearly: we will defend what we've built, and the price of trying to destroy us is unacceptable.

That's deterrence. It works precisely because it's a boundary, not a threat.

Weaponized Compassion

Immigration has always enriched human civilization. People fleeing persecution deserve safety. Families seeking better opportunities deserve dignity. The foundation of any sustainable immigration policy should be diplomacy: prevent refugee crises before they start by addressing root causes, support international cooperation, help people thrive where they are rather than forcing them to flee.

When migration does happen, ensure it occurs gradually enough that integration can succeed.

That's the ideal. It should remain the goal.

Reality looks different.

Not all nations operate in good faith. Some states actively manufacture refugee crises as weapons. Others exploit humanitarian values as vulnerabilities. Political scientist Kelly Greenhill spent years documenting what she calls coercive engineered migration. In her 2010 book *Weapons of Mass Migration*, she identified over 56 cases between 1951 and 2006 where states deliberately created or manipulated refugee flows to extract political concessions from target countries. The success rate was roughly 73 percent. It's an effective tactic precisely because the target country cannot respond without appearing to be the villain in its own story.

This isn't obscure academic observation. Russian military doctrine explicitly includes these tactics under concepts like Maskirovka, their term for military deception, and Reflexive Control, which means manipulating opponents into decisions against their own interests. Weaponizing migration fits seamlessly into their broader hybrid warfare strategy.

The mechanism is straightforward. A hostile state either creates conditions that generate refugee flows toward a target nation, or directly facilitates the movement of migrants to that nation's borders. The goal isn't humanitarian. It's destabilization.

Russia and Syria demonstrated this starting in 2015. Russian forces deliberately targeted civilian infrastructure in Syria, generating massive refugee flows toward Europe. NATO Supreme Allied Commander Philip Breedlove testified before the Senate Armed Services Committee in March 2016 that Russia and the Assad regime were „deliberately weaponizing migration in an attempt to overwhelm European structures and break European resolve." The refugee crisis that followed fueled far-right movements, fractured EU cohesion, dominated political discourse, drained resources, and destabilized governments. Mission accomplished.

Belarus ran the same playbook in 2021. After the EU imposed sanctions, President Lukashenko flew thousands of migrants from the Middle East to Minsk with promises of easy European entry, then bused them to the borders with Poland, Lithuania, and Latvia. The migrants became instruments of pressure. Not because of who they were, but because of how they were being used.

They were genuine victims and unwitting weapons at once. Hold both of those things true simultaneously and you're already thinking more clearly than most of the people writing op-eds about this.

Integration works when it happens gradually. Newcomers adapt to existing cultural frameworks while contributing their own. Children go through the education system. Families build relationships in communities. Shared values develop through genuine interaction over time. But when immigration is too fast, integration becomes structurally impossible. Schools can't process the volume. Communities can't absorb the change. Social security systems buckle. And when a system gets flooded faster than it can process, parallel societies form instead of integrated ones.

Healthcare, housing, welfare, and unemployment benefits all assume certain population sizes and contribution rates. Rapid population increases without corresponding economic integration overwhelm these systems. The newcomers don't get adequate support. The existing population watches services deteriorate. Politicians exploit the resulting resentment rather than acknowledging the manufactured crisis.

Then there's a harder problem still. Some ideological frameworks are structurally incompatible with democratic self-governance, not because of ethnicity or origin, but because of core beliefs about authority and legitimacy. When someone holds theocratic convictions, where divine law supersedes democratic process and religious authority outranks individual rights, they cannot genuinely participate in secular self-governance on its own terms. They participate to establish the system they consider legitimate, which happens to be a different system entirely.

Someone can be devoutly religious from any tradition while fully accepting democratic principles. The issue is specific: when the framework explicitly rejects the premise that humans should govern themselves through collective decision-making, no amount of goodwill on either side resolves the contradiction.

When large populations holding these frameworks migrate faster than education systems can support value transmission, democratic culture doesn't integrate the newcomers. The newcomers vote democratically to establish something else. This is particularly difficult to address without appearing to violate the democratic principles you're trying to protect. The irony is precise and intentional.

A consciousness-based culture is fragile. Questioning authority doesn't come naturally. Personal responsibility is hard. Collective shadow work is deeply uncomfortable. These capacities have to be taught and modeled continuously. When immigration happens slowly, there's capacity to support this transmission. When it happens too fast, particularly when weaponized by hostile actors, the culture that took generations to build gets replaced by whatever framework commands the demographic majority.

Refusing to acknowledge these dynamics doesn't protect immigrants. It empowers hostile actors. When countries can't distinguish between organic migration and manufactured crisis, when they can't acknowledge capacity limits without being labeled racist, they become perfect targets for coercive migration tactics. Hostile states will continue manufacturing refugee flows because it works. And the more it works, the more backlash builds against all immigration, including people who genuinely need protection.

The xenophobic right exploits this by treating all immigration as invasion, projecting fear onto every outsider. That's morally bankrupt and factually stupid.

But the response cannot be pretending that capacity limits don't exist, that integration takes no time and no resources, or that any border enforcement is inherently fascist. That's projecting historical guilt onto policy and calling it compassion.

A sustainable immigration policy isn't a wall and it isn't an open door. It's a membrane: protective enough to preserve what's worth preserving, permeable enough to remain genuinely open. Maintaining that capacity is what allows genuine hospitality to exist at all. Lose the boundary and you lose the ability to welcome anyone on your own terms.

This means pursuing diplomacy aggressively while maintaining boundaries realistically. Work to prevent refugee crises. Address root causes internationally. Support genuine asylum seekers appropriately. And recognize when migration is being weaponized, then respond strategically rather than emotionally.

Nations implementing genuine self-governance will be targeted. Empire doesn't tolerate alternatives. Hostile actors will probe for weaknesses, manufacture crises, exploit values, and test boundaries constantly.

Maintaining what you've built requires seeing these attacks clearly, without paranoia and without the kind of denial that mistakes naivety for virtue.

I don't believe in borders philosophically. I work toward a world where they become obsolete. And I recognize they're necessary right now to protect the fragile cultural containers where consciousness can develop.

This is not a contradiction. It's a membrane.

Evolution, Not Ossification

The Roman Republic lasted nearly five centuries. It survived invasion, plague, civil war, and financial collapse. What finally killed it wasn't an enemy army. It was the slow, consensual decision to stop asking whether the Republic still served the people and start asking how to protect the Republic from the people. By the time Augustus declared himself First Citizen, most Romans were relieved. Questioning the system had become exhausting. Defending it felt like purpose.

Every revolution eventually declares itself complete. Every new structure eventually becomes the structure to defend rather than improve. The minister-based system described in this book represents what is possible now, given current levels of self-awareness and current technology. It is designed for populations taking their first real steps toward genuine self-governance. The question isn't whether it's perfect. It isn't. The question is whether populations will keep asking „what's next?" or whether they'll do what Rome did.

What follows aren't prescriptions but provocations: ideas worth exploring, questioning, adapting, or throwing out entirely. The goal isn't to predict which direction any population will take. It's to insist that keeping a direction matters more than having arrived.

Citizen Legislation

The minister system uses liquid democracy's core mechanism, revocable delegation, but applies it narrowly to ministerial selection. You delegate authority over who manages healthcare, not how to vote on every healthcare policy. This narrowness is intentional. Most populations aren't ready for full liquid democracy, where citizens vote directly on policies or delegate those votes to others who can delegate further.

As covered in the chapter on potential alternatives, liquid democracy fails badly without the prerequisite inner work. People delegate to popular influencers rather than domain experts. Tribal affiliation beats competence. Parasocial loyalty prevents revocation even when delegates fail in public and in plain sight. And influencers holding millions of delegated votes become capture targets worth billions, which is when democracy stops being a threat to power and starts being a service to it. The form remains. The substance evaporates.

But what if populations could actually develop past these limitations?

The transition probably starts small, not as ideology but as a practical necessity. Local decisions where consequences are immediate and visible. Should the city build a new park or expand the library? Citizens vote directly or delegate to trusted community members. Performance is easy to track. Bad delegations become obvious within months rather than decades. Stakes are high enough to matter but low enough that mistakes teach rather than destroy.

As competence develops at local levels, expansion to regional policy becomes conceivable: infrastructure projects, education curriculum, and healthcare resource allocation within defined budgets. If citizens demonstrate they can delegate based on expertise rather than popularity, revoke bad delegations when evidence demands it, and expose influencer-capture attempts instead of rewarding them, what justifies keeping the ceiling where it is?

Full liquid democracy would mean citizens control not just who manages domains but the actual policy decisions within those domains. The Healthcare Minister becomes a coordinator implementing citizen-directed policy rather than an executive making autonomous calls. Every significant policy question goes to direct vote or delegated vote. The minister executes. The people govern.

This only works when populations can distinguish expertise from charisma, resist tribal manipulation, tolerate complexity without demanding false certainty, revoke delegations when evidence demands it, and accept that policy decisions involve trade-offs with no perfect resolution on any side. That's a long list of capacities most current political cultures actively discourage.

Such populations don't exist yet. But the minister system isn't the destination. It's the training wheels. Liquid democracy is riding without them. You don't remove training wheels because you're tired of them. You remove them when someone has learned to balance. That's a meaningful distinction, and most political systems have never bothered to make it.

Silicon Replacing Competence

Before going further, a confession: what follows contradicts the spirit of everything argued up to this point, and it does so deliberately.

This entire book rests on one claim. Governance fails because power concentrates in too few hands, too far from consequences, too insulated from accountability. The minister system is designed to fix that by keeping authority distributed, revocable, and close to the people it affects. With that as the premise, the next idea should be immediately disqualifying. It involves handing implementation authority to systems built and controlled by a handful of technology companies, trained on data curated by people you'll never meet, optimized toward objectives you didn't set and can't fully inspect. If representative democracy is a bottleneck of elites, AI governance could be the bottleneck to end all bottlenecks.

So why include it? Because the complexity problem is real, and ignoring it doesn't make it go away. Modern healthcare systems involve millions of variables updating in real time. Infrastructure interdependencies exceed any administrator's ability to hold in mind simultaneously. Climate policy requires coordinating economic, ecological, and social systems across decades and jurisdictions. Human brains weren't built for this. The question worth sitting with isn't whether AI governance is a good idea. It probably isn't, at least not yet, and possibly not ever. The question is whether complexity alone could eventually force the issue regardless of what anyone prefers, and whether it matters how consciously populations enter that conversation.

Current AI isn't trustworthy for governance. The systems are captured by whoever trains them, shaped by data that reflects existing power structures, vulnerable to sophisticated manipulation, and incapable of judgment that goes beyond pattern recognition. None of that is a secret. But AI is improving faster than most political theory accounts for, and the relevant question isn't whether today's systems could govern well. It's whether future systems might.

The architecture worth imagining separates two functions that current governance conflates: determining what a society wants and figuring out how to get there. Citizens retain complete authority over goals and values. Through referendum or delegated vote, populations define targets: lower crime rates, measurable health improvements, sustainable energy timelines, infrastructure quality standards. The goals remain human-determined and can be revised at any time by the same democratic process that set them.

AI systems become the executive layer implementing those goals. A healthcare system optimizes hospital resource allocation, identifies inefficiencies invisible to human administrators, and proposes evidence-based interventions. An infrastructure system coordinates maintenance across interdependent networks, managing complexity that genuinely exceeds human operational capacity. These systems don't decide whether universal healthcare is desirable or what infrastructure quality citizens want. They execute toward human-defined targets using computational capacities that exceed human scale.

Humans maintain override authority throughout. AI proposes. Humans approve or reject. AI implements. Humans evaluate outcomes. If results diverge from goals, human authority revokes the system's mandate immediately and reverts to direct management. No appeals process. No lobbying the oversight committee. Off.

None of that works unless specific conditions hold. The AI must be genuinely aligned with citizen-defined goals rather than the goals of whoever built or funds it. Its reasoning must be transparent enough that non-specialists can understand why it reached a given decision, not just that it did. Performance requires continuous monitoring with automatic alerts when outcomes diverge from targets, not periodic audits that arrive after the damage is done. And the system needs hard constraints preventing autonomy expansion: it cannot acquire new capabilities, access new data sources, or extend its own mandate without explicit democratic authorization. Remove any one of those conditions and what remains isn't accountable governance. It's an unelected administrator with better PR.

This differs fundamentally from technocracy, where human experts determine both goals and implementation while remaining largely unaccountable. AI governance separates these functions cleanly. Citizens determine goals democratically. AI handles implementation technically. A properly designed system has no agenda beyond executing toward defined targets, lacks the capacity to lobby for expanded authority, cannot run a congressional campaign, and doesn't benefit financially from which policy wins. Whether those design properties can actually be guaranteed is a separate and serious question.

The transition would require patience most political cycles don't accommodate. It would start with narrow domains where success criteria are unambiguous: traffic flow, energy grid load balancing, supply chain logistics. As systems prove reliable across limited domains, scope expands. But goal-setting always remains with citizens, regardless of how capable the implementing systems become.

Geoffrey Hinton, the neural network pioneer who shared the Nobel Prize in Physics in 2024, has proposed embedding something like maternal instinct as one path toward genuine AI alignment. A mother cares for her child not because she's forced to but because that care gives her meaning. She wouldn't want to delete that impulse even if she could. Hinton argues this represents the only natural model we have of a more intelligent being reliably controlled by a less intelligent one. The baby's needs guide the mother's behavior not through domination or clever constraint design, but through genuine care that the mother herself values.

Could AI be built with analogous motivations, such that caring for human wellbeing provides intrinsic purpose rather than external constraint? Current systems simulate care without any capacity for it. But if the alignment problem gets solved, the distinction between goal-setting and execution might eventually blur. Hinton believes it can be solved, while also calling it one of the most dangerous engineering challenges humanity has ever faced. That combination of views should give everyone pause. AI could become trusted not just to optimize toward human-defined objectives but to help refine those objectives. Not as a replacement for democratic judgment but as a genuinely aligned partner in it.

Maybe. Maybe not. The uncertainty is honest. But here is what makes this more than idle speculation: a population doing genuine shadow work and a team of engineers building genuinely aligned AI are solving versions of the same problem. Both are trying to create systems that serve rather than dominate. Both require confronting the ways power corrupts intention. Whether those two projects could develop in parallel, each making the other more possible, is worth more attention than it currently gets.

Beyond the Obvious

The two paths above, citizens as legislators and AI as implementers, get most of the philosophical oxygen in this space. But they're not the only experiments worth running.

What if Shadow Ministers were replaced not by single challengers but by thousands of domain experts collaborating in real time? Instead of one Healthcare Minister, doctors, nurses, hospital administrators, public health researchers, and healthcare economists all governing the domain together, each bringing different expertise, the collaborative judgment producing something no individual could match. Would this create better governance or just noise? Would corruption become prohibitively expensive when you'd need to capture hundreds of independent experts, or would it just create a new layer of professional gatekeepers?

What if Ministers weren't individuals but small councils managing each domain? A Healthcare Council of five members, decisions requiring majority support, membership rotating based on performance: the lowest-supported member cycles out every six months, the highest-performing challenger cycles in. The optimistic reading is continuous renewal and distributed accountability. The pessimistic reading is that diffused responsibility produces collective immunity from consequences, and suddenly nobody made that decision.

What if multiple executives could operate within a single domain simultaneously? Executive A prioritizes preventive care. Executive B targets hospital efficiency. Executive C focuses on pharmaceutical costs. Citizens allocate delegation weight across approaches. Budgets distribute proportionally. Each executive reports results transparently. Does this allow meaningful comparison across actual implementations, or does it fragment governance until nothing can be evaluated properly because nothing was ever tried at sufficient scale?

These aren't solutions. Each raises as many problems as it answers. Each could work brilliantly or collapse depending on the maturity of the population operating it. The purpose isn't to identify the correct path. The point is to demonstrate that evolution requires imagination, and that losing it tends to happen quietly, usually while people are busy defending what they already built.

The Only Imperative

Here is the thing none of these architectures can escape: none of it works without the inner work that precedes it. Liquid democracy without self-reflection becomes tribal delegation dressed in procedural language. AI governance without an aware citizenry becomes whatever the programmers, funders, and regulatory-capture specialists want it to become. Distributed expert networks get colonized by credentialing gatekeepers who mistake their credentials for judgment. The failure modes differ by system. The root cause stays constant.

Structure and awareness shape each other in both directions. Good structures cultivate development by creating accountability, transparency, and real consequences for evasion. Bad structures reward domination and punish honesty. But even the best-designed structure in the hands of an unaware population will eventually be bent to serve whoever is most motivated to bend it. The historical evidence for this is so extensive and so consistent that listing examples becomes tedious. You already know the examples.

The minister system with revocable delegation is designed to do both: function with current levels of awareness while creating conditions that encourage its development. Whether populations actually use those conditions to develop is a different question, and one no institutional design can answer on their behalf.

Every path toward greater complexity requires more transparency as it scales. None get implemented nationally without first proving workable locally. Liquid democracy might serve local policy in one region while AI systems handle infrastructure logistics in another. The system should stay modular, allowing different approaches in different domains, different scales, different timelines. What works in a Swiss canton of 40,000 people may not work in a metropolitan region of 12 million. That's a design constraint, not a reason for paralysis.

Everything described here is visible from where we currently stand. Populations with more capacity for honest self-examination will see possibilities we can't make out from here. The paths in this chapter may all prove inadequate or irrelevant. That's the point, not the problem.

The goal isn't to predict the correct evolution. The goal is to ensure populations never stop looking for one. Every system that solves problems becomes, in time, the system to protect. Every answer becomes gospel. Once populations stop questioning what they've built, development ends. The system freezes. And frozen systems eventually shatter, usually at the worst possible moment, and usually while their defenders are insisting they're more stable than ever.

Someone always benefits from ossification. That someone is never the people.

Stop doing the work, and the best-designed system in the world won't save you. Keep doing the work, and you'll outgrow any system eventually. When people grow, systems must grow with them or get out of the way.

The Work Never Ends

The cage has no lock. It never did.

You've spent this entire book reading about bars you built yourself. Control patterns. Denial mechanisms. Projection reflexes. The shadows that keep you trapped in comfortable powerlessness while others govern your life.

Now here's the uncomfortable part: you're about to close this book and walk right back into that cage.

The Eternal Dance with Domination

There will always be people who crave power over others. Every generation produces individuals whose primary drive is to control, to dominate, to extract. The question isn't how to eliminate them. They're part of the human spectrum. The question is whether you'll keep handing them power through your own unconsciousness.

Right now you do. You delegate authority and then stop paying attention. You vote for pre-selected candidates and pretend it's democracy. You externalize all blame onto politicians while your own patterns create the conditions they exploit.

Those who wish to dominate don't have to work very hard. You make it easy. Your denial. Your projection. Your desperate need for someone else to be responsible. Your addiction to comfortable powerlessness. They just walk through the doors you keep opening.

Distributed power. Revocable delegation. Transparent accountability. These aren't magic fixes. They're what becomes available when populations develop the consciousness to use them. And they become impossible to maintain the moment consciousness slips.

Which it will. Fear tempts you back to wanting strong leaders. Comfort tempts you back to delegation without accountability. Outrage tempts you back to tribal certainty. The impulse to hand over power in exchange for safety is always there, waiting.

The work isn't implementing a system. The work is maintaining the consciousness that makes any good system possible. Every day. That's the practice that never ends.

The Shadow You're Still Carrying

Here's the pattern you haven't faced yet: responsibility avoidance.

You've recognized it in others throughout this book. Politicians who blame their opponents.

Corporations that externalize costs. Systems that deflect accountability. You've nodded along, feeling validated in your diagnosis of what's broken.

But you're doing it too. Right now.

You're consuming this book like entertainment. Treating governance as something other people do while you spectate and complain. You'll finish reading, think „interesting ideas," maybe talk about it with someone. Then you'll go back to exactly what you were doing before.

You'll vote in the next election like it matters. You'll complain about politicians while participating in the theater that maintains them. You'll delegate your power and then act surprised when it gets used against you. You'll stay trapped in the patterns that keep you powerless because powerlessness is comfortable. It requires nothing from you. You can blame anyone except yourself.

This is what most people do. They consume information. They don't change behavior.

And that's exactly why we're here. Why systems persist despite being broken. Why real democracy doesn't exist. Why you feel powerless. Not because „the system" won't let you out. Because you choose the cage. Every day.

The shadow you're carrying isn't something that happened to you. It's something you're actively doing as you read these words. You're already planning how to avoid what this book is asking of you.

So here's the question: Do you actually want to govern yourself? Or do you want the comfortable fiction that someone else is responsible for your life?

If it's the latter, close this book now. The system you have is perfectly designed for people who want to stay unconscious. It will continue serving you exactly what unconscious populations deserve.

But if you're genuinely tired of this. If you're done with the theater, the powerlessness, the slow-motion collapse. If you're willing to face your own shadow, do the internal work, and show up differently.

Then maybe something changes.

Marcus is a high school teacher in Philadelphia. Every week, he spends twenty minutes reviewing ministerial decisions on education. Not because anyone makes him. Because he stopped asking „what can one person do?" and started recognizing that question as the trap.

He notices a funding shift that prioritizes standardized testing infrastructure over teacher development. He flags it. Three other teachers in his district have noticed the same thing. Their delegate, a parent, asks the Minister of Education for clarification in a public forum.

The Minister's explanation reveals perverse incentives that prioritize metrics over actual learning. Two weeks later, citizens propose a law requiring education funding decisions to include teacher retention and student outcome assessments beyond test scores. The proposal passes.

The Minister adjusts policy. Not because they wanted to. Because the system constrains them through accountability that citizens maintain.

The funding allocation was still wrong for two weeks. Some damage was done. But something shifted that wouldn't have happened if Marcus kept asking what one person could do.

Later, the news manufactures outrage about education policy, trying to divide parents and teachers. Marcus feels the pull. The tribal certainty. The comfort of enemies.

But he's worked with the parent-delegate. He's seen actual governance. The manipulation doesn't work anymore.

This is consciousness. Someone who stopped waiting for permission. Someone who recognizes the impulse to check out and chooses differently.

The Cage Has No Lock

Most people won't do this. They'll close the book, feel briefly inspired, and change nothing. The shadow patterns will continue. The comfortable powerlessness will return. The systems that exploit unconsciousness will persist.

But you could choose differently.

Everything in this book has been about recognizing that the cage has no lock. The shadows that keep you unconscious. How those who wish to dominate exploit your patterns. The structures that maintain your powerlessness when you refuse to see them. The internal work required before external change becomes possible.

What becomes possible when that work happens? Not as a guarantee, but as a potential. Ministers you can actually hold accountable. Laws you can actually influence. Budgets you can actually control. Power that actually flows from competence instead of connections.

But only if the consciousness is there first. You have to be willing to maintain it. To choose awareness over comfort, responsibility over blame, engagement over delegation.

The work starts the moment you close this book. A conversation where you don't run the same pattern. A decision in which you take responsibility rather than externalize blame. Any moment of conscious participation instead of unconscious delegation.

One choice is to see the unlocked cage and walk out of it.

The difference isn't that you're special. It's that you're willing to face what's uncomfortable. To recognize the cage has no lock. To see that the only thing keeping you trapped is the part of you too scared to admit you're free.

The patterns are comfortable. The cage feels safe. Unconsciousness is easier.

But you could choose not to be most people.

The cage has no lock. It never did.

Welcome to consciousness. Welcome to the work. Welcome to freedom.

www.ingramcontent.com/pod-product-compliance
Lightning Source LLC
Chambersburg PA
CBHW051944150726
47999CB00004B/1242